loose wire

jeremy wagstaff

loose wire

a personal guide to making technology work for you

Equinox Publishing (Asia) Pte. Ltd.
PO Box 6179 JKSGN
Jakarta 12062 • Indonesia

www.EquinoxPublishing.com

ISBN 979-3780-39-8

Loose Wire:
A Personal Guide to Making Technology Work for You
by Jeremy Wagstaff

First Equinox Edition 2007

1 3 5 7 9 10 8 6 4 2

This book contains articles which previously appeared in
Dow Jones publications, including *The Wall Street Journal Asia*
and the *Far Eastern Economic Review*. This material is the property of
Dow Jones Publishing Co. (Asia), and is being used with permission.

Printed in the United States.

to Mum and Sari

contents

part 3: getting what you need

part 4: getting out of trouble

foreword

I was present at the birth of "Loose Wire". It was February 2000. I was at that time managing editor of the *Far Eastern Economic Review*, Asia's most prestigious news weekly.

A group of the magazine's editors had gathered in a dingy, cramped conference room at our Hong Kong headquarters to discuss a series of changes we planned to make to the *Review*'s content and design. One of the changes was to introduce a regular column on technology.

This was at the height of the Great Dotcom Bubble, only we didn't know it. All we knew was that technology shares were going through the roof everywhere you looked. Everyone seemed to have an insatiable appetite for tech-related stories. The hunt for "killer apps" and "the Next Big Thing" was on. Net-savvy 25-year-old kids were going to take over the world.

One of the puzzles we wrestled with at that February meeting was what to call our new tech column. We knew it was going to be written by Jeremy Wagstaff, a young reporter who had worked for *The Asian Wall Street Journal*, a sister publication of the *Review*. He was based in Jakarta – an odd place, I thought, to locate our tech columnist, but that's where he lived.

Various names were thrown about. None of them caught fire. Then I said, "What about 'Loose Wire'?"

I was reading from an email Jeremy had sent me the day before. I had asked him to propose some names for his column. It was the one I liked most. It had a zany, unorthodox feel to it. It somehow suggested the need to reconnect something that wasn't quite right.

And if you said it fast enough, I joked at the meeting, it sounded very sophisticated, very *French*: Le Soir.

Well, the name stuck. And over the next five years, Jeremy's column would become one of the best read sections of the magazine, a veritable fount of practical wisdom, insight and advice about the everyday uses and abuses of technology.

When the *Review* ceased publishing as a weekly in late 2004, the column was transferred to *The Asian Wall Street Journal*.

Jeremy's approach to writing about technology is unique. I know of no other writer who quite matches his ability to enrich the ordinary person's understanding of the technology we use everyday with such clarity, wit, and sympathy.

Reading this book is like taking a marvelous journey through familiar and unfamiliar lands, but with a patient, amiable companion by your side, someone who is capable of annotating the landscape in ways that make you see things you never realized were there.

I had no idea at that meeting nearly seven years ago that "Loose Wire," our modest effort to meet a part of the growing demand for technology writing, would long outlive the dotcom bubble that gave birth to it. I am glad that it did. And you will be too.

David Plott
Deputy Director
Journalism and Media Studies Centre
The University of Hong Kong
September 2006

introduction

Technology is now so much a part of our lives that we no longer have much choice about whether we use it. It has probably always felt like that; I'm sure when the first spinning jenny came along the workers asked to use it were grumbling to themselves about "all this newfangled technology" and "wasn't it better in the old days when we'd do all our spinning on a spindle?" But in the past twenty years technology has invaded the workplace, the home and society in a way few of us imagined, and while it hasn't delivered all the benefits we thought it might, it's definitely forced all of us to be a little more, well, geeky, than we may have wanted to be. Who would have thought that we'd spend most of our lives interacting with computers – whether they're the traditional sort in our cubicle or in the den at home, the small variety in the mobile phone that is our constant companion, or in every appliance we use, from our toothbrush to the car?

This book is all about that interaction – what is happening, why it's happening, how it affects us, and how to make it work for us. It's written for ordinary people, based on columns I have done for different Dow Jones publications including *The Wall Street Journal* and its Asian, European and online editions, and The *Far Eastern Economic Review.* But just in case you're thinking to yourselves, "yes, I've heard that before. Everyone says they're writing for ordinary people and then I read the first two paragraphs and feel myself sinking into a quicksand of acronyms and technical blather. Whoever these ordinary people are, they're not living on my street," let me assure you: I'm no geek either. Really.

Judge for yourself. I was always hopeless at anything with numbers in. My math teacher used to sharpen his sarcasm on me, either verbally or with the soft end of a slide rule. (Note to people who have not used a slide rule or have no idea what one is: There is no soft end), while the science teacher used me as target practice for his particular brand of brutality, which usually involved Bunsen burners. By the time I reached my O Levels I was so traumatized I would come out in a rash whenever someone asked me a question with an equals sign in it, which probably explained why I failed math, physics and chemistry, and wasn't even allowed to do biology. I was quickly considered a basket case when it came to anything technical or scientific: My career counselor concluded I was, and I quote (I can remember it by heart), "probably completely unpractical". So I decided to become a writer (well, actually I wanted to be a pop star, but that involved cabling and an understanding of basic electronics). When the early word processors started appearing in the mid 1980s I was intrigued. I didn't have enough money to buy both synthesizers and word processor so I hung up my ponytail, threw my bandanna in a cupboard, sold my keyboards and bought an Amstrad. It was an emotional day.

Luckily they weren't that hard to master. A few weeks with a manual and I knew enough to hammer out a few pieces which got me noticed by a very small crowd in south London. But it wasn't enough, so I moved to Thailand, where I had to make do with a manual typewriter I had picked up in a mall on Phetburi Road. I snuck across the Burmese border a few times, wrote a few pieces, and, more through luck than anything else, landed a job with Reuters News Agency. The second half of 1988 was a heady time – Aung San Suu Kyi headed a people's movement against the Burmese generals, Indochina grappled with the unraveling of the Soviet bloc, and Khmer Rouge guerrillas nipped at the heels of the retreating Vietnamese garrisons in western Cambodia. The first few months of my job, however, was to sit in Bangkok, trying to get a telephone line to Rangoon.

This was harder than it sounds: At the time there were only half a dozen such international lines, all of them reached through prolonged conversation with Thai switchboard operators. Journalism is the art of the conversation, and persuading these poor harassed telephonists to keep trying to get a line on our behalf involved convoluted techniques, sometimes incorporating vague protestations of love and proposals of marriage, which stood me in good stead when I later interviewed ministers and generals across Asia. But technology was not, initially, my friend: When once I managed to get not only a phone line to Rangoon, but to the besieged Aung San Suu Kyi herself, my colleagues crowded round as I conducted an excellent interview with her, my whirring tape recorder leaning against the speaker phone and both hands clutching the hand piece with pride. At the end of the interview I puffed up my chest and played back the tape, only to realize I had managed to record half an hour of exclusive silence. My boss patted me on the shoulder, shrugged and walked back to his desk.

I learned a lesson of sorts: Technology can be your friend or your enemy. Don't allow it to let you down. Or something like that. News with the wires is a 24-hour thing and that gave me a chance to redeem myself. As the new kid on the block I always seemed to be on the late shift, shuffling like a ghost through the ramshackle office on the 12th floor of a building that had definitely seen better days. So had the prostitutes who worked the pool hall downstairs. The rain would leak through the sagging ceiling, caught in strategically placed buckets that doubled as ashtrays. The ticker tape printers would clatter away, spewing rolls of fast fading dispatches onto the floor. Occasionally a stringer would wander in, a woman or two in tow, some of whom looked vaguely familiar from rounds of pool. Journalists whose employers were subscribers to Reuters could come in and read our public wires, although some would also sneak a look at our private clipboards of raw copy, transcribed interviews and snippets we'd picked up; sometimes these nuggets would find a way into their copy. One of my tasks as night watchman was to make sure they didn't repeat such a heinous crime.

The late guy's job was also to monitor the official news wires from Laos, Cambodia, Vietnam and Burma, then exotic outposts where we had no useful correspondents and no independent access to news. These wire services would deliver their text by radio transmitter, which would appear on our teleprinter as mostly unintelligible gibberish splayed drunkenly across the page. Occasionally we could make enough out to write a story, mostly along the lines of "Vietnamese Communist Party Chief says Farmers Must Work Harder" or something equally moving. Rarely, just rarely, something big would find its way across the airwaves, and the lonely torpor of the shift would transform to a heady sense of immortality within one's grasp. But most of the time it was just something that had to be done while the rest of the city played or slept.

It wasn't entirely solitary confinement: Two Burmese exiles would wander in after dinner, beer and curry on their breath, to listen to the official radio broadcasts from Rangoon, and would then write out their laborious and usually indecipherable summaries in neat script on the backs of envelopes. They were lovely guys, and it was fun to sit around with them as they cooped themselves up in a tiny booth to listen to an ageing contraption as big as a fridge. There, vintage headphones akimbo, they'd twiddle the dials until a scratchy faint voice could be heard launching into some anti-Western diatribe, a close relation in all but name to the Communist propaganda issuing from Indochina.

This was all easy enough to stay on top of. Anybody could rip the paper streams up with a ruler and read the backs of the Burmese envelopes. The real problem lay in a separate room, chilled to 20°C, where the engineers kept their servers. There, among the cabling, the racks and the buckets was one small PC, hooked up via modem to a telephone line. Twice a day we were allowed to dial into the U.S. Embassy to collect their translation of propaganda from across Thailand's western and eastern borders – anything from three-hour speeches by increasingly unhinged Burmese generals to tightly phrased editorials in Vietnam's army daily *Quan Doi Nhan Dan*. Nowadays that paper has its own website, but in the late 1980s it was like being given gold dust – a chance to look inside the heart of one of Vietnam's most powerful institutions. The U.S. embassy was doing us – and all Western wire services – a huge favor by letting us do this, although, of course, they had already creamed off anything they didn't want us to see. And it was hardly secret: Most of this stuff eventually found its way into the public domain via a longstanding monitoring agreement with the British. And it has to be said that the reams of these documents were breathtakingly dull. But sometimes they weren't. One piece might carry vital news, and we needed to make sure we got it, and get it before or at the same time as our competitors.

I don't know who set up the system to give us access to all this, but it required a bit more technology than most of us hacks had at our disposal. It was in the world before Windows, so we used a DOS program called Xtalk, meaning we had to type a command to dial the embassy computer, and then a number of other commands to get the feed to start downloading. Then we had to capture it to our computer, which required remembering to type in a command before the text started churning itself down the screen in a storm of digital rain so fast you couldn't make out more than a few words. Then, once it had stopped, another command was needed to save the text stored in the buffer; forgetting to do either of these commands would result in an empty file. And there was no second chance: to foil snoopers, each news agency was allowed in only twice a day. It was not my favorite part of the evening, and put me in a sweat I hadn't had since the whole Aung San Suu Kyi phone call debacle.

I quickly realized three things, two of which were useless, and one of which would change my life: a) I was out of my depth here. This wasn't word processing. This was something else, with something suspiciously like numbers in it, b) I was going to screw up again, just as my math and science teachers told me I would; if not today, then at some point in the future, and c) none of the other journalists really knew what they were doing either. There was some kind of crib sheet, which, like all crib sheets, revealed that those using it would just slavishly follow the instructions, line by line. This last realization – that my colleagues were probably all journalists for the same reason I was – made me feel a bit better, made me aware that there was a slim possibility that I could actually have something useful to contribute, right up until one night when I lost a vital evening's worth of monitoring because I forgot to set the capture on. The boss gave his usual shrug, but I knew if I struck out again, my brilliant Reuters career might be over before it began.

It was then that I discovered I had to master this technology thing before it mastered me. I found an Xtalk manual and rewrote the crib sheet. I started playing with sending stories from remote locations using modems. I started dialing into bulletin boards to ask other people for help. I even started saving some of the monitoring to my own computer, building up a database of sorts that made finding out whether the last congress of the Lao People's Revolutionary Party called Marxism-Leninism a "good thing" or a "darned good thing" (important to the Laotian equivalent of Kremlin watchers.) My stories didn't really get any better, but I learned that a little bit of technology really helped. I was able to write a better cribsheet for capturing the CIA stuff, and eventually devise a better procedure for getting it. In Indonesia in 1993 I was able to get useful insight from overseas academics starved of information about what was happening in Jakarta using email. In East Timor I was able to send out my story before the other guys because I had figured out how to get around the limitations of the local phone system before them; in Afghanistan I tweaked a satellite phone so it talked to a modem so the Reuters bureau there could, for the first time in weeks, actually send their story as text rather than dictate it. When the Web came along I embraced it like a long-lost friend, realizing it did all the things I had been trying to do for years.

It's not that I had turned into a geek. I still didn't know very much about technology. (Read this book and you'll realize I still don't.) But I had realized that I didn't need to know everything. All I needed to do was to know enough to make it work for me and to offer some help to colleagues: To do the job, to get things done. And, I guess, to rest the ghosts of math class and science lab. Technology still drives me nuts, but that's usually only because much of it has been so badly designed. Now, after all these years of fiddling and messing about, technology has become less like an intimidating teacher and more like an exasperating friend.

I hope this book might do something similar for you.

Jeremy Wagstaff
Jakarta, September 2006

a lexicon for luddites

It's unsurprising, given the kind of people who design and play with computers, but I've always felt there to be a chronic shortage of terms to describe what we actually do with our technology. So in 2003 I came up with some of my own. And, in case I was to be accused of merely adding words to the English language, I'd used existing words, in this case from the villages of the United Kingdom (I make no claim for originality here; the late author of A Hitchhiker's Guide to the Galaxy, *Douglas Adams, did it first with a marvelous book called* The Meaning of Liff. *I also offer a nod in the direction of* Harry Potter's *J.K. Rowling).*

Here's my contribution (these are all real place names, so my apologies in advance to offended residents):

appledore (*n, Cornwall*) Someone who touts the superior benefits of Macintosh computers at parties, even after the dancing has started.

aynho (*n, Northamptonshire*) Someone who forwards inane jokes, hoax virus alerts and cutesy emails to everyone in their address book, however much they're asked not to. *Who is the aynho that keeps sending Saddam jokes?*

biggleswade (*v, Bedfordshire*) The process of scouring through tons of Word files, spreadsheets, and emails to find a crucial document. *I've been biggleswading all afternoon and I still can't find the dang thing.*

branksome (*adj, Dorset*) A temperamental Internet connection. *The Net's been really branksome today.*

chettle (collective *n, Dorset*) The debris, such as crumbs, dead insects and lint, that gets stuck inside your computer keyboard.

chew magna (*v, Dorset*) When your floppy or ZIP drive, instead of reading a disk, grindingly destroys it.

chipping norton (*n, Oxfordshire*) The point a PC reaches when it requires the use of an error-fixing program such as Norton Utilities. *I'm sorry, guv, but your computer's chipping norton.*

crackington haven (*n, Cornwall*) A website that is home to ne'er-do-well hackers, crackers and credit-card fraudsters.

cridling stubbs (*n, Yorkshire*) The stunted, misshapen fingers and thumbs of teenagers who have spent too long sending text messages on their mobile phones.

devizes (*n, Wiltshire*) Gadgets you bought, used once and then, realizing they took up more time than they saved, threw in a drawer.

fiddleford (*n, Dorset*) A person who jabs away on a personal digital assistant in public places.

fladdabister (*n, Shetland Islands*) A sore or bruise that appears shortly before the onset of cridling stubbs.

foindle (*v, Highland*) The (usually) unconscious act of stroking a much-loved gadget in public.

fugglestone (*v, Wiltshire*) Frustration experienced after failing to master an item of hardware or software. *I've spent three hours on this dumb program and I'm completely fugglestoned.* (Not in polite usage.)

gnosall (*n, Staffordshire*) A person who frequents newsgroups and appears to know the answer to everything, while having no apparent qualifications or job.

hayling (*n, Hampshire*) The gesture made by someone answering his mobile phone during a meeting or meal, signifying it's important and they'll be with you in a minute.

hordle (*v, Hampshire*) The noise a modem makes when it is trying to connect to the Internet. *My modem isn't working. I can't hear it hordle.* (*see also* **millom**)

inchgrundle (*v, Angus*) To assist, reluctantly and grudgingly, a customer with their recently purchased computer.

keevil (*n, Wiltshire*) A small icon residing in your Windows system tray, the purpose of which remains a mystery.

lostwithiel (*n, Cornwall*) The remote area not covered by your mobile phone operator. *I would have called you, boss, but I was in lostwithiel.*

melbury bubb (*n, Dorset*) The noise of people talking on their mobile phone on public transport, unaware they are driving fellow commuters to distraction. *How was your day, dear? Fine, but the melbury bubb on the train home was awful. What's for dinner?*

melplash (*n, Dorset*) An annoying window that pops up on your screen when you're trying to do something important.

millom (*n, Cumbria*) The period of blissful silence when, after hours of fiddling with settings and wall sockets, your modem no longer hordles and connects to the Internet.

much wenlock (*n, Shropshire*) The belated realization that you've been typing with the cAPS lOCK oN.

odstock (*n, Wiltshire*) Gadgets and peripherals you can no longer use because you've lost the cables, software or power adaptor for them.

padstow (*n, Cornwall*) The place where all your mousepads mysteriously head for when they go missing from your desk.

puncknowle (*n, Dorset*) A geeky teenager who knows the answer to all your computer problems but never seems to actually get around to fixing them.

scrooby (*adj, Nottinghamshire*) When a computer screen starts behaving oddly for no apparent reason. *Jeremy, can you come round and take a look at my computer? It's gone all scrooby again.*

swaffham bulbeck (*n, Cambridgeshire*) The pseudo-authoritative spiel delivered by computer-store staff in the hope of browbeating a sale. *I tried to find out which was the best computer to buy but the guy just gave me a load of swaffham bulbeck. I'm not going back to that store again.*

tibshelf (*n, Derbyshire*) The area near your computer where you keep software and hardware manuals you never refer to.

ufton nervet (*n, Berkshire*) The suspense experienced upon rebooting a crashed computer, fearing that valuable data has been lost.

upper tooting (*n, London*) An insister error beep, the source of which cannot be identified. *I have no idea what the problem is, the thing just keeps upper tooting.*

wantage (*n, Oxfordshire*) The shortfall between your present computer's capacity and that required to run the program you just bought.

whitnash (*n, Warwickshire*) The pain in your shoulder at the end of a long laptop-carrying trip. *The trip went fine, but I've got serious whitnash and need a bubble bath.*

If you don't know what any of these terms are referring to, then it's a good thing you bought this book. Thanks for that.

More definitions can be found throughout the book, flagged with a ☞. *I should stress that usage of them in public will not necessarily elicit knowing nods and smiles unless the person you're talking to happens to have read this book.*

PART ONE

getting connected

mobile phones

We go on about the Internet, cyberspace, the information superhighway, the blogosphere and all those terrible clichés we find ourselves uttering even though we know we shouldn't. But nothing encapsulates the changes of the past 20 years better than the mobile phone. While it has been spotted in the wild since the mid 1980s (relatively easily, since it was then about the size of a small house) it wasn't until everyone had one that we began to notice how much it was changing us. Just watch any movie before the mid 1990s and see whether the plot – with people missing each other on the stairs, rushing to a payphone, leaving voice messages and standing waiting in the rain – would have survived if it had been transposed to the mobile phone age. Our lives have changed utterly. This was how I saw it in January 2002:

Few of us stop to think just how revolutionary the mobile phone is. It enables us to be always on call and always in touch with those important to us, it frees us from the confines of office and home, but perhaps most importantly it gives us something to fiddle with during awkward moments at meetings, parties, funerals, etc. And the revolution is only just beginning.

Mobile phones have redefined the concept of personal space, of what is meant by communication, as well as allowing us to send messages to each other – mostly consisting of such vital data as smiley icons, jokes and "you owe me rent."

☞ **audlem** (*n, Cheshire*) An office with too many mobile phones ringing. *It's audlem in here. I can't get anything done.*

Mobile phones, in short, have altered the way we behave. The phone has become an extension of our bodies, and we feel lost without it. It's the first thing we park on the table at restaurants, bars, desks, pulpits, etc. As cultural observer Sadie Plant, in her entertaining treatise "On The Mobile", has observed, whether we have one, how we use it, how many names we have stored in its memory, all define what kind of person we are, indeed, whether we are anybody at all.

As mobile phones change us, so in turn we feel compelled to ensure they say as many good things about us as possible, short of hanging a placard around one's neck saying "really nice guy, cool but not aloof, interesting job but even more interesting hobbies involving water, rocks and rugged footwear." We buy the latest model and parade it until another model comes along, after which we sheepishly stuff it in our pocket. I was mortified when my Nokia Communicator, a bulky but state-of-the-art number incorporating keyboard, big screen, tumble-dryer, etc., was mistaken for one of those brick-sized monstrosities of yore.

Smaller phones don't necessarily mean less intrusive: In fact the fancier the phone is, the smaller it is, which means the more prominent it should be. To assist visibility, buy a snap-on cover sporting designs from Snoopy-esque to racing cars. The next stage, of course, will be for the phones to actually be shaped like a Disney character or a packet of cigarettes, which might well mark the end of civilization as we know it. In the meantime, Nokia this month unveiled a subsidiary called Vertu to produce mobile phones encrusted in precious gems and sporting luxurious metal finishes. Sadly, tackiness and mobile phones seem a good fit.

As if that wasn't enough, ring tones show no sign of getting tasteful. A new generation of palm-sized devices which double as phones will use ordinary sound files as ring tones. In the future, expect to hear more melodious stuff or, more ominously, recorded voices of Hollywood characters uttering personalized messages along the lines of: "Sebastian,

☞ **mamble** (*n, Worcestershire*) A mobile phone conversation that isn't really going anywhere but neither side seems about to terminate. *There was someone mambling the whole trip, I couldn't get any sleep.*

you have a call from your mother."

Of course, mobile phones have wrought broader change. The overthrow of Philippine President Joseph Estrada is an oft-cited example of the broadcasting power of short messaging, or SMS, but protests have been coordinated by mobile phone for much longer. Many middle-class students involved in the anti-military uprising in Thailand in 1992 had the bulky units of the day stuffed into their jeans, which must have been painful when their soldier captors forced them to crouch or crawl.

But more importantly, it's no longer a revolution confined to the elite. In poverty-stricken Indonesia, for example, mobile phones will outnumber land lines this year. Transvestite prostitutes wandering the streets near where I live all seem to be sporting the latest silver-plated Nokia, and when the shoeless busker who accosts your car at a junction pauses in his rendering of "Olé Olé Olé" to answer his Siemens you know the mobile phone has broken out of its traditional socioeconomic limits. This is no bad thing. The more of us have these dang things, the quicker we can agree on how they are used and, most importantly, what to do to people who use overly glitzy phones with annoying ring tones. Make them eat the precious gems, I say.

Since I wrote that, mobile phones have gotten smaller, more sophisticated and more functional by including calendars, contact lists, GPS devices and cameras (more on all this later). I haven't studied the impact of this on the tranvestite prostitution business but I imagine it's been as revolutionary as in other professions. But what is perhaps most surprising about all this is that the mobile phone's popularity, at least outside the U.S., is largely down to a very simple tool that no one – including the people who invented it – considered as something that might catch on. Here's how I saw it in May 2001:

I felt pretty dumb the other day when my friend John – a man whose technical savvy extends to figuring out which remote to use with which appliance – triumphantly walked me through some of the finer points of the

☞ **beeby** (*n, Leicestershire*) A ringtone that is a little too over the top for the person using it. *She's so cultured I was a bit surprised when her phone rang with a beeby.*

short message service (SMS). For those of you even dumber than me, this allows mobile phone users to send simple text messages to one another.

OK, this is nothing new. SMS has been around for a while; the first such message was sent in 1992. But it is only recently that the service has begun to take off in many parts of the world, mainly because operators have been slow to allow users to send messages to friends using a different operator. The service got started this month in Indonesia, for example, quickly boosting traffic by half and transforming my assistant's mobile phone into a permanently buzzing message center.

This is all rather ironic, given that by now we were supposed to be using our phones for something more sophisticated than sending each other silly messages all day. Less than a year ago we were promised a vision of Internet access, email and seamless communication between mobile phones and other devices using buzzwords such as WAP (wireless application protocol).

Very little of that has happened, in part because these technologies are way too fiddly for your average Joe. It is a fine, sobering example of consumer power: give me something I can use to communicate with and I will use it. Anything that leaves me twiddling my thumbs or requiring a manual and I will almost certainly ditch it.

So SMS is marching on, and shows no sign of stopping. Billions of such messages are being sent each month.

The awkwardness of tapping out a message on a key no larger than a Q-tip has been made easier through an ingenious technology called predictive text, which tries to anticipate what you are going to tap in as you tap. Hit the keys marked 4/GHI, 3/DEF, 5/JKL, 7/PQRS, for example, and it rightly assumes you are tapping in 'HELP'. This software, developed by Tegic Communications (www.t9.com) and now owned by America Online, works in 29 languages and is in about 180 kinds of mobile phone.

I suspect the enduring appeal of SMS is its simplicity. Intended originally as a messaging service for technicians, it is flexible enough to cope

☞ **warbleton** (*n, East Sussex*) The noise a mobile phone makes when placed close to an audio device.

not only with text but with other binary data, such as sending ringtones. It also supports broadcasting, so one person can send large numbers of people the same message. This opens the door to third-party services, such as stock quotes or sports scores. Users can send messages cheaply internationally (provided the operators agree to swap SMS messages), as well as between phones and Internet-based messaging services such as ICQ (www.icq.com).

Of course, the explosion of SMS brings with it some downside. The main fear: viruses. I have received several emails in the past week from people fooled by hoaxes. Just to put minds at rest, there is so far no evidence of a global system for mobile communications, or GSM, virus, say antivirus software manufacturers, although there have been isolated reports of text messages somehow locking up keypads or address books.

Still, this is probably the area that could cause the most headaches. Because of its capacity to broadcast multiple copies of an SMS, it is easy to send junk mail, or spam, to large numbers of mobile phone users simultaneously. An SMS bomb against one person could load him with extra charges from his operator, crash his phone, or ruin his weekend as he spends time deleting all the unwanted messages.

This technique, however, isn't just for the bad guys. Faced with a wave of mobile phone theft, Amsterdam's police force earlier this year started bombing stolen phones with short messages by using the unique identity number assigned to most GSM phones, rendering the phones useless. The result: phone theft, which previously accounted for 75 percent of street robbery now accounts for only 30 percent, according to Elly Florax, the Amsterdam police's communications director.

That isn't to say talk of mobile phone viruses is all hogwash. The more sophisticated phones apparently are vulnerable: Japan's DoCoMo i-mode system was attacked last year by a message-borne script that dialed an emergency number without the user knowing. As mobile phones get more sophisticated and more widely used, they become a juicier target

☞ **warbstow** (*n,v, Cornwall*) The place on your desk where you put your mobile phone so that it doesn't make a warbleton.

for hackers. According to Joe Hartmann, director of antivirus research for Trend Micro Inc., virus writers have already challenged each other to come up with a mobile-phone virus.

In the absence of any big new technology to replace it, expect SMS to edge its way further into your life. The introduction of phones with extended messaging service, or EMS, later this year, will add different typefaces, images, melodies and animations to the basic SMS text format. While most of us aren't likely to be wowed by being able to add funny noises and dancing Father Christmases to our messages, it means we can get Internet-style content without the sluggishness of WAP. It should be easier to master, too, but I am still counting on John to talk me through it.

Another great example there of me sort of getting it right, but mostly getting it wrong. EMS and its cousin MMS never really took off, although it has become possible to get Internet content on your phone, after the early missteps of WAP. But SMS is still the most popular form of non-verbal communication, apart from glaring and sulking. At the time of writing this, for example, an East Timorese minister submitted his resignation via SMS, while two famous soccer players – teammates in the English league, foes in the World Cup – settled their grievances via texting.

The combination of voice and short, pithy message has changed the way we relate to them – and to other people – in ways that even Sadie Plant might not have imagined. Here's how I saw it in 2004, in a piece called "My Mobile, My Master":

We all know that mobile phones, cellphones, handphones, whatever we want to call them (and shouldn't we all be calling them the same thing?) are changing our lives. But it takes a good old-fashioned survey to wake us up to the glaring reality: They have changed who we are.

If someone had said to you 10 years ago that, in 2004, the majority of people would consider their mobile phone to be an "extension of their

☞ **birling gap** (*n, Kent*) The distance from the bottom of a BlackBerry or smartphone screen to the end of the text of an email; that area never read by someone.

personality," you would have been forgiven for looking skeptical and saying: "What's a mobile phone?" And yet that's exactly what German electronics giant Siemens found in a recent survey: Across Asia, sizeable percentages of folk believe their mobile phone and its contents – music, games, contacts and messages – form an extension of themselves. Heaven only knows what we'll be saying in five more years. Perhaps we'll be sending mobile phones to represent us in meetings, on dates, and make speeches on our behalf at the United Nations General Assembly.

I've talked before about how the mobile phone has changed the way we behave. But perhaps we don't realize how much we have become its slave. Consider other elements of the Siemens Mobile Survey: With the exception of Australia, in every country surveyed the majority polled said they would go back for their phone if they left it at home (in Australia it was a respectable 39%). If you've endured the traffic in Indonesia, Philippines and India, you'll know what kind of sacrifice some two-thirds of those polled are making. I can't think of anything I would go back for – except my wallet, maybe, or my clothes.

And even if we remember to bring it, we're still not happy. Many of us get antsy if it hasn't rung or a text message hasn't appeared for a while (a while being about an hour). Once again, of those polled, Indonesians (65%) and Filipinos (77%) get particularly jittery. Australians are more laid back about this (20%), but every other user in Asia seems to be glancing at the phone every few seconds. This statistic, I have to say, is highly believable, and the instinct highly annoying. There's nothing worse than chatting to someone who constantly checks his or her mobile phone. Except when I do it, of course.

If you want proof that we're not in control of our gadget, ask the question: Would we drop everything to answer its call? Sadly, yes. Most Chinese users (81%) would. In fact, the majority of users in every country polled, except Australia, would pick up their mobile if it started ringing. Perhaps this shouldn't surprise us: Nearly two-thirds of China's users

☞ **belluton** (*n, Somerset*) Bluetooth earpieces that look like dead beatles squashed in the user's ear. *You can spot him easily. He's the guy with the belluton in his ear.*

polled plan most of their social activities via mobile phone, and a quarter of Indians surveyed yak on theirs while having a bath or a massage. Is nothing sacred?

All this is taking a toll on our relationships. More than half the Indonesians polled would ask their loved ones who the text message they had just received was from. Again, this is unsurprising: Mobile phones are making flirting risk-free. Nearly a quarter of Indians polled said they would often send a message to an unknown number hoping to meet someone new. Interestingly, Indians are also the most likely to use their camera-phone to take a photo of someone without their knowledge. Meanwhile, a lot of folk save cherished text messages, though whether it's for memory's sake or legal purposes is not clear. Mobile phones allow us to be in constant touch with our loved ones, which can mean different things depending on the state of your relationship(s). More than half the Filipinos polled send text messages to or phone their loved ones "plenty of times a day." The figure is only slightly lower elsewhere. Call me unromantic, but I can imagine constant beeping from one's loved one might wear thin after a while.

Then there's the fact that mobile phones are not only enslaving the user, they're trampling the rights of everyone else. Around a third of folk polled acknowledge they get so engrossed in mobile conversations that they're often unaware of speaking loudly while discussing their private lives in public. At least most of us agree on one thing: With the exception of China, Hong Kong and Taiwan, the increasing usage of mobile phones has led to a decline in courtesy and considerate behavior. You bet.

The bottom line here is that we are more than a little bit out of control. Mobile phones are great, but if we allow them to dominate our lives to this extent – interrupting conversations with those around us to take a call, staring at our phones rather than relating to the world and people around us, sending flirty text messages to random numbers – then I can only assume that in another 10 years, society as we know it will no longer exist. All we'll see is a blur of digital data going out and having all the fun, socializing, falling in love and taking sneaky pictures of each other.

☞ **toller fratrum** (*n, Dorset*) Life before BlackBerrys.

Part of the problem with mobile phones, in my view, has been the awful hype we've been subjected to about what they might be able to do for us. Drowning in a soup of acronyms, we were told at the turn of the millennium that we would be able to access the Internet so fast on our mobile phones that we wouldn't need computers and we'd never have to go past a Pizza Hut without knowing what their specials were. This, perhaps thankfully, hasn't happened. But tracking the trajectory of their hype and our expectations reveals just how far, and how little, we've come since I started writing about this kind of thing. At the heart of all this hype is something called Bluetooth, which was launched in 1999 and yet hadn't, by 2002, done much to merit the attention, as I wrote in August of that year:

By now you've probably heard of Bluetooth technology, but chances are you're not quite sure what all the fuss is about. I don't blame you. If its name – better suited to a dentist specializing in unhappy teeth – isn't enough to put you off, then you might be forgiven for wondering, "Just how is this going to improve the quality of my life?" I'm not about to suggest you go Bluetooth-crazy, but I reckon it's worth getting a handle on because one day Bluetooth will make linking your PC, gadgets and telephones a lot easier.

First, let's get the name out of the way: Bluetooth was the nickname of a Danish king called Harald. Through his impressive communication skills – no one is too specific about this, but I suspect that as a Viking they didn't involve throwing baby showers and Tupperware parties – King Bluetooth united Norway and Denmark in the 10th century. Hence Bluetooth is a wireless standard that allows users to unite through communication. Get it? Gadgets with no fuss. Or cables. In short, one gadget with Bluetooth built in – say your mobile phone – should link up automatically with another gadget – say your laptop – without you doing much more than putting them in the same room.

This works using the same free part of the radio spectrum that WiFi,

☞ **toller whelme** (*n, Dorset*) Life with BlackBerrys; the feeling of never quite being in control of your life.

or Wireless Fidelity (p.38), devices use. But while WiFi connects devices over longer distances, Bluetooth gadgets only hook up within a 10-meter range. Where WiFi evangelists dream of large networks without wires, Bluetoothers dream of little informal clusters of computers, printers, personal digital assistants, mobile phones, headsets, cameras, floppy and CD-ROM drives all connected wirelessly. Unlike infrared they don't need to be pointed at each other, and they'll also work through a door or wall.

It's a great idea, so why isn't it happening yet? Well, when Bluetooth first appeared in 1998-99 the hype raised expectations to a silly level, particularly since there was only a handful of products with Bluetooth built in. But three years on, there are still problems: There are now dozens of Bluetooth products, and more in the pipeline, but Bluetooth chips are still too expensive, meaning that few of these gadgets cost less than $100. That's too pricey for most people.

But mainly the problem is that it's still too fiddly for prime time. So while some pundits say Bluetooth has arrived, I'd suggest some caveats: Buy with care, don't expect too much, and be ready for a bit of pain. The future may have fewer wires, but there are still plenty of strings attached.

Since then, Bluetooth devices have gotten cheaper and easier to couple, so much so that it's the normal way to link a wireless earpiece with a mobile phone. But that's a more modest achievement than the original goal inventors and hypesters of Bluetooth had in mind for us. Still, it works, and it means we aren't strangling ourselves in a sea of cables. This is also linked to the rise of the intelligent phone, better known as the smartphone. Here's a piece I wrote in 2003 about them:

If you're anything like me, you hope the next gadget you buy will solve all the problems with your existing one – phone, palm-held device, lawn-mower – only to find that in most cases, you're forced to settle for something that may be better, but not necessarily in the way you imagined, or hoped. Call it Feature Disconnect.

☞ **baddesley ensor** (*n, Warwickshire*) People who make a miscall and then still call the same number.

Take my new mobile phone, for example. I needed something that didn't keep switching off mid-call, where the keys didn't stick, and which had some extra features such as a decent calendar, contacts list, etc. After much deliberation I settled for the Nokia 7650, a beast that combines camera, digital assistant and phone.

Two weeks on, I like half the features and am somewhat disappointed over the other half, but in most cases the things I like about it are not the reasons I bought it. I've had to abandon synchronizing my data with Microsoft Outlook because the Nokia slows to a crawl with all my contacts aboard, while the short messaging (or SMS) feature, while comprehensive in terms of storing and displaying messages, is actually more fiddly than its predecessor. On the other hand, I'm addicted to taking pictures of people and linking the picture to their contact details, so on the rare occasions they call, their visage appears on the screen. Completely pointless, I know, and certainly not why I bought the thing, but it makes me happy.

I suspect similar problems with Sony Ericsson's P800, another supposedly smartphone. As I'm sure you know, Sony Ericsson is a trial marriage of Japanese electronics-giant Sony and Ericsson, the Swedish mobile phone manufacturer. They've been dabbling for a while in handsets and with their most recent model appear to have hit something near the jackpot. It looks a lot like a normal phone, but flip open the keypad and you get a screen the size of Hungary, an interface to die for and an almost fully fledged digital organizer. It's a marvel of engineering, delightful to hold and look at, but sadly it's still vulnerable to Feature Disconnect.

The problem as I see it is this: As all these gadgets get better, we demand more out of them. Then we want all those features in one device. Seeing the P800 – the closest anyone's come to an all-in-one gadget – I can't help wondering whether we'd be better off keeping some things separate. With a keyboard and Bluetooth, today's Palm or PocketPC can, under certain conditions, do a very good job of mimicking a laptop, something that wasn't really intended when they first appeared in the mid 1990s.

☞ **belchamp walter** (*n, Essex*) People who wear Bluetooth earpieces when they're not on a call.

Mobile phones now are messaging devices – transmitting not just voice, but messages, pictures and whatnot, storing music and taking photos – something that certainly wasn't envisaged with the launch of their brick-sized ancestors in the early 1980s. All these features, in my view, make it less likely – and indeed, less preferable – to have an all-in-one device. So long as they communicate well with one another, I think manufacturers should focus on combinations of devices, allowing us users to mix and match according to our whim, however quirky. That way we might get what we want and not lose the features we like every time we upgrade.

Now keep still while I take a picture of you in case you call.

Once again, half right and half wrong. It turns out people did like to have everything in one device; it's just that we've got a lot more choice about what those things are. Nowadays we demand a camera in our phone, but won't start thinking about having all our music in our phone until it can store a year's supply of it. So we're still carrying lots of separate devices around with us, but only because technology hasn't quite caught up with our fast-moving expectations. So smartphones were smart up until the point we asked them to live up to the hype, when it turned out that they weren't really smartphones as much as Smart Alec phones: They did some smart things, but they were punching above their weight since they lacked the processing power, the screen size and the overall wallop necessary to really do what they were trying to do. (Most Nokia phones since, in my view, suffer from this problem in that there are noticeable lags between command and function. It's a bit like asking a teenage son to clean his room and watching his painful, slow-motion rise from the bed.) But when PDAs started to acquire phone functions then we started to see smartphones with enough muscle to be able to handle what was being asked of them. And I was completely wrong about cameras – now every phone has one and everyone uses them – and as for combinations of devices, the less said about that the better. Even I succumbed to the charms of a Palm Treo and realized, in a July 2005 piece, that there was an art to loving your smartphone:

☞ **ditchling** (*n, East Sussex*) Someone who discards their gadget when a new model comes along.

I thought being a technology columnist had cured me of gadget love. After years of testing gadgets large and small, good and indifferent, functioning and unworkable, I thought I had weaned myself off the irrational but persistent belief that having a new gadget would somehow make life easier, make me feel more content and make me more attractive as a person. Sadly, I have just found out that I am just as sick as I ever was. It all started when my wife gave me a Treo 650 for my birthday recently.

Treos are nothing new. They're a so-called "smartphone" made by Palm, and I usually run a mile when someone calls something "smart." But I had played with its immediate forebear, the 600, and those with good memories might recall me recounting how I used it to write a column from a Javanese beach while checking my email and scheduling a massage. The unit was on loan from the company, however, so I knew I had to return it one day, meaning I had no great incentive to master its intricacies or customize it. To make gadgets like the Treo work, you've got to "own" them.

It's like this: Gadgets are great to play with. The malls of the world are full of office workers wandering around during their lunch hour hoping to stumble across some gadget that is fancy enough to hold their attention but not so outrageously overpriced or impractical as to attract the opprobrium of a spouse. We need gadgets in the same way we needed to bring along our favorite toy to every social function as kids, from the dinner table to kindergarten cocktails.

My theory about the way personal digital assistants, or PDAs, took off isn't so much to do with their ability to accept text via stylus but because they're only slightly bigger than a model car or action figure. There's no mistaking the similarity in the way (mainly) men line them up alongside the cutlery in restaurants in the same manner they would plonk down a favorite fire engine or police car on the table at mealtimes as kids. (Sometimes, if they think no one is looking, you can catch chief executives driving their handheld around the table making "vrrrmmm" noises.) The same is true for mobile phones. And now, smartphones. Such gadgets give

☞ **sturry** (*n, Kent*) The constant state of anxiety your boss has displayed since being issued a BlackBerry. *He's in a total sturry.*

us the same buzz. And, of course, after a while, the buzz wears off and we're left with a feeling of emptiness and a gnawing sense we just spent $600 on an overpriced toy firetruck.

It needn't be like this. Having my wife buy me a gadget – and the sense of guilt that I only got her an Aveda token and a measly six gigabyte iPod Mini for her birthday – has forced me to squeeze as much out my Treo as I possibly can. I'm determined that this won't be one gadget where the buzz will wear off. So, I'm pushing the Treo 650 as far as I can in the week since I've had it to see whether a) it's as smart as it claims to be, and b) a gadget can be more than a shiny new toy. It's early days, but this is what I've done, and the lessons I've learned.

First off, get some extra storage: I'd recommend buying a 512-megabyte expansion card that plugs into the top of the unit and suddenly boosts all the extra software and files you can bring along with you by a factor of 10. Also, get a Bluetooth headset, which makes receiving and making phone calls a lot easier. (After years of nightmare experiences matching Bluetooth gadgets I was pleasantly surprised that my Logitech earpiece dovetailed quite well with the Treo.) Lastly, get a keyboard – I use Palm's own Wireless Keyboard that isn't actually designed for the Treo, but works well enough, especially if you strap the phone into the cradle using a highly sophisticated device called a rubber band.

All this is still gadgetophilia, of course, but it sets you up for the next bit: turning the Treo into a serious multimedia device and organizational tool. The Treo comes with a good word processing and spreadsheet package, which is a good start. But there's more you can do. I've been playing with a to-do list organizer called Bonsai from Natara Software. In fact, calling it a to-do list doesn't do it justice: Used properly, it's a great way to organize more or less anything you're doing, both on the Treo (or any other Palm-powered device) and your Windows personal computer.

Then there are RSS, or Really Simple Syndication (p.251), feeds of information from blogs and other sources that have become hugely and

☞ **bramham cum oglethorpe** (*n, West Yorkshire*) The crowd that gathers around a booth at a tech show supposedly displaying some hot new gadget.

deservedly popular of late. I use something called QuickNews (www.standalone.com/palmos/quick_news/) to import a dozen or so of my favorite feeds to read on airplanes, in traffic, or anywhere I've got a minute or two to spare. You can update the feeds either via the phone's Internet connection or when you synchronize your Treo with your computer.

Related to this are podcasts: The Treo is a great place to listen to these MP3 files of radio-style broadcasts, especially if you have the extra storage card I mentioned above. Just load the files and fire up the built-in Real player. Finally, if you have a blog (a Web log, or online journal, p.239) of your own you want to update, you can either use the built-in email program to post updates to your blog (assuming your blogging host supports this option) or else download one of several blogging tools, such as HBlogger from www.normsoft.com, which specialize in doing this kind of job. Bottom line: You can manage your blog from your phone.

It needn't stop there. You can use the built-in camera as a barcode scanner, or hook up a Bluetooth GPS module and mapping software to see where you are in the world.

I'm not saying all this is new, or that it's easy. Some of it's fiddly and not worth the effort. But if you persevere you'll find, as I have, a new depth of gadget love that makes it slightly less likely you'll be ditching your latest toy for a new one in a few months' time. The lesson is actually a simple one: You get as much out of a gadget as you put into it (or attach to it).

☞ **white notley** (*n, Essex*) The tangle in iPod headphone cables.

wifi

WiFi is now so common that it's hard to believe that four years ago most folk hadn't heard of it. That didn't stop some readers pooh-poohing the article below, published in July 2002, arguing that I had just discovered something they'd been using for years. Perhaps I shouldn't have sounded quite so explorer-like in my discovery, but at the time WiFi connections outside the U.S. were as rare as homemade sambal *on restaurant tables.*

Embracing new technologies can be hard. My first Walkman, in 1981, earned me looks of undisguised bafflement on the London Underground, and my first mobile phone 15 years later was considered a highly amusing oddity in the newsroom where I worked. Back then hands-free sets looked ridiculous to people who now swear by them. Now, even my Neanderthal friend John now dabbles in the black arts of SMS text messages, something that would have had him thrown out of the Hairybacked Minstrel Pub a year ago. It's the price you pay for pushing the envelope – or at least giving it a good prod.

I'm here to trumpet another imminent change: WiFi, or wireless Internet. I've been risking arrest or worse to test the technology, mainly by trying not to get arrested for loitering as I wandered around hotel lobbies in Washington, flicking open my laptop and nosing around the potted palms trying to find a signal. The risks are high, but the reward is great: super-fast, cable-free Internet access.

WiFi, in case you haven't heard, is short for wireless fidelity and is a radio-frequency communication standard. In the past year or so it's taken off, particularly on the United States west coast, allowing any computer with a WiFi card to connect to a network. These include networks set up by well-meaning individuals providing a free public service, by universities avoiding expensive cabling, or by companies hoping either to make a buck by selling you a coffee while you surf, or through pay-as-you-go 'hot spots' to use between office and home.

This is one of those rare technologies that really make sense. It's not like 3G, or WAP, or Cornish pasty-flavored cappuccinos, where an idea is years away from being implemented or desperately looking for a market; WiFi more closely resembles SMS, the text-messaging service of GSM mobile phones, which has grown out of all proportion to the forecasts of its creators. For one thing, WiFi is relatively easy: Once you've got your card – expect to pay up to $100 for one – you're pretty much ready to go. The latest version of Microsoft Windows, XP, will tell you whether there's a wireless network where you're standing and should connect to it automatically. Then you open your browser, or email program, and you're off, usually at very respectable speeds.

Hence my perambulation through downtown Washington. More or less as soon as I'd plugged my credit-card-sized WiFi card into my laptop, the software was sniffing out networks. Of course, a lot of these are office networks which are not accessible to law-abiding folk, but within a block I was in the lobby of the Sheraton Four Points Hotel and on the Internet, courtesy of a service called Boingo (www.boingo.com) which bundles together such hot-spot access points and bills your usage accordingly. From then on I was hooked, scouring the capital for more connections.

I should stress it's not always plain sailing. My first two insert cards didn't work on Boingo. I replaced them with Lucent Technologies' Orinoco PCM card, which worked like a dream. Boingo's proprietary software works neatly, informing you of nearby networks and connecting

☞ **firle** (*n, East Sussex*) The antenna on a WiFi router.

seamlessly, though when I tried to connect in the lobby of the Wyndham Hotel City Center, nothing happened. The manager told me he had never heard of Boingo, or of a WiFi service operating in his lobby, and walked off to make some calls. I left confused.

Such minor qualms aside, WiFi is the future of connectivity. Soon most laptops and PCs will come bundled with wireless cards, and it'll only be a matter of time – a few months, in the case of places like South Korea, Japan and Hong Kong – before we can whip out a laptop and surf while drinking coffee, waiting for a flight or doing the laundry.

This may give next-generation mobile phone operators the heebie-jeebies. It needn't: WiFi gives users fast access in places where they can sit and work – cafés, lounges, parks – while data-ready mobile phones will give them short bursts of information and email in transit – in cars, trains, and while hiking up mountains.

And as WiFi providers begin to proliferate, users will be willing to pay a premium for reliable service in places where they need it. As Alan Reiter, president of U.S.-based consulting company Wireless Internet and Mobile Computing (www.wirelessinternet.com), puts it: "Suddenly we've got something that people are willing to pay for. I can't remember when we were last able to say that with a straight face." Hallelujah.

Actually, I'm not sure I got that right. Nowadays, at least in the U.S. and places like Taiwan, free WiFi is de rigeur. *And most computers now come with WiFi built in, which makes it a lot easier. Perhaps that's why it's taken off in the home. Here's how I saw it in August 2003:*

When I wrote about WiFi a year ago I was all breathless about this great new thing that lets you surf the Net without cables from your local Starbucks. Now nearly everyone's heard of it (including, I'm proud to say, my mother, although she still calls it "wiffy" – Mum, it rhymes with hi-fi). But has it really taken off in the way we expected?

One of the beauties of WiFi is that unusually for such tech stuff, it's a cinch. No really. I have a small cable network in my apartment (called a

LAN) which was no fun to set up, and no fun when it goes wrong. So the idea of mussing it all up by adding another element kept me out of the WiFi department much longer than was healthy. When I finally took the plunge, I begged the store owner to man his phone for the weekend in case I called for help. I needn't have worried. Plug the access point (about the size of a cigar box with a cute little antenna sticking out of the side) into the connection box, or hub that links your computers to the network, type a few commands into your browser and you're off.

This kind of simplicity is to be praised. Hooking things up is also relatively painless: Palm's Tungsten C, for example, has some excellent software aboard that automatically hunts out WiFi connections and sets them up for you. Even Windows XP is straightforward enough, although I struggled with its portable cousin, Pocket PC 2002. Apple, who basically invented the 802.11 standard which they call AirPort, worked like a dream when I tried WiFi out on one of their PowerBooks.

I'd recommend that anyone with a home network, even if it's just two computers sharing an Internet connection, immediately invest in a WiFi network. I don't know why, but there's something very liberating about checking your email on a Palm Tungsten when you're in the bath. But what about if you're out there in the real world? Is WiFi as easy?

Well, yes and no. There's certainly no shortage of WiFi hot spots – public places where you can hook up your gadget to a wireless network. But a recent visit to Singapore revealed some anomalies: While Changi Airport has long had useful, and free, WiFi spots, complete with the gadgetry necessary to get hooked up and some helpful assistance, hotels seem to remain in the Dark Ages. The business-oriented hotel I stayed at in the city center, while offering excellent cable Internet access from the room, was all nonplussed when I asked to try out the much-advertised lobby WiFi network. After much legwork I still ended up with no connection. The assistant manager confided in me that "not many people" requested the service, and suggested I use the Internet connection in the room which, he

☞ **ormesby** (*n, North Yorkshire*) The range of your WiFi network. *What kind of ormesby do you have on yours? I can get a signal in the rotunda.*

assured me, was better because it "used electricity."

Which perhaps gets us to the crunch. WiFi is crossing over from a nerds-only, early-adopter, we're-doing-this-for-the-greater-good approach to finding a way to be sustainable. While everyone from your corner café to McDonalds has been rolling out in-house WiFi networks – some for free, in the hope you'll stick around and buy more coffee, some as a paying service – not many will survive. For them to do so, they need to be properly supported – combining security, so someone can't snoop at what you're doing, as well as having someone around to make sure the connection is working. Which means that in one form or another they become a payable service, either directly (through subscription, or over-the-counter cash) or indirectly (the price of the WiFi is built into the coffee). Either WiFi remains a gimmick, or it's something folk can rely on, and base their decision on whether to dine, wash clothes, drink coffee or walk their dog at that particular establishment because they know the connection will be working.

In short, WiFi is a great thing. Eventually it will cover whole districts, as it does in San Jose, California, and whole airports and airplanes, as it threatens to do with a small American airline called Southeast. But for it to be anything more than a gimmick it must work, and someone's head should be on the block if it doesn't. Indeed, it's likely to end up being a service just like your mobile phone: You don't grumble too much if you can't get a signal in the Bering Strait, but when you can't use your mobile phone at the mall you're baying for blood. WiFi, one day, will be that reliable. In the meantime, sellers shouldn't expect the immediate rewards to be that high, and us users should expect some teething problems.

Now, please excuse me, I need to run a bath so I can check my email.

A few years and bathtimes later, and WiFi has largely replaced cable connections in the home and office. But bigger dreams have replaced simple WiFi, including something called WiMAX. I'm always skeptical of cute-sounding abbreviations, but thought I'd take a closer look while I was on trip to Singapore in April 2006:

You might be forgiven for considering WiMAX, which in theory allows computers to hook up to the Internet wirelessly over large distances, more of a question than a technological standard. As in: Why Max? Sure, we asked "WiFi?" and got quite a good answer: Connecting our computer to the Internet without wires in our home or office turned out to be quite useful. But WiMAX? Isn't WiFi enough for home-size wireless connections, and short-range wireless connectivity standard Bluetooth enough for connections between, say, mobile phone and earpiece? Why max out with another standard?

This is what I'm pondering as I sit in a car in an otherwise empty Singapore parking lot with two strangers, one of whom, a laptop on his lap, obsessively tweaks something on the dashboard that looks like a one-eared bunny, but which is in fact a WiMAX receiver. If the bunny is moved "just a fraction like this, we get a signal," says the fiddler, Low Chin Yong, managing director for Southeast Asia, Australia and New Zealand for Singapore wireless networking company QMax Communications Pte. Ltd. The bunny's light goes from red to green. I have just seen my first WiMAX signal. For a revolution, it looks kinda fragile. So what is WiMAX? The name is a clever marketing term for a standard called 802.16 which, like WiFi before it, was assigned by people with no sense of humor (in this case, the IEEE 802 LAN/MAN Standards Committee, the "premier transnational forum for wireless networking standardization," who I'm sure throw great parties). The problem is that, as with all technologies driven by hype, WiMAX – Worldwide Interoperability for Microwave Access – hit the early adopters too soon for it to be ready and, after the usual delays, hit us ordinary mortals after we'd already lost interest. My skepticism about it was fueled by a conversation a year or so ago with a self-confessed spammer, who cheerfully told me he was getting out of the junk email business and into the far more lucrative WiMAX one. "It's going to be huge, dude! The whole of Florida could be one big WiFi network!" Where spammers sniff, the smell of snake oil may not be far away.

☞ **brightwell-cum-sotwell** (*n, Oxfordshire*) The two flashing lights in your system tray indicating network activity on your computer.

Indeed, there's been a lot of hype about what one can expect from WiMAX. In a nutshell, the idea is simple enough: WiMAX really is just a more powerful form of WiFi, using transmitters and receivers to beam signals wirelessly over longer distances – a few kilometers, say. But in practice, who, apart from retired spammers, is getting excited about this?

Well, not everyone. Most of the players have scaled back the claims that arose when WiMAX first started doing the rounds a few years back. Nowadays you're less likely to hear talk of countrywide coverage and more likely to hear about helping cellular operators handle those parts of their traffic that currently use expensive cabling, or about replacing leased-line Internet and telephone connections to small offices.

A more enticing vision is of using WiMAX to bring fast and decently priced connections – Internet and telephone – to developing countries that previously didn't have many of either. If there's no prior investment in cables, tunnels and the like, there's nothing to stop a communications company starting from scratch. Take Cambodia, for example, where San Francisco-based SOMA Networks Inc. has helped install a WiMAX network. "With wireless it's really happening," says Greg Caltabiano, company president. "If you don't have anything (by way of telecommunications infrastructure), in this day and age you can go for the latest...because it's actually cheaper."

But it could also work in places where networks already exist. For many people, the beauty of WiFi isn't just that you can sit in the garden, kitchen or bathroom with your laptop, but that you don't have to first install yards of cabling around the house. WiMAX, the argument goes, extends this cablelessness out of the house and down the street. But WiMAX will have to be as fast as existing services, such as DSL and cable, to compete.

This is what my two new Singapore friends are betting on. Their attempt to show me WiMAX in action now sees the three of us on the roof of a nondescript mall in suburban Singapore, staring at what look like public loudspeakers, but are actually base stations. These pump out the signals

☞ **oving** (*v, Buckinghamshire*) Wandering around the office/house/neighborhood trying to test your ormesby (p.41).

to the one-eared bunny in what is Singapore's first commercial WiMAX deployment, a joint venture between network operator QALA Singapore Pte. Ltd. and the island state's most famous techie company, Creative Technology Ltd. Given that Singapore is one of the best-connected places on earth, Why Max, I asked my new friends? The answer, it seems, is a mix of mastering the technology before anyone else does, and an attempt to entice those Singaporeans still accessing the Internet through their telephone line. Says QALA director Alex Tan, the other of my parking lot and roof companions: "Hopefully we're the white knight coming to their rescue."

Indeed, this might be the future of WiMAX. It offers, for the first time, the promise of a cheap, accessible and fast Internet connection to those who didn't have one before. Beyond that, there's a new standard, ratified last December and already being deployed as WiBro in South Korea, which not only improves the quality of WiMAX connections – less twiddling of the bunny ears to get a signal – but also, in theory, makes it mobile. It could mean not only extending WiFi beyond the range of Starbucks or your front lawn; it could also mean replacing expensive cellular phones and accessing high-quality music and TV on a train, boat or speeding car.

That's further down the track. For now the WiMAX promise is an Internet connection for people beyond the reach of cable and DSL. Huge? It will be for them, dude.

voip

One of the most exciting technologies of the past few years has been Voice over Internet Protocol, or VoIP, a fancy way to say "talking to people via your computer". Exciting because its benefits – free or very cheap phone calls – have spurred otherwise skeptical users into installing software, plugging in headsets and registering online, things I could never persuade them to do under other circumstances. I must confess, though, I was a bit late to the party myself, as I explained in this December 2004 piece:

I've been a bit nervous about using the Internet to talk to people because of past experience. Every time I've tried it, the other guy sounds like a frog trapped in a well. Or, as a colleague of my friend Jim so eloquently puts it, "men sound like chipmunks. Women sound like men. And it's not very reliable." All true. Or at least it used to be. But has using the Internet to talk to people, known in the trade as voice over Internet protocol, or VoIP, gotten any better? And if it has, what does that mean for us?

To answer these questions I hooked up a few weeks ago in Boston with Andy Abramson, a wine lover, public relations consultant, broadcaster and a follower of VoIP. At the annual Voice Over the Net conference Andy kindly walked me around the exhibits, talked me through the lingo, introduced me to a few folks and steered me away from others. The bottom line: VoIP is already big for lots of people, and it's going to get bigger.

VoIP, simply, is using the Internet (or a network that uses the same standards or protocols), rather than the telephone, to talk to someone. The difference? Telephone networks use something called circuit switching – where a continuous electrical circuit is set up between the two people talking. VoIP uses something called packet switching – where what one person says is broken down in real time into little packets of data, and then passed to the other guy.

The advantages of VoIP? It's cheaper, because once the IP infrastructure is installed – whether it's the Internet, or an office network – there's no extra equipment needed, such as expensive switching stations and whatnot.

None of this is particularly new, so why have things suddenly gotten better? Andy points to several reasons. Firstly, a lot of people now use broadband, instead of dialing through their telephone, to access the Internet. This means faster connections, which make all the packet-making and packet-sending bit faster and easier. Secondly, a lot of people (at least in North America) have ditched their landline telephones for mobile phones. This means people are ready for other ways to make phone calls. Thirdly, and crucially, computers are better. The chips that make a computer work can handle doing much more stuff, and since talking over the Internet requires a computer to convert what we're saying into a digital form that the Internet can understand, the better the chip, the less like a chipmunk you or your interlocutor are going to sound.

On top of that, the headsets and handsets that people use with their computers are getting better. "You're starting to get better sound going in and out," says Andy, adding, after a pause: "And telephone is all about sound."

If all this is news to you, I suggest you try it out through a service such as Skype. Skype allows you to chat with other registered Skype users for nothing, and it also lets you call people on their normal telephone. For this latter option, of course, you have to pay, but it's a lot cheaper than an ordinary call.

I tried calling my itinerant friend Jim, who always seems to be in Liberia, on his mobile phone. We yakked for nearly 20 minutes about very

☞ **blawith and subberthwaite** (*n, Cumbria*) Two people who dominate any kind of online discussion, whether it's a Skypecast call or an IM session.

little for $4. (Users pay for airtime to particular countries via credit card, although Skype says it is working on alternative ways to buy airtime for those places where payment can't be made by credit card.)

It sounded even better when I used a special $100 Internet telephone handset from Clarisys, called the i750, which plugs into your USB port and looks like a normal handset except for the fact that the cable seems to come out of the top rather than the bottom. Neal Shact, the man behind the handset, asked me not to ask why that is because apparently everyone asks that, so I didn't. The point is, that a USB phone converts what you say to digital before it goes anywhere, improving the sound quality. (You could also use a PC headset so long as it has a microphone. Plantronics do a great range of USB headsets. For basic chats, there's even the option of using the computer's built-in microphone and speakers.)

For sure, VoIP has some way to go before it really works for us, but besides the obvious savings it will bring those of us paupered by hefty phone bills, it may also allow us to make more use of our phones, configuring them into being a bit smarter about what they do before they bug us with a ring. Until then, I've suddenly started talking to people on the other side of the world – some of them complete strangers – just because VoIP means I can. And very few people think I sound like a chipmunk.

Skype is, at the time of writing, big and getting bigger. And it wasn't just about making phone calls to Mom. Something more was afoot, as I wrote in a piece in May 2005:

Is something we're not sure how to pronounce changing the way we communicate with each other?

The thing is called Skype, and for the few of you who haven't heard of it, it's a way to make free – or very cheap – voice calls over the Internet. If both of you have the free Skype software installed on your computer (and a headset with microphone, and a decent Internet connection) you can talk to each other for free. If you want to call an ordinary telephone, or be reached via Skype from one, you need to buy some credits from

Skype. But it's peanuts compared to most calls, which may explain why up to 3 million people are using Skype at any given moment. Oh, and it's pronounced not Skypy, Skypé or Skypee, but Skype, to rhyme with hype. But is it? (Hype, I mean.)

I don't think so. True, the marketing has been pretty savvy, building on a buzz that stretches back to its launch in late 2003. Skype has made co-branding deals, partnerships and affiliate agreements (this week it officially launched a program rewarding websites that carry Skype sign-up ads). And there are those who point to its closed standards and peer-to-peer mechanism as sinister and backward. All this may be true. But I think it misses the point. Skype has already changed the landscape. And this revolution has only just begun.

Consider this: Skype – at least the free bit – doesn't care where you are, where the person you're calling is or how long you talk for. Want to improve your language skills? Find someone on Skype who is happy to chat. Far from your family and can afford to call only once a week for 10 minutes? Now you can yak indefinitely. Got nothing much to say, but just feel lonely? Leave Skype open and listen to your loved ones bumping around in the background many thousands of kilometers away.

For business, it's just as useful: Lose your mobile phone on a business trip? Find a WiFi spot and use your 'SkypeIn' number, which lets people without Skype call you. Want to stay in touch with clients, colleagues or consultants? Skype lets you see whether they're online, send them a text message, and, if required, switch to voice.

That's just the obvious stuff. Niklas Zennström, co-founder and CEO of Luxembourg-based Skype Technologies, says he's blown away by some of the ways people have used his tool, from real-time music collaboration to radio.

And this is just the beginning. Skype lets other people into enough of its software for them to make add-on programs, and dozens of them have

☞ **slad** (*n, Gloucestershire*) someone who uses call waiting to put you in your place. *He called me, then put me on hold and then said he'd call me back. Clearly he found someone more important to talk to. The slad.*

already emerged, from software that records phone conversations and voice mail to programs that turn your Bluetooth mobile phone into a handset for taking and making Skype calls away from your computer.

Indeed, Skype isn't just about sitting at your PC or laptop making phone calls. Already, many users make Skype phone calls from their mobile phones, their WiFi-connected handheld organizers or good old-fashioned plug-in-the-wall telephones. Says Mr. Zennström: "We're pushing to break out of the PC." So, expect gadgets to have the option of switching to the much cheaper Skype option if there's a connection that supports it.

Skype is also working on video conferencing, which for those of us who have tried that kind of thing before, doesn't sound all that exciting. Skype is being coy, but some early testers say it's good. Mr. Zennström says to expect something this year.

All good stuff, and attracting a huge following. The number of new users is growing by 150,000 every day. That's a lot of people.

And a great market. "Everybody's missing the point," says Bill Campbell, who contributes to an independent blog covering Skype issues called Skype Journal (www.skypejournal.com). "I don't think you want to look at the application per se, but that Skype is building a network that people would die for." Mr. Campbell isn't alone. California-based Charles Carleton, who runs an online Skype community called Jyve (www.jyve.com), sees the Skype world as a chance for professionals to sell their services online. Users would contact them over Skype and Jyve would handle the transfer of fees.

Mr. Carleton has big plans, having registered some 800 Skype-related domain names, which illustrates the range of his vision. However, folks anxious to sign up for skypebikinimodeling.com, skype-flirting.com and skypedatingcoach.com may be disappointed – he says registering the more salacious domains was a "defensive move" to deter rivals. Expect to be able to talk to a lawyer, medical professional, real estate agent, financial consultant and, perhaps, a dating advisor, anywhere, anytime.

☞ **baulking** (*v, Oxfordshire*) Method of speech adopted when using Skype and other VoIP tools over a poor connection. *It was great to talk to Mum for the first time in ten years but we ended up baulking at each other for twenty minutes, the connection was so bad.*

Skype isn't perfect: It's still somewhat cautious and wooden about what it says publicly. Its payment system is still choppy. Its critics do have a point that we might all be ditching our hated monopolistic long distance carriers for another monopolistic carrier, albeit a cheaper one.

But a lot of things about this smell right. Skype is ridiculously easy to install and use. Most of my friends have figured out it's worth installing, and these are people who have never downloaded anything in their life. And it really is global: while the U.S. is the single largest country in terms of users, nearly half of total Skype users are based in Europe, and more than a quarter of them in Asia. After the U.S., the second largest Skype adopter is Taiwan, followed by Poland, Brazil and China. This is not your traditional geographical adoption pattern.

Some suggest that Skype may not be up to the challenge with so many users and so many big enemies. But that's not the point. Users are out buying headsets and installing software. They suddenly realize the Internet isn't just about email, browsing and illegally downloading music. It's also about talking to people across the street or across the globe – and soon it will be about seeing them too. Whether it's Skype that continues to carry this new banner or some other upstart we haven't heard of yet, in the words of Andy Abramson, "The genie is out of the bottle."

If you haven't done so already, I suggest you scoot off to buy a headset ($5) and download Skype ($0) and grab yourself some of that genie.

Skype, since bought by online auctioneers eBay, isn't the only player in town although it's still the biggest. "Skype has not got the whole playing field," says Louis-Philip Lenir, who runs a website about Skype called SummitCircle (www.summitcircle.com). Its challengers range from telephone companies angry about the loss of business, to other companies hoping to offer something better. Skype's Mr. Zennström claims that some telephone companies and Internet service providers have tried to either block Skype or reduce its quality, but he declined to go into specifics.

☞ **trull** (*n, Somerset*) Someone who ambushes you on instant messenger or Skype as soon as you come online.

Meanwhile, there are other providers of VoIP, most of them relatively small players. One cool one to try: the switchboard (www.theswitchboard.ca), which uses Java to do pretty much what Skype does, but without actually installing any software. But, as Mr. Lenir pointed out, the biggest challenge to Skype is probably going to come from the big Internet names like Microsoft, AOL and Yahoo!, who already have huge networks of users of their instant messaging services. Since I wrote that piece they've all improved their voice services and begun offering limited calls between their instant messaging services and ordinary phone numbers. Microsoft and Yahoo! promise to allow calls between their services too. But Skype is still pretty well entrenched, so if you haven't started yet, that's the place to go.

usb drives

I've always loved USB key drives – those little matchstick-lengthed flash drives you can put on a key ring – and being so small and handy they are the traveler's best friend. For some reason I only seem to have started writing about them in June 2003, with this piece called "How to Steal CIA Secrets: It's as easy as USB":

I got some flak last time I was rude about how implausible technology is in Hollywood movies, even supposedly authentic fare such as *Minority Report*, *The Bourne Identity* and *Mary Poppins*. One comment was "grab a beer and chill out, dude, it's only a movie," though that doesn't count because it was from my mother.

But I can't help venting my spleen, if that's what you do with spleen, after watching *The Recruit* with Al Pacino and Colin Farrell. It's a thriller revolving around a recruit (no, really) to the Central Intelligence Agency trying to smuggle a top secret program out of CIA headquarters at Langley. There are some neat gadgets in there, such as biodegradable bugs and a program that hijacks nearby television screens. But the premise is that it's well nigh impossible to steal data from the CIA since none of its computers have floppy drives, printers or (presumably, if we're going to get finicky) infrared ports or Bluetooth dongles. In short, how do you transfer data if you can't download it? I wanted to shout out suggestions but my friends, alerted by previous visits to the cinema, had gagged me beforehand.

Anyway, not a bad idea and not a bad movie. Except (skip the rest of this paragraph if you intend to watch the movie) someone succeeds in downloading the top secret program by plugging a USB drive into a USB socket on a CIA computer (USB – Universal Serial Bus – is a commonly used port that allows users to connect gadgets to their computer). She then hides the said drive – about the size of a lighter – in her aluminium coffee mug. I mean, duh! I can't believe they have USB sockets in Langley and that the X-ray machine confuses a gadget for coffee dregs. Tsk.

Anyway, it made me realize that Hollywood really, really needs my help in making their scripts believable. So here are some ideas for future movies, all involving existing USB gadgets:

- Our hero penetrates high-security installation, wanders nonchalantly up to floppy-less computer, and accesses USB port (inexplicably left on computer despite it being responsible for massive security breach as revealed in *The Recruit*). Uncoils USB cable from watch strap, plugs into USB port, downloads data into USB watch from German company LAKS (www.laks.com).

- Our hero wanders nonchalantly up to floppy-less computer, plugs USB drive into USB port (amazingly still there despite aforementioned movie and pioneering column from tech writer), and accesses own email via newly released PocoMail PE (www.pocomailpe.com). Okay, this doesn't sound that wild, but it's a great plot twist if you're using someone else's computer and they don't have an email program you need, or, in the case of our hero, you don't want to leave any trace of yourself (say at an Internet café or a public library).

- Our hero has made off with the data on a USB drive. But he's caught by the bad guys. Being avid readers of this column, they know what to look for and quickly locate the USB drive. But our hero's drive is a bit different: Made by Singapore's Trek 2000 International (www.thumbdrive.com), his ThumbDrive Touch has a silver pad that requires the user's thumbprint before data can be accessed. Unfortunately for our hero, but great for a plot twist, the baddies simply cut off his thumb and plonk it on the biometric pad.

- Armed with a $100 MP306 USB drive from Azio Technologies (www. azio-tech.com), our hero fails to access the CIA computer because his nemesis has installed a SecuriKey Computer Protection System, Personal Edition (Griffin Technology at www.securikey.com/personal/). This looks just like a USB drive but in fact works like a key: If it's not plugged into the computer, then the computer locks up. Confounded, our hero sucks his remaining thumb and admires the silver metal mini-briefcase that the SecuriKey dongle comes in. Resigned, our hero reaches for his Azio USB drive, dons earphones, kicks back and listens to MP3 music files stored on the drive. Fiddling with the built-in equalizer for improved playback quality, he hears footsteps and quickly switches the USB drive to recorder mode to eavesdrop on two CIA officers passing by, griping about their canteen lunch.

Okay, so not all these plots will win prizes. But one thing I'm willing to bet my DVD collection on: USB drives will replace floppy drives, those flat disks of old, as PC manufacturers add USB ports to new models and remove external disk drives. Prices will drop further, meaning gadgets smaller than lighters will carry gigabytes of data for peanuts. Already you can buy a 1-gigabyte model for $300: Expect to pay half that in a year or less. They will be so cheap people will give them away: Visitors to a recent launch in Britain of Microsoft's Windows Server 2003 were given freebie press bags with 32-megabyte USB drives inside.

In future, folk will carry around all their programs and data aboard one dongle and run it from any computer they come across, effectively personalizing the computer for however long they're sitting at it, but

☞ **ord** (*n, Highland*) A collection of USB cables you cannot match with any device. *The cable is probably somewhere in the ord but I haven't got the energy to look for it.*

without leaving any trace. Wait for the futuristic movie where everyone's life is stored on a USB drive and every computer in the world is for public consumption. Interested? Call my agent.

Unsurprisingly, I didn't get any calls. But I did feel a warning note was worth striking about flash – the technology inside these devices – after a couple of bad experiences. Here's what I wrote in May 2004:

I left you last week in the capable hands of Ethel Girdle, the fictitious octogenarian who took her accusations of built-in obsolescence to the technology giants. One of her beefs was about so-called flash drives – small devices that store data, for example as memory cards for MP3 players, digital cameras or personal digital assistants, or as ultra-portable drives which can plug directly into your computer's USB port. These little things have taken off in a big way. Nowadays it's hard to find a gadget that doesn't use them – even your mobile phone uses the same technology – or a keychain that doesn't have a thumb drive dangling off it. But Ethel (OK, it's really me) found that two out of five memory cards in my possession have given up the ghost within a year or so of buying them. So what gives? Are flash drives the future or, if you'll excuse the phrase, just a flash in the pan?

Flash memory has been around for a while. Invented in the 1980s, it really started coming into its own in the past few years. Its trick is twofold: Unlike a hard drive, or even a floppy drive, it has no moving parts, so it is more rugged, uses less power and doesn't make noise. It's also nonvolatile, which doesn't mean it's less likely to fly off the handle than other, more moody, memory devices, but that it will retain data after it's been switched off. (Compare this to the RAM memory in your computer, which will not retain anything unless the computer is powered up.) Both of these tricks mean flash memory also works much faster than other devices – you can save stuff to it or delete stuff from it much more quickly than, say, your PC hard drive, or a CD-ROM, or a floppy drive.

Another plus: This memory is small. The different kinds of flash memory you're likely to see are not much bigger than a postage stamp;

others are in the form of USB drives, sometimes called thumb drives or keyring drives, which do exactly the same thing but in a different casing. As they get more popular, they get cheaper and their capacity gets bigger: Semico Research reckons there will be about 60 million USB drives sold this year with an average capacity of about 200 megabytes. In four years they expect more than three times that many drives with an average capacity of 1.7 gigabytes, or eight times what they are now.

But what you may not be told is that there are downsides. First, devices need power to read these memory chips, and so will suck juice out of your camera, MP3 player or whatever if you leave them in. Secondly, they all have bits of metal that connect them to the gadget, called contacts, and these contacts are vulnerable to dirt, wetness and other normal things you might encounter in your day. Also, memory cards do not like being removed in the middle of writing, so make sure your gadget, whether it's a camera or your computer, has finished writing to or downloading from the memory card before you whisk it out. Doing this before it's finished risks corrupting the data, says Terry O'Kelly, technical communications manager for Memorex.

And the rugged claim? Not exactly a myth, but Gordon Ung, senior editor at *Maximum PC* magazine, did some tests of some USB drives, which included putting them in a washing machine, a dryer and dropping them two storeys. Conclusion? "The washing machine didn't actually kill them. Nor did the dryer. But the drop tests did most of them in," he recalls. You needn't even be that brutal: Ung warns against leaving the cards, or keys, on your car dashboard. Also: "It's OK to put them in your pocket but you should be aware that static shock can jumble the files on a card or wipe out a section of the card that contains information on where the files are stored." Which kind of begs the question: Where else would you put a keyring but in your pocket?

☞ **adlestrop** (*n, Gloucestershire*) Strap attached to USB drive which breaks on first use. *Day one the adlestrop fell off so I just stuck the drive in my pocket. Which is probably why I lost it on day two.*

That raises another question: How long do these things really last? Ten years seems to be the rule; but that's clearly not true in the case of my two devices. If things do go wrong, all is not necessarily lost. If you really want to try to save valuable data from the card, you could try using third-party software, such as RescuePRO from Florida-based LC Technology International (www.lc-tech.com). But be warned: Recovery isn't guaranteed, and it didn't work in either of my cases. David Bernard, managing director of New York-based consulting firm DB Marketing Technologies puts it bluntly: "There is little chance that you can retrieve information from a damaged flash card."

If you're not too bothered about the data but want to just save the card, try reformatting it. Remember, you'll lose anything you have on the card if you do this. You're in with a good chance that you can at least re-use the card. Unless, that is, you happen to be me, in which case both memory devices refuse to play ball.

My experience has driven home to me some important lessons. One is that the experts don't really know very much. They'll say this flash-memory thing is wonderful, and they'll say the devices last longer than you need to worry about. It's true that they are very, very useful, but it's not true that they last so long. That brings me to the second lesson: Keep the drives and cards in a safe place, and keep the contacts clear of dirt, electrical charges or the tops of tall buildings. Finally: Don't rely on flash-memory sticks to store really important stuff without a back-up (p.194). If you're taking pictures with a digital camera, upload those pictures to your computer as soon as you can. If you're using a thumb drive to move data around, don't assume that just because it's in your pocket you – or it – are safe. Keep a back-up somewhere.

The bottom line is: Flash memory is great, but it can go in a flash, too.

The following year I went back to the cinema for inspiration about USB drives, which had started to become the all-singing, all-dancing devices I thought they might be a few years earlier. Here's what I wrote in March 2005:

If you need to know whether a new technology is here to stay, go no further than your local cinema. For all its glitz and glamour, Hollywood is a pretty conservative place, so if you see some gadget onscreen it's likely that it already has taken root elsewhere. Take, for example, that well-explored plot device, the Diskette With All the Bad Guy's Secrets on It. In many thrillers, the villain keeps one in a drawer, or chases the good guy to get hold of one, or was unwittingly using one as a coaster. (No one seemed to have thought of making a copy, and everyone seems to have access to a computer that can instantaneously read the disk, irrespective of format or whether it had been dunked in water, blood and acid.)

But in the past few years I've noticed a shift. Hollywood's plot-device data has moved from diskette to small sticks called, variously, key drives, thumb drives or USB drives. These devices, like diskettes, store data, but they do it on a small rewritable memory chip, called flash. In the 2003 thriller, *The Recruit*, starring Al Pacino and Colin Farrell, for example, one character smuggles data out of the CIA on a USB drive. More recently in *Collateral*, Tom Cruise jabs one into the taxicab's guidance display to find out who else he has to rub out after his tablet personal computer containing his hit list is crushed under a truck. It's official: USB drives have arrived.

That's a good thing because they've actually been around a while. At least one company, Singapore's Trek 2000 International Ltd., has been making them for five years. Indeed, they're easier to find nowadays than the floppy disks they have pretty much replaced (I tried to buy a floppy in several computer stores recently and was laughed out of each shop). They come in all shapes and sizes, from small-capacity freebies given away at expos to sticks no bigger than your little finger that can hold up to four gigabytes of data (that's about 3,000 floppies' worth). Some double as MP3 players, others as WiFi hubs. Some can also take photographs; some are shaped like rubber duckies. And, crucially, prices have fallen as capacities have risen. Five years ago you would have paid nearly $2 per megabyte of storage. Nowadays it's about 10 cents. Expect it to drop further this year.

☞ **blunham** (*n, Bedfordshire*) The noise your computer makes when you plug in a USB device.

These drives are versatile too: Plug them into a Mac, a computer running Microsoft Windows XP or even a Linux machine and they're ready to go. Use them to keep backup copies of valuable files, move stuff between one computer and another, or store favorite music files or photos.

But why stop there? USB drives are fast (well, faster than a floppy drive). They're reliable. And most important, the key drive is the first bit of cheap(ish) hardware we can actually put in our pocket while leaving room for other stuff, like handkerchiefs, real keys and coins. People are beginning to figure out that instead of just storing files on them, why not whole programs? As long as there is a computer within reach, you use your own email program, your own browser, even your own word-processing program, along with all your customized settings and files. Think of it as PC Piggybacking for the Peripatetic.

That isn't all. Programs that run from the USB drive needn't leave any footprints on the host computer, so when you leave the building, your data goes with you. This is especially useful for public computers at Internet cafés, in libraries, at work or at your Mom's house.

In fact, all this isn't that new an idea. Some programs designed specifically to run off a USB drive have been around for a while: Email program PocoMail PE, from Poco Systems Inc. (www.pocosystems.com), is now into version number three and works like a dream. Adventurous people have developed versions of the popular open source browser Firefox, its sister email program Thunderbird, as well as whole operating systems, to run off USB drives (for an attempt at a full list, see loosewireblog.com).

Iomega Inc. has been peddling its own Active Disk technology, which allows users to run dozens of compatible programs from one of its external disks (including their very cute Micro Mini drives, which look like a well-groomed thumbnail.) Iomega says more than 10,000 Active Disk-compatible programs are being downloaded every month. Active Disk, however, is a proprietary technology, which means that while the programs that use it will run on Iomega disks, they won't run on other brands.

This is partly why late last year two companies, M-Systems Flash Disk Pioneers Ltd. and SanDisk Corp., joined together to promote what they hope will be an industry standard, called U3, to make it easier to develop applications that run on all USB drives. "We think we're taking it to the next level," says Nathan Gold, director of the U3 Developer Forum. So far several companies have signed up, including the instant messaging pioneer, ICQ Inc. This could be the start of something.

Downsides? Well, a lot of system administrators won't be delighted to have people plugging their drives into the corporate network. (While it's possible to block key drives from office computers, it isn't that easy at the moment, although Microsoft Corp. plans to change that in future versions of Windows.) And while most computers nowadays come with USB ports, they aren't always accessible, especially if the computer itself is locked up in a cupboard.

I've had a few USB drives die on me, so don't believe anyone who says these things are indestructible and last forever. And finally, if the computer you're using is infected with a virus, assume the stuff on your USB drive will become infected too.

I'm not suggesting that this is the future of computing, although it might be. I do like the idea of free, connected computers all over the place waiting for us to plug in our own customized USB drives. But even if that doesn't happen, a drive containing all your favorite programs and data is a great back up for when your laptop runs out of juice, you can't find a WiFi connection, or you're away from your own computer and no one else seems to have installed the mind-mapping program you need. It's a great comfort to know you, just like Tom Cruise, have one more option in your pocket.

A year later I was back with more good news. Either that or I got the impression that the kind of people using these things remained somewhat limited. Here's what I wrote in June 2006:

I'm here to sell you (again) on the idea of the world's most portable computer.

Loyal readers of this column (hi, Mom!) may recall I wrote 15 months ago about USB drives ("Keeping your drive," March 11, 2005), those little cigarette-lighter size sticks that have pretty much replaced the floppy disk as a way to move data between computers. My point then was that companies were beginning to explore the idea that they could not only store data, but software programs too, so that you and I could carry everything we need around in our pockets. Just plug the drive into a personal computer or laptop and all your software and data magically pop up on the screen like mushrooms after rain.

Well, not exactly mushrooms. Installing the software and then getting it to run wasn't as straightforward as it could be. So I'm here to give you three pieces of good news: Things have gotten easier, software-wise. Secondly, you don't need to use a USB drive if you don't want to. You could just as easily use your iPod or other MP3 player – or your smartphone. The third bit of good news is that as memory prices fall, these devices are costing less and less. I bought a 1-gigabyte drive for less than $25 the other day; a year ago it was four times that.

Why bother? Well, see if one of these scenarios rings a bell: You're going away for the weekend, you don't want to take your laptop, but you know you might be able to snatch an hour or two on your father-in-law's computer; however, you also know he hasn't got any decent software on it. Or: You don't like taking your laptop into the office, but you really like the English-Sundanese dictionary on it and it would be great to access it. Or: You have six or seven computers and don't want to have dozens of different versions of documents sitting around on each computer. Or: You just don't want to install programs on your office computer, and may not want to leave any trace of your activities on a computer if it's not your own.

You get the picture. USB drives give us the potential to feel we're parting company with our work while giving us the peace of mind that comes from knowing we've got not just the important documents we might need but the programs to run them. Until recently, the problem was that the last part had lots of caveats riding with it. Not just that it was difficult, but that when companies came out with software that made installing and running programs easier, they did so with limitations. U3, for example, is a consortium of companies that has developed software for users to load and

☞ **berden** (*n, Essex*) The noise your computer makes when you unplug a USB device.

install programs. Fine, but the drives need to be U3-compatible, and of course those U3-ready drives tend to be a bit pricier, to take into account the licensing fee the manufacturer has to pay. They are also limited to about 100 Windows programs, which may sound a lot until you realize there are thousands and thousands of Windows programs out there, some of which actually make your life easier.

But there's another way, and I like it. The software is called Ceedo (www.ceedo.com; a free trial version is available), and it allows you to do what U3 does – install programs on a USB drive. But the program, built by Israel-based Ceedo Technologies Ltd., goes further than that. Firstly, it will work on any drive; just download the software, install it and you're off. Secondly, while it offers you a list of compatible programs to install, it's a badly kept secret that most other programs will work on it, too.

Thirdly – and this is where I think it gets cool – Ceedo isn't restricted to keychain drives. I tried it on my iPod and, using third-party software, my Treo's external memory card, and it worked fine. You could also run it off a USB hard drive or a PDA. So long as the device can be read as an external drive, your pocket computer can be more or less any shape. Finally, the software itself is a treat. Once it's installed on the external drive, and the drive is plugged into a PC, Ceedo will run as a sort of Windows Start Menu look-alike. (Ceedo marketing manager Ofir Shahar told me off for calling it that; he says it's a Compact Bar and Easy Access Menu.)

Downsides? Both U3 and Ceedo only work as program launchers on Windows. And don't expect programs running off an external drive to be as fast as if they were running off the PC itself.

Lastly, get into the habit of carrying your USB drive around with you. Ones that attach to a key ring are not always sturdy; the clasp on mine broke after two days. Better to go for something like Imation Corp.'s models, which build the drive into chunky clips that attach to your bag, or into rubber wristbands.

A rubberized wristband. Now there's a computer.

traveling

In my early days in Asia I carried no gadgets because there were no gadgets to carry. A camera, maybe, but one of those old ones that didn't require batteries. A Walkman perhaps. Sometimes, if I was feeling particularly nerdy, I'd carry a small electronic typewriter. All of it squashed into a backpack. Call it The Pre-Laptop Bag Days. Back then, in the mid 1980s, there was very little chance of establishing contact with the head office except by expensive phone call or telex chats, removing the need to check in regularly, or to carry modem gear around with us.

Things have gotten more complicated since: Indeed, in the past five years travel has been changed by the arrival of high-speed telephone connections, or ubiquitous WiFi. But not everywhere. I still use my AT&T dialup account from time to time. Here's a September 2004 dispatch from South Korea, a place that has more and faster broadband Internet connections than anywhere else in the world:

On a recent visit to Seoul, supposedly the most wired (and wireless) place on Earth, I couldn't help noticing the irony that my hotel room in Seoul had no broadband, no WiFi, not even a telephone socket within lassoing distance of the desk. In fact, no power outlets that were accessible without a commando-style foray behind the refrigerator. The default setting on the

☞ **affetside** (*n, Greater Manchester*) The disappointment you have when the empty seat beside you is filled.

television appeared to be pornography, the walls were made of paper-maché and while my dinner "burger" (I use the term loosely) didn't come with French fries, the morning omelette did. Somehow I had landed in another dimension that just happened to be in the center of cutting-edge Korea. This got me thinking: a) Why does my boss hate me so much he puts me up in this 1960s throwback of a hotel? And b) Why are hotels so patchy in their grasp of the needs of the early 21st-century traveler?

First, I realized things aren't so bad that they can't be worse. A lot of my friends travel to offbeat places, and report back that star ratings don't necessarily mean hi-tech. Matt reports that "most of the places I stay, I'm happy if they've got electricity and no bed bugs or rats." And also languid hostility to surfers: "Most receptionists won't even let me borrow their phone line to quickly check email, as their phones 'cannot be used for the Internet'," he reports. Jim, who goes places other people avoid, is more specific: "If the Le President Meridien in Luanda, Angola, can put on free plug-and-play Internet access in one of the most Internet-challenged countries I've been to in recent years, why is there no Internet connection at Brussels' airport?"

Clearly the world's an uneven place, and it pays to carry extra cables, plugs and adaptors. It's also worth emailing in advance to find out what facilities a hotel has. Mine had a business center, for example, but it was only open on weekdays at 9 a.m.-5 p.m. Look for hotels that offer a bare minimum of extra, and accessible, power and telephone sockets, and, if possible, in-house broadband access and a decent desk and chair. The M Hotel in Singapore has particularly good workspaces. Some hotels now offer WiFi in the room. And, as lawyer and software developer Buzz Bruggeman points out, small WiFi access points like Apple's Airport Express can turn even a broadband connection into WiFi.

Indeed, hotels should already be offering this kind of service. If they're not, you have a right to grumble. Inflight Internet, too, is beginning to take off: Ultimately, all airlines, airports and hotels will have free WiFi access. But for now you'll need to sniff around to see what's available. To help, get the WiFi Seeker, a $30 keychain device that locates wireless hot spots.

And don't tell anyone I told you, but you don't always have to be in a business-class lounge to use their connection: As Buzz tells me: "I have learned that, while traveling, all I have to do is find where the Delta Crow Room or United Red Carpet Lounges are and sit across from them and tap into the WiFi." Good luck, and don't forget to ask for fries.

Mind you, just because a hotel says it has WiFi doesn't mean your troubles are over, as I found during a trip in March 2006 to Singapore, king of efficiency and communications:

As a seasoned traveler and technology columnist, I'm wise to various tricks, so when the guy at the hotel reception told me as I checked in, on a trip to Singapore, that I could set up my Internet connection from my room, I didn't believe him. Too many times I've traipsed up to my room, bone-weary from budget air travel, to find that "connecting from my room" means that the computer may be in the room, and the connection may be in the room, but the process whereby a guest actually registers and logs on is back down in the lobby, in the hotel reception guy's drawer. The problem is simple: For a lot of hotels, particularly those not in the high-price, luxury bracket, there is still a perception that an Internet connection is, for most guests, an afterthought. It isn't: Nearly everyone needs Internet these days, and they need it to be as accessible as their TV set, kettle or shampoo.

In my recent experience at several Asian hotels, the procedure, if that's the right word, for getting on the Internet goes something like this: Crawl up to reception, laden down with baggage. Confirm that hotel has Internet connections in the rooms. Receive assurances that this is so. Relax a little. Check in. Have nagging suspicion. Confirm that by "an Internet connection," hotel means "an Internet connection" and not "a telephone line," an Internet-through-your-television-set service or dial-up access at the hotel's ambitiously-named Business Center. Receive assurances that

☞ **stisted** (*adj, Essex*) The expression people adopt in an elevator when no one knows anyone else.

Internet connection is in the room – my room – and can be conveniently and effortlessly arranged from my laptop. Take assurances with pinch of salt and, gradually, ascertain that Internet time must be bought in advance, like lottery tickets, from the very guy I'm talking to.

I've learned all this the hard way. In Hong Kong, for example, I was seduced by the attractions of a self-styled "cyber-hotel," which promised free Internet access in every room. In fact, this involved obtaining printouts the size of cash register receipts, featuring enigmatic codes like "7Yd54dHj" that had to be typed into my computer before a connection was established. These codes also had to be renewed every day, involving a trip to the lobby and a lot of signing of forms. The Internet access may be free, but the saga of getting it isn't without heavy cost to shoe leather, patience and inner calm. Especially when, in one Manila hotel, the ticket-issuing printer broke, meaning, I was told, that there was no more Internet access available. It was bit like telling me that breakfast wasn't being served because they'd run out of napkins.

One hotel in Singapore seems to have improved on this Indiana Jones-style approach to Internet access by ditching the cash register receipt in favor of writing down each code by hand. But making the whole process slightly more complex is the fact that the hotel only allows you to sign up for chunks of access time lasting 15 minutes, one hour or 24 hours. Forget it if you're the kind of person who might work in three- or four-hour bursts – like, say, most normal people. Being unceremoniously disconnected halfway through a chat, email exchange or surf isn't fun – and it's made worse by the fact that the system isn't clever enough to reconnect you with the logon page if your time expires and you want to sign up for another session. Don't even think about saving minutes by logging off and on again: The parcels of time are continuous, meaning that your one hour of Internet time can only be used in a single big chunk.

This isn't the case in all hotels, but I've come across it often enough – and we're talking mostly about four-star places here, not flophouses – that I've found myself starting to get into the Zen of it all. First off, I tried to blow the reception guy's mind by asking for dozens of single parcels of 15-

minute and one-hour sessions, quickly reducing him to a blubbering wreck as he wrote down reams of 10-digit codes. (I was still ahead financially, thanks to the hotel's somewhat odd pricing structure that didn't seem to reward buying the longer periods.)

Then I found that not having a permanent Internet connection actually made me more productive: Arranging my Internet sessions into 15-minute and one-hour packets made me more focused about what I was doing. So my day started falling into a pattern, dictated by the scribbled codes by my laptop keyboard: Up in the morning for a 15-minute email download while I ran my bath, plus another 15 minutes of uploading responses. Out shopping – sorry, working – and then back for an hour's research and writing, out again for another foray and then perhaps a three-hour online blitz. Another trick I learned is to use a plug-in for my Firefox browser called Countdown Clock (free from www.mercille.org/extensions/CountdownClock.php) that lets you set a timer so you know when your connection is about to end. It's better to know – trust me.

I readily acknowledge that not everyone has the same sort of problems as I seem to with hotel Internet access. But smaller, less costly hotels should stop treating their Internet-seeking guests like they're trying to buy cocaine or enriched uranium or something. It's time to realize that the first thing most of us do after checking in is to check our emails. Make both easy for us and we'll stay again.

Travel, of course, isn't just about getting connected. It's about getting comfortable, something technology can also help with. Here's an October 2004 review of a gadget I still love:

If you've ever had problems sleeping on a flight, let me introduce you to Bob Duncan, a formerly sleep-deprived Alaskan Airlines pilot and reluctant inventor.

After six years of commuting between home in Washington state and his flying base at Anchorage, he was arriving home too exhausted to play with the kids or sustain a conversation with his wife. Things were tense at

It's just a flat pile of rubber with an air-hole, about the size of a bolster or large cushion, and the temptation is to blow into it until it's inflated like a Lilo or inflatable bed. Don't. The idea is to let it fill in the gaps between you and the seat, so that you can lie straight, head to toe.

So, a few firm breaths are enough to get you going. You then put the Sleeper behind you in the seat so the top is about level with the headrest. You should sit as far forward on the seat as you can without falling off or damaging yourself. Then strap yourself in tightly over the hips. Then, keeping your behind in position, just allow your upper body to lie back.

That's when you start to figure out you're on to something: Instead of the usual gap between your back and the seat, a soft cushion of air welcomes you. Your head rests on a special spot at the top of the Sleeper device (usefully marked "place your head here"). You may need to adjust it a little by yanking the Sleeper up a little higher, or blowing a bit more air into it so you get good support for your back. That's pretty much it. Now you should look like a very straight person resting atop a blue cushion of air, your legs out in front of you, appearing to all the world like a piece of timber.

I wish I could report back that I was in seventh heaven for the whole flight. However, this approach requires ditching a few old habits. One is moving around as you sleep: With the Sleeper it's best to get comfortable and then stay there. I had some problems with this, and found myself several times during the night sleeping sideways, alternately wrestling the Sleeper and cuddling it, depending on the kind of dream I was having. None of this buttressed my credibility as a sane fellow passenger.

Getting the optimal air content into the Sleeper was also something I didn't really want to play with. Blowing air into something in the middle of a night flight is going to get you funny looks. Then there's letting air out: The device makes a quiet, but noticeable, whistling sound which could unnerve anyone of a nervous disposition.

Eventually, when I did get the hang of things, I hit a limitation that Bob Duncan can't really help with: my height. I'm a little over six feet tall, and so in a correct prone position as suggested in the manual, my toes dangle over the luggage bar of the seat in front and inevitably perform what Bob tells me is officially termed "footsie" with the passenger in front of me. This caused both of us some surprise: Me because when I went to sleep there was no one sitting in front of me, and her because she had probably already seen enough inflating and deflating to want some distance between us.

All this would require some practice, but there's no question that once you're used to it, the Sleeper is an excellent solution to the problem of trying to sleep in economy-class travel. And if people give you weird looks, ask them how much sleep *they* got.

There's another part of travel where technology can help: packing. Here's a piece from June 2005:

The world is full of people carrying all sorts of different stuff around with them. If you don't believe me, look at the hundreds of photographs people have submitted to Flickr.com, the online photo gallery, of the contents of their bag (www.flickr.com/photos/tags/whatsinyourbag). No two bags are the same, and neither are their contents. And that is as good a starting point as any for exploring the question: What, technology-wise, should you take with you on a trip, and how should you take it?

Bag. This is important. Without it you'd just be stuffing everything in your pockets and dropping it everywhere. Actually, more important than the bag is the strap. I learned that lesson in 1990 when I used to ride to work in Bangkok on the back of a motorbike taxi, which would weave through the mostly static traffic on my behalf, shaving at least an hour off my commute (and most of the hairs on the inner part of my legs).

One day we were perched in pole position on a main intersection, engines revving across six lanes of traffic, my trusty Compaq LTE/286 laptop nestling in a trendy new bag across my shoulder. When the lights went green, we surged ahead of the pack, bouncing over the uneven

☞ **ingst** (*n, South Gloucestershire*) The feeling of loneliness you get as a telecommuter being free from office politics and watercooler backchannel chat.

surface in a cloud of fumes. As we passed over a particularly impressive bump, I felt the computer bag strap rise above my shoulder – but not come down again. That is because it had broken, and the bag, with my Compaq inside, was bouncing around on the road behind me. Without a thought for myself, the speed the bike was going, or the traffic bearing down on me, I leapt off and, waving like a lunatic, ran back.

I wasn't run over. I picked up the bag, not daring to look inside, the traffic roaring by in a symphony of horns. In the office I emptied the bag on to my desk. Amazingly, the laptop was intact. One corner was black, and badly dented, but it booted up fine and my sobs of anguish turned to sobs of joy. Bottom line: Don't buy expensive stuff unless you are willing to splash out on a decent bag.

Some makes to check out: Eagle Creek (after a few years in the computer bag wilderness, they are back); Mountainsmith (I'm still using the one I bought nearly a year ago); for the hip and bike-oriented, check out the Crumpler; for the fashion-conscious, try WaterField Designs, which aren't only great to look at (and, like Crumplers, don't look like computer bags) but are voluminous. For the more sober look, take a look at Briggs & Riley or RoadWired, both of which have impressed Phil Baker, a San Diego-based inventor and consultant who travels frequently to China and Taiwan.

Of course, it's what you put in your bag that is going to make or break your trip (and your back). Weight is an issue. I started carrying around a laptop in 1988, a charming Olivetti M15 that weighed 5.7 kilograms. Nowadays laptops weigh much less – the IBM ThinkPad I'm writing this on weighs 2.25 kg – but this doesn't necessarily make our load lighter. We just tend to carry more things. A look at the Flickr pictures confirms this.

The trick, in my view, is to replace what you can with something smaller that does the task better. And then, where possible, find something that does two tasks, removing the need to carry two devices. A simple example: a USB drive that doubles as an MP3 player. It may not look as snazzy as your iPod, but it'll play music and store your files. Indeed, if it's a short trip, you might consider the USB drive as an alternative to bringing your laptop with you, or else use your PDA or smartphone in conjunction with an external keyboard. The new palmOne LifeDrive, with its four gigabytes of storage, could fill this gap quite nicely.

Another alternative: bulkier phones that can, at a pinch, replace a laptop. Indonesian economist Kahlil Rowter has returned to his Nokia 9500 Communicator after experimenting with smaller, slicker gadgets that, in his view, lacked the 9500's long battery life, a decent keyboard, and built-in faxing. An added advantage, he says is that Nokia is ubiquitous, meaning "I can borrow chargers if I forget to bring one."

Indeed, power adapters and chargers are always a headache. Some pack extra batteries, and that makes sense if you know you are going to be away from power points for any length of time. But you can cut corners by using something like Targus' universal power adapter, which can simultaneously run or recharge PDAs, phones and laptops. You could also save space and duplication by getting some retractable USB cables for connecting external drives or synchronizing (and recharging) phones and PDAs. Sydney Low of Australian email service AlienCamel swears by a good old-fashioned extension board: "My favorite accessory is a power board with six sockets, then I only need to carry one adapter for the local power socket."

There are some things people will take even if they aren't vital. A lot of the people I chatted with carry around a mobile WiFi router, a cigarette-packet-size device that plugs into any hotel Internet socket and turns it into a wireless WiFi network. Uses? For Singaporean technologist and road warrior James Seng it is an escape – "it's great when you are in a hotel and you can do your stuff on your bed instead of on the horrible chair they give you" – whereas for me it's more about sharing the Internet connection with others in the room. Other devices worth the extra load? A WiFi finder, which lets you check out the presence and strength of a WiFi signal without having to get out and boot up your laptop. And I love my Logitech cordless optical mouse and my Sennheiser headset.

Communication. Think about how you're going to stay in touch with the world, your spouse and the boss before you pack. Nowadays there are

☞ **lumley thicks** (*n, County Durham*) The feeling that crashes in on you when you wake up in a hotel and don't know which country you're in.

myriad ways of doing it, but it pays to figure out a couple of good options ahead of time. WiFi is growing, but don't depend on it. I've often found myself in airports lending Ethernet cables (the wires you need to hook up to an Internet connection if there's no WiFi) to people who haven't brought one. (Get a retractable one: They take up less space). And being prepared means you can make connections in the most unlikely places.

Dina Mehta, an Indian researcher who runs a popular blog, was last month wandering the hinterland of Uttar Pradesh when she came across a mud-and-straw village that lacked electricity and a working landline. After chatting with some of the villagers and taking photos of a new well, Ms. Mehta says, "I got into my taxi and blogged right from there" of her visit – using a fast mobile phone connection and her laptop.

How to pack all this gear? Some swear by carrying everything on the plane. I never go on trips that are short enough (or the places hot and informal enough) to travel so lightly, so I pack quite a bit of the gadgetry in the hold. Eagle Creek again comes to the rescue, with some small padded cubes that have kept accessories safe, but you have to be careful. External drives and anything with moving parts should probably come with you, but if you have to put them in checked luggage, be sure they are well protected.

Lastly, security. This mightn't seem very sensible advice, but try not to be too attached to your computer; chances are it will get stolen. Don't believe me? Laptops get filched from cars, lobbies, rooms, hands, desks all the time (mine was stolen from my office desk while I was on my lunch break). Folks will tell you about using secure locks, but the sad truth is that most won't deter thieves. As one guy showed recently on a video circulating around the Internet, one quite common lock can be broken with a toilet roll, some duct tape and a pen. This doesn't mean all locks are useless, it just means you have to assume they are.

Bottom line: Encrypt. "The laptop is never valuable. The data is," says

☞ **acton turville** (*n, South Gloucestershire*) The feeling when you realize that all the other passengers have left with their luggage, you've seen the same three cases do five laps on the carousel, and that there's no chance in hell that yours have arrived.

Tom Raftery, a technology and Internet consultant in Cork, Ireland. So, encrypt your data on the hard drive using a strong password – a combination of uppercase letters and lowercase letters with numbers (p.336). Back up your data onto an external drive before a trip. Mr. Raftery recommends practicing this a few times so you don't panic as the plane is about to leave.

Indeed, practicing packing for a trip isn't a bad idea. Make a list of what you need, and what you can leave behind. See whether it will fit snugly, and whether you might be carrying too much. Then, when you're ready, check the straps.

In the end, travel and technology are a personal thing. Some folks like to carry a lot of stuff; some don't. Bring what you can't bear to be without and ignore the strange looks if that means bringing an inflatable igloo with you.

☞ **acton pigott** (*n, Shropshire*) The person next to you who turns up at the carousel after you and gets all their luggage before any of yours has arrived.

contacts

Getting connected is not just about hooking up to communication networks. It's about getting connected to other people. That's what the Internet is all about. But this involves organizing personal information – something I've wanted to do, like paragliding, but never gotten beyond buying all the right gear and admiring myself in the mirror. I've tried a lot of different approaches (I'm talking about organizing personal information now) and I must confess I never like software that orders me to insert first, second and third names in separate fields, and each line of the address in a separate box. It's all a bit too much like Boy Scouts camp for me. Besides, personal information rarely fits into these neat categories, especially the details of the kind of weirdoes I know. The same is true of events: Why should I have to limit myself to categories of event, or how long an event lasts, or whether it's in a restaurant or meeting room? How would I fit my secret cake-eating binges into such narrow formatting straitjackets? I know it is supposed to make it easier to transfer to our phones or to other programs but that never really worked for me either: Sometimes the fields would duplicate themselves, or the names would appear in the wrong field, or, weirdly, telephone numbers would lose a digit or two at the end so you'd be calling a number that no one would ever answer, at least in our lifetime. Here's how I saw the problem back in January 2001:

The latest Holy Grail of Internet start-ups: online contact management software. And, like all Holy Grails, there's a lot of trudging around trying to remember why you're trudging around.

Briefly put, we're talking programs which allow you, the harried executive, to juggle names, addresses and phone numbers whether you're working from your desktop PC, your laptop, your Palm-like device or an Internet café in Nowheresville. It's a nice concept: easy access to your address book (and other data) with or without gadgets, and a way to back up important stuff if a gadget dies on you. What's more, some offer the possibility of merging all that information with other crucial tasks, such as automatically sending your boss roses on her wedding anniversary, if that's the kind of person you are and she is.

Of course, there's a catch. Well, several, actually. One is that this sort of data is sensitive and most people will think twice before uploading it to some website, whatever the promises of privacy and security. Another catch is whether you entirely trust the company in question when it says it won't ever, ever access the data itself or, gasp, sell it to some sleazy marketing company that bombards you and all your business contacts with offers of a free leg wax.

But to me, the biggest catch is this: Does all this actually help? Too many of these kinds of programs seem to be technology searching for an idea.

All services assume you have a contact list somewhere on your computer, that you have a Palm or something similar where you also store contacts, and an Internet connection. Contact Networks, for example, is a free program to replace your Microsoft Outlook or Palm address book. You can back up all that data to an Internet site – meaning you can then access it from any computer that's running the Contact Networks software. What's more, it offers the future prospect of dovetailing all that data with your mobile phone and other gadgets.

But what may make Contact Networks appealing to some (or make others run) are the interactive possibilities. If I choose, I can make some of my details available to others, meaning that when I, say, get promoted, my snazzy new title is automatically added to the address books of other

☞ **aldwincle** (*n, Northamptonshire*) A name in your address book whom you cannot for the life of you remember anything about.

Contact Networks users. Other more revealing information can also be conveyed: photos, conversation topics, gift ideas will allow users, Contact Networks promises, to "see what really makes people tick." My question is this: what kinds of people are going to store potential conversation topics online, and are they the kind of people you want in your address book?

I don't want to sound too negative about Contact Networks. It's still in beta, meaning you've got to expect the unexpected, but I found it a viable alternative to Outlook's address book or the software that comes with the Palm, even when it decided to duplicate all my data during one synchronization session. And it's free.

In the meantime, this particular Holy Grail – finding a good way to hold all your contacts in one place and see them all seamlessly synchronize with each other – still feels a long way off. More promising, I reckon, is the idea that contact software will get better at extracting people's contact details from emails, websites, namecards and other sources. The vCard standard, for example, is making some headway: the latest version of Palm's desktop software, for one, effortlessly reads vCard data into its address book. Meanwhile, my money is on an ingenious and unsung piece of software called Syncplicity, available from Cognitive Root, which will magically extract names, positions, address and other contact data from any text and pass it on to your Palm Pilot. OK, so it's $10, but it works well, and it genuinely saves time.

My conclusion: Maybe the Holy Grail isn't a cumbersome start-up, but a simple idea that works.

Well, Syncplicity didn't survive, but I think both they and Contact were actually onto something. They just might have been a bit ahead of their time. I was wrong about people wanting to store their data online; as the PDA evolved into the smartphone, it started to make more sense to store or back up your data there. But while we got better at organizing our contacts in programs like Microsoft Outlook, we were still having problems exchanging personal information with each other, as I found in April 2005 when I wandered around a Hong Kong trade show:

Why do we still use business cards? This occurred to me the other day as I traipsed around a technology-related trade show in Hong Kong. It was vast, and my supply of name cards was small, and as nearly every stall holder I glanced at proffered one and demanded one in exchange, I soon ran out. Stall holders then asked me to write down my details in their ledgers. But because my handwriting is awful, I haven't heard back from any of them.

The next day, still name-card-less, I tried a different way. Firing up my Palm PDA I activated its business card function. This allows you, at the press of a button, to "beam," via infrared, your personal details to anyone with a similar device. When challenged, I offered to beam, only to be greeted with suspicion. This at an expo sporting devices from dehumidifying shoe stretchers to radio-frequency identification Bluetooth pens. Clearly business cards are a tenacious technology. But why?

Well, part of the answer is that, at least in Asia, business cards aren't just about exchanging telephone numbers. They have a pedigree stretching, according to some accounts, back to 13th-century China. High society in 18th- and 19th-century Europe made them a cornerstone of complex social interactions and, the books of Jane Austen and her contemporaries are dotted with references to calling cards, as they were then called. The etiquette hasn't been lost. In places such as Japan and South Korea, it is polite to use both hands to give and receive, although elsewhere you can generally get away with one. It is the ritual that goes some way to explaining why we're still doing this: You want to show you are someone by proffering your card, and you want someone to acknowledge your presence (and rank, if you have one) by receiving it.

But that's only part of the story. After all, it isn't just the social interaction but also the exchange of data that makes a business card important. These guys at the Hong Kong expo don't want my business card just so we can mutually acknowledge each other's existence but because they want to send me stuff. And I want to know when their shoe stretcher or inflatable

☞ **bawburgh** (*n, Norfolk*) A friend who always seems to be on line but who you never want to talk to. *I wanted to share news of my promotion but all I could find at that hour were a couple of bawburghs.*

DVD player is available. So hasn't anything better come along, in this age of Google, smartphones and WiFi, that makes finding, sharing and transmitting personal information easier and more productive?

Well, the short answer is no. The longer answer is, sort of. Back in the 1990s there was something called a vCard, which was a standard format that would allow you to exchange your personal details digitally via email or on a website. Actually the vCard is still around: If someone had agreed to accept my beam at the trade show, they would have been receiving a vCard. Similarly, some people still attach their vCards to email messages that can be automatically saved into Microsoft Outlook or other programs. But this hasn't really lived up to its promise. First off, email attachments aren't popular because that is how many viruses get inside your computer. Second, software such as Outlook hasn't been kind to the vCard, allowing users to only import them one at a time, making it impractical for moving clumps of addresses around your computer. Lastly, a vCard created in one program may not always work when you move it to another program.

So has anything better come along? Some people think so. One initiative, called Friend Of A Friend, or FOAF, allows users to save their personal data in a similar way to the vCard, but using a more modern standard. Another option is i-name, a sort of permanent personal Web page that you can direct people to who want your contact details.

Neither of these has quite caught on, perhaps because their benefits aren't easily explained. Other more commercial efforts revolve around sharing and updating your contact details from a central source online: Services such as Plaxo (www.plaxo.com) do this, while others such as LinkedIn (www.linkedin.com) focus as much on building new contacts as keeping an accessible record of your own. All tackle a corner of the problem, but don't really solve the big one: finding a way of exchanging personal details with others that is simple, protected from scamsters and spammers, and not beholden to any one company's proprietary standards.

So what's the answer? I admit there's something to business cards. They're portable. They're a tangible record of your interaction (which you can annotate, although don't do that in front of your Asian hosts; business cards are to be digested and admired, not scrawled on). You can design them to reflect your personality (check out VistaPrint.com), or, if you're daring, Hugh MacLeod's blogcards (gapingvoid.streetcards.com) can put your details on one side and one of his trenchant cartoons on the other.

But cards are best used in conjunction with other tricks. For example, you may want to try PenPower's WorldCard Office card scanner (www.penpower.net), which is about the size of a small mobile phone and does a better job than its predecessors of scanning business cards into your computer and subsequently saving them into Outlook or whatever contact program you use. Another tip: It's a good idea to include in emails those contact details you want to share. Lastly, to harvest these signatures from other people's emails try Anagram (www.getanagram.com), which tries to assign these details to their correct fields in your contact manager.

It would be great if all these tweaks weren't necessary. It would be great if vCards, or something like them, moved around as easily as their cardboard cousins. Maybe then we could work on a social etiquette for exchanging them via Bluetooth or something, while politely inspecting the other person's wallet full of family snaps. Until then I've got a new batch of business cards, printed on the back with, "Next time, beam me."

It's not just about sharing personal details. How about sharing events? Here's how I saw the problem in May 2005:

A few weeks back, I wrote about the trials and tribulations of replacing business cards with something that better suits our new digital lifestyles. But that problem pales into insignificance when we start trying to digitally share our calendars. Why is swapping schedules, appointments and to-do lists still so hard? Weren't we supposed to be beaming these kind of things to each other's hand held device, or synchronizing a group/family/congregation Web page calendar with our home and office computer? In short, weren't missed appointments supposed to be a thing of the past?

I'm sure my company's no different, but there's no such thing as an electronic group schedule in the office. If there's a meeting everyone should attend, the details are emailed around to all staff (except me, for some reason). We then usually a) print out the memo and stick it on our computer, b) forget all about it and hope a colleague reminds us or c) copy the text into our calendar software using a program like Anagram (www.getanagram.com). I usually find out there's a meeting going on because the office suddenly seems quiet.

And as for beaming appointments to one another from our smartphones or other handheld devices: do you know anyone who does that? Or do you know anyone who saves an appointment from Microsoft Outlook and attaches it to an email to send to others? Or does their bit to keep a shared online schedule up to date? The Internet is full of online calendars started with the best of intentions, all of them so outdated that other civilizations monitoring us via our online world might conclude humans either have really, really short life spans or that we just don't have very much going on.

So what should we be doing? Well, in a perfect world my boss would send around a calendar file as she would a round-robin email, which would automatically update my Microsoft Outlook and alert me to the fact I've got an important meeting on Thursday afternoon, not the goofing off I had scheduled. Some may argue this is already possible, via proprietary solutions offered by big software guns like Microsoft. But how about if I then wanted to tell my family about the appointment and juggle the schedule in our family calendar? Not so easy, because the standards may well be different. The same applies if I then needed to juggle my doctor's appointment as a result of the new office meeting; chances are I'll have to pick up the phone rather than just shuffle my appointment around on the doctor's online calendar.

This is not rocket science, but it's also not as easy it sounds. Dave Thewlis works for an industry organization called the Calendaring and Scheduling Consortium (www.calconnect.org), which is trying to sort out some of these issues. He explains that setting up a standard for calendar-sharing isn't quite as easy as agreeing on a standard for emails, for example. It's not that folk didn't work on this: There is a standard called iCalendar, which Mac users are very familiar with, but Mr. Thewlis says that it's only half finished. "The net result is that nobody has implemented all of iCalendar, and some bits have been done differently or interpreted differently by different vendors," he says. Bottom line: One iCalendar file won't always move happily from one program to another, which is why your doctor isn't confirming your appointment via email with an iCal file attached.

This hasn't stopped people from trying. In the late 1990s a raft of startups offered ways to store and juggle events online, but for one reason or another few of those worked out. That's not stopping a new generation of startups from trying again: Check out AirSet (www.airset.com), Trumba (www.trumba.com) and Planzo (www.planzo.com), all of which offer variations of online calendars, reminders via text message or email and synchronization of calendars on your desktop computer, handheld or laptop. All of them have their merits, but they all rely on a couple of things that may prove as hazardous to the makers' profits now as they were a few years back: People are lousy at keeping their calendars updated enough to make using them a habit, and second, any service that doesn't seamlessly work with another service isn't popular. If I use Trumba, in other words, can I still synchronize all my stuff with my brother who uses Planzo? Without standards, Mr. Thewlis argues, these startups "are, I think, treading water."

I agree with Mr. Thewlis (who stressed he was offering his own opinion, not those of his employer, a motley collection of software companies and universities). I'm not going to invest all that time uploading my stuff to some company's server and get my family, friends and masseuse to do so if I know it's going be either only compatible with their software or really fiddly to move to someone else's service later.

Someone with a more realistic approach is Brian Dear, who has set up an online event calendar called EVDB.com, which allows users to add, find or stay updated with events anywhere in the world. He has no illusions about the futility of locking customers into one service: "We don't expect we're going to write the One App(lication) That Rules Them All (and in the darkness binds them)," he says. Rather, Mr. Dear plans to offer bits of

☞ **bawdrip** (*n, Somerset*) When you go online wanting to chat and there's no one there you want to chat to.

software that plug in to other applications "and let people find one they prefer to use."

That's one solution. But I'm for simplicity. Do we really need complicated calendars with hundreds of different fields to fill in (I counted more than a dozen potential fields or options for a single appointment in Outlook)? The simple life is espoused by Jason Fried, founder of 37 Signals, a company that has recently launched an online scheduler and task manager called Backpack (www.backpackit.com). This – and its even simpler cousin, a to-do list called Ta-da List (www.tadalist.com) – are beautifully simple, elegant and intuitive tools that make an Outlook screen look like the software equivalent of a torture chamber. "Life is more random and chaotic than a calendar," says Mr. Fried. "Backpack is built for that chaos."

For now, I suspect that's the way to go.

Interestingly, this is a corner of the Net that has taken off in the past year. Google, Microsoft, AOL and Yahoo! have all launched their versions of online, sharable calendars and they've made them a lot easier to enter information. Eventually these calendars will develop standards – known as microformats – so you can move data between them, removing one of my bugbears about them. Secondly, calendars have become more public: Event websites like EVDB.com are dealing with a slightly different kind of scheduling issue than a family or office calendar. These sites cover public events, drawing traffic from people who want to go out and check out an art gallery, for example. But the challenges are similar: Making an attractive interface, getting the data to the people when they need it, and, most important for these kind of websites, putting enough information in there to make the site worth visiting.

All this is happening because more people are online, and online longer, and have faster connections. This in turn feeds other parts of connecting to other people, in particular something called presence. This is one area I do get genuinely excited about, because I think it takes us beyond merely using technology to speed things up and make us more efficient, but adds a layer of social and personal usefulness we didn't have before. Here's how I try to explain it in a piece from September 2005:

It wasn't a particularly unusual interaction, but a connection I made with a stranger halfway around the world that defines this week's topic better than a boring dictionary might. The topic is "presence," and for some it is the future of communications. Well, if not that, it might just mark an end to disruptive phone calls.

While trawling around Google and the online bookmarking website Del.icio.us (http://del.icio.us) for interesting people to talk to about the idea of presence, I stumbled upon Martin Geddes, a consultant and resident of Scotland's Edinburgh. His blog, Telepocalypse (www.telepocalypse.net), contains not only a wealth of observations on communications but also a little Skype icon (Skype, for those of you who aren't paying attention, is an Internet phone and online chatting service). The icon allowed me to not only add Mr. Geddes to my Skype contact list but also indicated that he was online, if not actually at his computer. Clicking on the icon, I sent him a brief Skype text message requesting an interview. Upon his return from a vigorous walk along the city's Royal Mile, Mr. Geddes replied to my note. We started the interview with a few online text messages – what is usually called instant messaging – before deciding to switch to voice. All this happened within about 10 minutes of my reading his blog and figuring he would have something interesting to say about presence.

He did. But the way we connected was also about presence. I knew how Mr. Geddes preferred to be reached, and I knew instantly that he was reachable. Not just that. He also had added a line to his Skype name indicating what town and what time zone he was in, so I knew I wouldn't be waking him up. Lastly, by leaving him a short text message, I didn't have to make an intrusive phone call. This was more convenient for him since he could answer it once he'd removed his boots and sou'wester. In short, I knew all I needed to know to ensure we hooked up with as little hassle as possible from the Skype icon on his blog. That's presence.

For those of you used to Skype, or to instant messaging, this doesn't

☞ **ainderby mires** (*n, North Yorkshire*) An email from someone you haven't heard from for years – and now you remember why you didn't keep the contact going. *I got an ainderby quernhow and now it's an ainderby mires. What should I do?*

sound very unusual. Anyone using an instant messaging program such as ICQ or MSN Messenger will know when their buddies are in a meeting, offline or available for a chat. Compare that with ordinary telephone communications, where you have no idea whether the person you want to reach is at his or her desk, at lunch, on holiday or deceased. Getting through to voice mail doesn't narrow it down because that might merely mean they're on the line, or have switched it over so they aren't disturbed. Phone tag is a boring sport but one still being played in offices all over the world.

Presence, theoretically, changes all this. In a world where the cost of the actual phone call is rapidly falling to nothing (my chat with Mr. Geddes via Skype didn't cost either of us a penny), some see presence as the best hope for the communications industry. As Douglas A. Galbi, by day a senior economist at the U.S. Federal Communications Commission, but by night something of a presence guru, puts it on his website www.galbithink.org: "To avoid disaster, the telecommunications industry needs to shift from providing telephony to providing means for making sense of presence."

How? Well, no one is quite sure at the moment. As Stuart Henshall, a consultant who runs a blog called SkypeJournal (www.skypejournal.com) says, "I think we're all struggling with this." Even the big players are wondering how this is going to develop, he says.

So perhaps it's better to first take a step back. Mr. Galbi traces the idea of presence to pre-biblical times, but perhaps his most important contribution is illustrating presence in everyday communications. "What makes a letter a joy, or voice from an object (a telephone headset) a comfort, rather than a horror, depends on the sense of another's presence, despite that person's physical absence," he writes. Anyone who has had a telephone call with someone where, for long pauses, neither speaks, will know what he is talking about: You can feel the other person's presence, whether they are speaking or silent.

Feeling another human being's presence is what, at heart, communication is all about, and yet technology has done an uneven job of helping us in this. Hearing a loved one breathing, or bustling about, at the other end of the phone is comforting, but consider a future where we can decide not only how and when people can reach us but also easily share with those people where we are – photos or videos of our environment, our clothing, the room we're in, the view we're enjoying, the website we're reading, the movie we're watching. More prosaically, imagine opening a document and seeing not only who else has worked on it but be able to see immediately where they are and whether they're available to discuss it. Imagine a corporate network that told you immediately who else was in the office, and where, through an easy-to-access Web page or desktop program. Skype's decision last week is a step in this direction – now, anyone can build Skype's presence feature into their software program or Web page to indicate their availability. In the words of Janus Friis, co-founder of Skype: "It's a very cool thing, even more important for telephony than for instant messaging."

Of course, there are privacy implications, too. And there are the usual caveats about some software companies not wanting to let their customers hook up with others. But these people will be swept aside. Google, a player to reckon with, recently moved into this space with its new chat and talk software, Google Talk, and with a commitment to hook up to other networks. I'm not sure it's going to happen as fast as we'd like, but I see a future where the concept of presence becomes so mainstream that we are able to connect with each other easily, more satisfyingly and less disruptively. One day a phone ringing at an empty desk will seem a quaint historical absurdity.

The lesson from all this? Sharing and updating contacts and other personal information is a great idea, but it's all aimed at pretty much the same thing: reaching people. Presence, more than fancy contact organizing software and web sites, really solves the problem. So next time you want to ring-fence your workday so you can control who can and can't interrupt, try instant messaging or Skype software, and let people know via a "presence" message when you are contactable. Trust me, it's the best productivity tool there is on offer.

☞ **ainderby quernhow** (*n, North Yorkshire*) An email from someone you haven't heard from for years (*see* **ainderby mires**). *Just got an ainderby quernhow from Johnson! Can you imagine!*

selling online

Selling online has changed a lot in the past few years. Now we can buy and sell more or less anything, with anyone, anywhere in the world. Without having to deal with spotty-faced staff who try to intimidate you with their alleged expertise. But what I find intriguing are the implications for buying and selling that such technologies offer. Like this piece I wriote in January 2005 called "Virtual Mall":

Here's my prediction: In the future we won't have possessions anymore, we'll have semiliquid assets.

Let me explain. Most of us have bought stuff from Amazon.com, the online bookseller, but have you ever sold stuff through them? If you're a customer, you might have noticed some odd messages on their website, along the lines of "(Your name here), make $151.31. Sell your past purchases at Amazon.com today." Follow the link and you'll see listed all the loot you've bought from Amazon, along with the price those goods are being sold for secondhand by other customers.

The service is called Marketplace and it's not a bad ruse for Amazon, which has the pleasure and profit of not just selling you stuff, but getting a commission when you decide to sell it again later. The company is quick to stress it's not pushing people to get stuck in a rapid buying/selling binge, however. Rakhi Parekh, Group Product Manager for Amazon.co.uk, says the service is just pointing out that people could be making cash out of past purchases they may no longer need: "Individuals may not think they've got an item to sell," she explains.

Indeed. It's part of a broader move that Amazon is aiming to be not just the biggest shop in the mall but the mall itself. Nowadays Amazon not only sells everything from books to babies' bibs, but acts as a store directory for products held by rival online stores; it not only sells DVDs but it rents them too; it not only sells new books but also lets anyone, ranging from you and me to big stores, sell stuff secondhand via its website.

Some analysts don't like all this because they think it's getting away from Amazon selling stuff. But that's because they don't really get it. Amazon is a brand that most people have heard of and many use and trust. That trust is now a key thing in an age of growing online credit-card fraud. By turning into a mall, Amazon can leverage this trust into being gatekeeper for all sorts of transactions, taking a percentage without having to open cavernous new warehouses.

This is the beauty of the Amazon Marketplace, a service that's open to sellers in Japan, North America and parts of Europe, as well as buyers across the world. While it's been around for a few years already, I get the impression it's only recently beginning to capture people's imagination (Amazon declined to offer specific figures on how such services are performing). As Ms. Parekh points out, you and I may not consider recent purchases as things we'd like to sell quickly. Nor would we necessarily think about selling unwanted presents we've received for Christmas to be things we'd sell online. But why not?

Of course, selling online is nothing new. There are hundreds of thousands of people, probably millions, out there selling stuff on eBay, its 25 local sites and eBay clones. But eBay is just a shop window: The company leaves the details of the transaction up to the buyer and seller, which can sometimes lead to misunderstanding and disaster.

Amazon, on the other hand, handles the payments too. So say I buy

☞ **bozeat** (*n, Northamptonshire*) Assistant in shop that doesn't know what they're talking about but insist on telling you anyway. *I wanted to buy a camera but the guy in the shop was a complete bozeat. I almost hit him.*

a secondhand book from Joe Blogger, Amazon will charge the credit card I have registered on my Amazon account and will credit Mr. Blogger's credit card after taking a cut. If there's any problem, Amazon will stop the transaction, inform both parties and investigate. Both parties can sleep better at night.

I've tried it and have to say it's pretty good. And painless: If you're selling, enter the ISBN (International Standard Book Number) that most books have nowadays (usually on the back cover), its details will pop up, along with a picture of the cover, just like an Amazon book page. Check the details, choose from a list of various conditions (such as New to Acceptable, enter any other details you care to) and then choose a price. Amazon helps you by listing what other people are charging for the same tome. Then you're done.

Should anyone be interested, you'll get an email from Amazon and you're obliged to dispatch within two days of getting the email. Amazon will include in the price a few dollars to cover postage, before taking its cut (which works out at about 20% of your take).

I listed a bunch of books I had sitting around the house, along with some from my father's collection. Within a day I was getting orders, and in less than a month sold about 15, making about $100 profit from stuff that was just taking up space. It was actually quite good fun, and took me back to the days when I worked in bookshops: The last was in London's King's Road, which quickly went bust despite (or perhaps because of) the patronage of some relatively famous actors and pop stars.

Amazon's Marketplace service got even easier when I tried out software called Readerware (www.readerware.com). It's a simple cataloguing system, which not only dovetails neatly with sites like Amazon but includes a free barcode scanner that allows you to swipe the ISBN from the book with one smooth swish. That saves a lot of typing.

Indeed, this kind of inventory software seems to be increasingly popular: California-based Socket Communications have this month launched the Socket OrganizeIT Suite (www.socketcom.com), which can scan and catalog DVD and CD information into PCs, Pocket PCs and

Palm devices. North Carolina-based Intelli Innovations also this month unveiled its IntelliScanner Express (www.intelliscanner.com), which can scan and inventorize everything from your wine collection to books.

Which brings me back to the liquid assets thing. To me these kind of products and services blur the line between what you have and what you want to sell. I've got shelves and boxes loaded with books, and up until Marketplace and services like it came along, I had no idea of whether any of them were valuable.

Now, with a swish of my barcode scanner, I can find out. And while I might not care whether I sell them, why not list them anyway? If someone wants to offer me more than I think it's worth to keep it, why not sell it? Forget just buying stuff online. Try selling. The Internet will turn us all into hustlers and traders, ready to sell our grandmother if the price is right.

If you want to sell your books online at Amazon, by the way, there's a catch: You need to have an invoice and credit card address in one of the countries where Amazon has a website (in Asia, that's Japan). If you live in Asia and don't have a Japan address, you may have to opt for a local auction site. Another option is the Advanced Book Exchange (www.abebooks.com). Koh Soo Wei, a student in Singapore, has used ABE to sell two to three of his unwanted books each month to customers as far afield as the U.S., Finland and Latvia. The downside: ABE's $25 monthly listing fee is "not quite feasible for a small-time seller like me," he says. But there's no doubt that people who wouldn't have considered this kind of transaction a few years ago are beginning to bite. I canvassed my customers to see a) whether I'd done OK and b) why they chose to buy secondhand from a complete stranger over the Internet, and was pleasantly surprised by the kind of people I was corresponding with: a 50-year old senior manager with an interest in crime; a 53-year old head of safety and environmental protection at a Scottish university; a Greek lecturer in communications policy; a former art student and "home alchemist"; and a 60-year old actor who records audio books. Most said they had only recently started buying secondhand books online, and seemed to have had mostly a positive experience. Perhaps they were being polite.

That's the consumer to consumer model. But what about the ordinary online shop? What surprised me was not so much what had changed in the transition between offline and online, but what hadn't. Here's how I saw it in December 2005:

Why does buying stuff online still look so similar to buying offline?

First, websites still use the whole browsing-shopping basket-checkout metaphor, an approach that even real world shops are trying to get away from. Then you have in-your-face promotions, top 10s, on-sale items, buy-two-get-one-free offers, which to me don't sound that different to your average supermarket gimmicks. Amazon has made some steps forward, such as pointing out that purchasers who bought a certain product have also bought other products, and allowing users to search for text inside books. But these are hardly huge leaps. After all, couldn't we look inside books in a bookstore, or ask an assistant for suggestions about similar books?

U.S. clothing retailer the Gap recently overhauled its online website. The changes amounted to being able to see more quickly what other colors were available of an item, or reducing the number of mouse clicks between selecting items and checking out.

While I guess this is all innovative, isn't this the wrong way around? Shouldn't retailers be thinking about using what the Internet offers to make buying online a completely different experience?

Like how? I hear you ask. Well, take a look at one online retailer, Etsy.com, a website where people can sell their handmade products. It's only been going since July but it's racked up almost 30,000 listings, and nearly $100,000 worth of items have been sold.

What is interesting about Etsy is the way Robert Kalin and his three co-founders have introduced some new ideas to the way shoppers can look for things. Don't know what you're looking for exactly, but know what

☞ **speen** (*n, Buckinghamshire*) Approach adopted by PR person trying to avoid overly spinning a client but which ends up sounding hopelessly fake and shallow. *Their pitch was so lame they started complimenting me on my choice of tie. It was total speen.*

color you're after? Move your mouse over a "Shop by Color" grid and see dozens of bubbles of color float under the cursor. Click on a color you like and small boxes will appear, each one a different product that matches your chosen color. Click on the box you like the look of and details of the product will pop up including price tag, the retailer in question, and a link where you can get more information. It isn't a revolution, but it's different – and an improvement on bricks and mortar. Ever tried saying to a shop assistant "I don't know exactly what I'm looking for, but please line up all the products that are this shade of turquoise?" Expect a blank look at best, a surly brushoff, or a "We're closing now. Bye!"

This innovation is well suited to the kind of things Etsy is selling (from a customized computer joystick shaped like Pac man to amigurumi dolls – Japanese crocheted dolls that are, according to Mr. Kalin, the site's biggest selling item). But it could just as easily apply to Amazon. I know: I worked in a bookstore for a few years and if you gave me a dollar for the number of times people came in looking for a book identified only by the color of its dust jacket, I wouldn't have had to work in bookshops quite as long as I did. Of course, it could be some time before someone comes up with the innovation that would help customers who know only that the author sported a hairpiece, or the cover had a picture of a cheese slicer on it, but I leave that to the guys at Amazon to figure out.

It isn't the only innovation Etsy has. You can browse via a sampler of random colors, each of which throws up a gallery of products – nice if you aren't quite sure what color you're looking for, or want to randomize your browsing. You also can search via a cute chronological spiral of recent purchases by other visitors, clicking on little boxes that recede into the distance, each box a product that has recently been bought.

Mr. Kalin walks me through an innovation the site is planning in coming weeks, where friends can browse the website together, collecting items they like the look of and showing them to each other as they browse. Useful if you're shopping for a present for a mutual friend, say, or you

☞ **langton herring** (*n, Dorset*) The long process to order or register for something that ends in failure. *I was taken on a total langton herring that took hours before it rejected my credit card.*

just hate shopping alone. You also can search via geographical location of sellers on a globe that, despite a bias toward North America, illustrates the site is catching on overseas, too.

Indeed, while some of these features may be more cute than functional, they highlight how staid the bigger online selling sites seem to have become in recent years. Nowadays, reckons Mr. Kalin, it is more about being responsive to users and experimenting with new ideas that draw shoppers, as well as helping sellers gain an edge. Take Lee Chu Ling of Singapore, for example, who is making $50 a day from selling her homemade stained-glass pendants online at Etsy. "Each time I thought of something they could improve on, they had already found a better solution that I would never have thought of," she says.

Of course, it isn't just Etsy that is trying to innovate. Wists (www.wists.com) allows users to bookmark pages visually via a small image and summary, which can then be shared with other users. This sort of thing makes sharing wish lists of goodies with others easier, for example. Kaboodle (www.kaboodle.com), launched last month, does something similar, allowing users to share bookmarks via small icons, and appears aimed primarily at anyone browsing shopping or auction sites. Both these approaches have merits, but suggest that innovation has tipped toward the consumer end rather than the outlet side. Sites such as eBay and Amazon, meanwhile, haven't changed a lot since we entered the 21st century.

I wish Etsy luck. I'm not a great buyer of amigurumi dolls or customized joysticks, but that isn't the point. For one thing, Etsy sees the world of crocheted dolls as a beachhead into a larger market. For another thing, the more innovation we see by smaller players in this sphere, the more we're likely to see the bigger players forced to compete by lowering their charges and raising their game. Now, Amazon, can you help me locate a yellow-spined book with an orange dog on the cover written by a guy with a Starsky afro?

customer support

Selling online has never been easier. But as a consumer the Internet hasn't done away with big retail companies; nor has it done away with the fiction of customer support. My big hope had been that the Internet would make reaching a real person easier, but I've long been disappointed. The Internet has wrought changes, it seems: just not the ones we expected. Here's how I saw things back in May 2001:

There are a lot angry consumers out there, and I'm ashamed to say I'm one of them. But not anymore.

That's because, in the age of the Internet, your customer-courtesy past can quickly catch up with you. If you doubt my word, take a hike to www.techcomedy.com/calls/calls.htm and listen to the telephone abuse technical support staff have to put up with. My personal favorite: a computer support lady who exhibits Zen-like patience while a customer informs her he owns Apple Inc., is a big wheel in the CIA, NATO and the G-7 and even as we speak, is about to send in his agents because his computer is "secret, higher than the Pentagon". Listen to that and you will vow never to give customer support people a hard time again, if only because you don't want to end up alongside eccentrics like Mr. Apple.

That's not to say that customer support doesn't sometimes need a

☞ **billinge** (*n, St. Helens*) An attempt by your phone company to bill you for services you didn't have or ask for. *I think they're trying to billinge me.*

good kicking. One can sympathize with some of the angrier callers at TechComedy. Spare a thought for the poor student who has lost her midterm paper because her computer wouldn't start up, or the woman who had been on hold for an hour.

Yet sadly, despite some early promise, the Internet hasn't really helped hook up customer and staff in a way that satisfies the customer faster and slows down the hair-graying rate of the staff.

A survey by CustomerAsset, an Internet customer services company, concluded that major retailers "fail the most basic test of retailing online: establishing a relationship with the customer." An email I recently sent to the British arm of major U.S. courier service DHL International Ltd. over a bill got lost somewhere between customer service and billing inquiries. Even those companies that have worked hard to support customers, such as book retailer Amazon Inc., have been forced by the dot.com slowdown to lay off customer support staff, leaving, in my view, a visible hole in their otherwise impressive customer relations record.

If your preferred language isn't English, you are in even bigger trouble. A recent survey by WorldLingo, an online translation service, concluded that more than 90% of the world's largest companies respond incorrectly to foreign language email inquiries. Among their findings are that many companies didn't even realize they were receiving a foreign language email, instead replying (in English) that there was something wrong with the original email. Still, at least they bothered: More than two-thirds of the companies didn't respond at all.

Well, if you aren't a massive company you should just check that you have an email address on your homepage and that the mailbox gets checked every few hours. International Communications Research, an Internet consulting firm, says customers vastly prefer email over other forms of communications, but they don't have much patience: men are willing to wait 2.8 days for a reply, while women want a response within a snappy 1.8 days.

There are alternatives; what the marketing types call customer interaction management tools. These are programs that allow customers home. You'd think that pilots would know how to sleep on aircraft, but Bob found otherwise: "The first 15 minutes of a flight was the only time I could ever sleep because the airliner would be climbing," he says. "This would allow my head to lay back and stay back. When the flight leveled off, my head would flop forward and sleep would be over." Sound familiar?

Bob tried every position and every accessory to get more sleep: Once he took 27 pillows and formed them into a mattress which he placed across three seats. Then he tried stuffing 11 pillows behind his lower back. This was the Eureka moment. With his hips pushed forward, he could straighten his legs. With the seat belt stopping him sliding, his legs relaxed. "The next thing I knew, it was two hours later. I missed the meal, the drinks, everything," he recalls. Worried it was just a one-off, he tried it on his next commute, but he had problems finding more than a few pillows. He needed something he could bring with him.

From the local Kmart he bought a child's orange inflatable life-vest. He stuffed it with two of his children's purple rubber balls and wrapped the whole thing in duct tape. It seemed to work. Now all he needed to do was to make something that would deflate when he didn't need it. He tried out different materials, settling on urethane-backed nylon – the same material used in scuba suits – welded together using the same process as life rafts. Voila: The 1st Class Sleeper (www.1stclasssleeper.com). A smart, neat solution, but I wasn't going to be convinced until I'd tried it out.

Bearing in mind all the odd looks Bob Duncan had endured during his experiments, I turned up at the airport prepared. I was flying from Jakarta to Melbourne and realized I wasn't going to be able to do this on my first go if I was wedged between fellow-passengers scrutinizing my every move. "I'm a technology columnist and I have this inflatable device I want to try out on the flight," I was going to tell the check-in clerk, but fortunately it wasn't necessary. With an expression that said nothing and everything, she blocked me off a whole row.

Once the flight was settled, I removed the sleeper from its blue bag.

☞ **tincleton** (*n, Dorset*) The faint muzak playing in the office lifts.

to interact via instant messaging with customer support. It works like this: Say you are looking through a site and want advice on what is the best bag to buy, just click on a special button. A customer support person will magically appear typing text and answer your query. Think of it as having shop assistants who actually assist.

That's the theory. And sometimes it works. I had a very pleasant online chat with Gabi from Human Click (www.humanclick.com), one of these services. However, I had less luck with FaceTime Communications Inc. (www.facetime.com), who told me to come back Monday to Friday 6:30 a.m. to 5 p.m. Pacific Standard Time in the U.S., except holidays. I couldn't raise Atmyside, a U.K. company, either, even during European office hours. In short, another great idea that gets lost somewhere in the implementation. Surely if you are going through the trouble of having an Internet presence, you are angling for international business, and for big companies – and especially those touting the technology that offers this kind of product – that means showing signs you think your customer base resides outside the San Francisco area.

Unfortunately that isn't yet the case. Which brings us to the next bright idea: automated customer service. Active Buddy (www.activebuddy.com) combines these online customer service widgets with instant messaging – programs such as ICQ, which allow users to swap instantaneous text messages online. The idea behind Active Buddy is that users can type in requests for specific information – a stock price, the weather in San Diego – and get an intelligent, but automated, response. Apply this to retail websites and one could use Active Buddy to respond to the online equivalent of "how much is that doggy in the window?"

I'm skeptical about all this. To get it right, I think companies have to follow basic rules that employ fewer fancy widgets and more, and competent, staff. Offer easy access to a "contact us" page, send an automated acknowledgment immediately and then get back to the customer in less than three days if it's a man, less if it's a woman. Then, maybe, just maybe,

☞ **brough sowerby** (*n, Cumbria*) Someone entering a computer shop about to demand a refund.

you may avoid receiving irate phone calls from mad megalomaniacs, weeping students – or me.

My skepticism proved well-founded. A year later I found not much had changed, and that to get a bit of attention I had to don tights, blue rinse and a hat, at least digitally speaking, in a piece my editors called "Tea, Sympathy And Service":

If you want good customer service online, try impersonating a little old lady. It worked for me.

Frustrated by the poor response to my own email enquiries to big companies – I'm not naming names here, except to say I'm still waiting for replies from the likes of 3Com, Fujitsu and Linksys – I figured things might work better if I metamorphosed into Ethel M. Girdle, a septuagenarian who claims to have typed her way through World War II while flying Spitfire fighter aircraft and is a dab hand at growing roses and laying on tea parties for the local pastor.

First stop for Ethel was fixing her Zanussi dishwasher. "Hello, young man (or lady)," she wrote to the customer-service center in Britain. "My washer makes a noise like one of those newfangled leafblower things and my crockery doesn't get clean. Can you send one of your nice young chaps round to fix it, I'm having the vicar for tea on Friday and if he sees the china in this state he'll think I've gone over to the other side. Yours, Mrs. Girdle." Zanussi responded with impressive speed and grasp of the gravity of the situation. "Dear Mrs. Girdle," they wrote. "Sorry to hear of the problems that you are experiencing with your dishwasher, if you would kindly let me have your postcode I will be able to look up the details of your nearest service center for you so that one of our engineers can come and repair your appliance so that your china gets nice and clean again."

My own experience of airlines and the Internet has been woeful, so I was interested to see how my fictional friend got on. She wanted to visit her grandson and fired off emails to several airlines: "I'm coming to Hong

☞ **bilting** (*v, Kent*) Your refusal to pay for a service you think is the result of billinge (p.95).

Kong/Sydney/Tokyo/Singapore to see my grandson, who is doing a grand job running one of your banks. This is not the first time I've flown (I used to fly during the war, don't you know) but it's been a while. Is it OK to bring my cocker spaniel, Poppy? He won't be any trouble, unless you've got rabbits on the aircraft! And may I bring my own teapot on board? I do like a cup of tea in the afternoon."

Ethel's still waiting to hear from Japan Airlines and Qantas, while British Airways' website had no functioning email address for ordinary folk. Singapore Airlines offered a form letter, Cathay Pacific was somewhat intimidating: "Please kindly note that domestic animals of any description are not permitted to be carried in the passenger cabin on any Cathay Pacific flights." But Virgin Atlantic rose to the occasion well: "I can assure you that our crew will make sure you receive a nice cup of tea on the flight or more than one in fact! It would not be necessary to take a teapot with you. Unfortunately Virgin Atlantic do not have a license to carry pets of any description, even though I am sure he is no trouble."

Next, Ethel decided to buy a computer. "I need the following," she emailed IBM: "A nice keyboard (if possible an electric one, the manual ones tire me out) and a nice screen to look at. Could I use my TV instead, and save a few dimes? It's a big one, though black and white and takes forever to warm up. My grandson says I need a CD drive but I think I can just drag the stereo over and plug it into the computer, yes?"

IBM were very helpful. "Please note that all our NetVista (desktops) come with a standard keyboard. However, we are unsure of what you mean by "electric" vs. "manual", they wrote, before gently pointing out that hooking up her black-and-white TV and CD player to the PC was a no-no.

Encouraged, Ethel went back for advice on the Internet: "Do I need some sort of passport, or special goggles, or something? My grandson says the connections are very fast these days, I don't want to mess up my hair." IBM was reassuring, saying a passport wouldn't be necessary.

☞ **broughton hackett** (*n, Worcestershire*) The member of staff deployed by computer outlets to deal with customers with brough sowerbys.

Overall, I was impressed. Customer service online has a long way to go – shame on those companies that didn't reply – but at least there are some bright and helpful folk at the end of those email addresses. And for those of you not getting customer satisfaction online, feel free to impersonate Ethel. I know I will.

Customer service, it seems, was still down to the initiative of one or two individuals. Blogs, those great soapboxes of the Web, have helped narrow the gap, creating what some people call "a conversation" between customer and company, but I'm still not 100% convinced. Here's what I wrote in March 2006:

Nowadays the mantra in the online world is that "markets are conversations." The idea, simply put, is that those selling and making stuff need to get back to talking to their customers – engaging them, as it were, in a dialogue that respects customers enough to hear and absorb what they're saying. The days are over, the argument goes, when companies could just throw their products out at customers and expect them to mutely accept them. Nowadays many companies run blogs, often with contributions from senior executives, as part of efforts to engage customers and users. They tend to still be a bit gushy, full of phrases like "we're really excited about this new feature we're working on that lets you compare dental floss preferences with your buddies – please let us know what you think," but it's a start.

This is half of the Web. The other half (and it's a big half) still seems to behave toward visitors and would-be customers much like foot-in-the-door aluminum-siding or brush salesmen. They use tactics that I thought had gone out with the likes of, well, aluminum siding and brush vending.

Take online music website Napster, for example. Once the bad boy of music sharing, where users could and did swap gigabytes of music with each other illegally, the only similarity to its old self nowadays is the logo

☞ **burrill with cowling** (*v, North Yorkshire*) The tactics employed by a broughton hackett to fend off brough sowerbys, using a combination of useless jargon (*burrill*) and bureaucractic stonewalling (*cowling*).

and name. Napster is now one of several sites selling music online legally, either by the song or, increasingly, through a subscription model. It's a treasure trove of music with some nice features, and now glistens with corporate respectability and professionalism. But a brief brush with it about 15 months ago, and the tales I've heard since of similar experiences, have convinced me that if markets are conversations, they can sometimes be one-sided.

Christmas 2004 found me in a computer shop in the United Kingdom that sold Napster vouchers. For about $25 you could download a certain number of music files from Napster's U.K. website. Excited to try it out, I redeemed the voucher online. Then it got complicated. On the company's website, I found that when I tried to enter the code on the voucher, the page would keep luring me to what it called a "free trial" of the $25-a-month full service. All that was required, it said, was my credit card. Three times this offer popped up as the default choice before I started to get a little ticked off. After all, the voucher had cost good money, and I wasn't in the mood to start giving away credit card details as well. Eventually I was able to use the voucher without divulging my card number, but it was a frustrating experience, and I posted something to my blog (www.loosewireblog.com) about it.

And this is when the real conversation began. Someone named Peter posted a comment below mine the same day, saying he had signed up for the free trial and had to spend more than half an hour on the phone trying to cancel his account. Later someone named Larry posted a comment begging for a Napster phone number; he couldn't find one on the company's website. A month or two later someone named Rynna said she had spent the best part of a day trying to cancel her account, which she said "was created in error."

To be fair to Napster, when I recently did sign up for the full service as a test, I was able to cancel it the same day without any problem. Napster says it has provided a toll-free number for canceling accounts since October

☞ **buxted** (*v, East Sussex*) The state of unsuccessfully seeking a refund from a computer outlet (*see* **broughton hackett**). *I went in to get a refund but I got buxted.*

2004, and a guide to canceling since September 2005; Dana M. Harris, Napster's vice president of corporate communications, says she doesn't know why the posters to my blog were unable to find the number. The company says asking for credit card numbers "allows customers to continue to enjoy uninterrupted access to Napster when their current subscription or trial is over" without Napster having to ask them if they want to continue, the company having got the whole difficult business of asking for credit card information out of the way at the start of the free trial. The company says that the average waiting time in February for customers indicating they were calling to cancel was less than seven minutes.

The situation is a common one on the Web, though. Try to download a free firewall program, a free antivirus program or a free online video and audio player, and you'll have to negotiate your way through the thicket of misleading signs trying to persuade you to cough up for a "free trial" – which of course requires your credit card information. Tactics like these don't succeed: They earn short-term, resentful customers who will, however good the actual service, easily explode into anger if they face obstacles trying to cancel later.

Companies that make it difficult for customers to get in contact are shutting themselves out of a discussion that will happen with or without them. My blog is just a tiny example of similar spontaneous gatherings of the disaffected, easily found on the Web. As customers who have battled to get through to a company gather and compare notes elsewhere, so that company's reputation can suffer. Even a good aluminum-siding salesman could do better.

Folk are still writing to my blog complaining about this kind of thing, so I'm not holding my breath. Some companies, it seems, don't care too much about the negative press they might get. Still, if you want to borrow Ethel's outfit to get a bit of attention, feel free.

PART TWO

getting stuff done

email

Email is the main event for most of us: It's where we receive stuff, send stuff, write stuff and where we can waste hours trying to corral our digital lives into some sort of order. But when it comes to organizing our email, advice – does it matter what program we use? How do we deal with spam? Should we organize things in to folders? – always seems to be thin on the ground. Here are some tips I've offered over the years, most of which still hold good. In a piece published in August 2004, I tried to offer some tips about organizing the inbox, all of which I still adhere to:

Given the amount of time we spend handling our email – checking it, reading it, writing it, occasionally clicking on attachments we suspect we probably shouldn't – you'd think we would do a better job of organizing it.

If you're anything like the rest of the world, nearly every email you've ever received sits in your inbox, gathering dust, cobwebs and the digital equivalent of bedsores. Some of them appear to date back to the Magna Carta. Your basic attitude towards email is to read it when it comes in, and then, if you work for the government or any company with more than 10 employees, forward it to as many colleagues as possible in the hope that you won't actually have to do anything more about it. The same applies to outgoing email: You write it, usually with a revealing and helpful

☞ **eshott** (*n, Northumberland*) An email you sent that you didn't mean to. *I think I just did an eshott. Oh my God.*

subject title like "Meeting" or "Proposal" and then send it, retaining only the haziest idea of whether you still have a copy of it and, if so, where it might be.

In medical circles this is called Chronic Email Bloat and the only known cure for it is to Get a Grip On Your Inbox. Here's how.

First, whatever kind of email program you use – or even if you access your email via a browser using services like Yahoo! or Hotmail – you should think of your inbox as a sort of waiting room or lobby. At the end of each session it should be empty of stuff. That means you should either be deleting everything you read or, more practically, moving stuff from your inbox to another box, or folder. So take some time to set up some folders and sub-folders and move messages from your inbox as soon as you've read them. I have about two dozen folders and that works pretty well for me, although I am seeking treatment for being something of an Email Hoarder. Here's a tip, courtesy of David Allen, the productivity guru: Have a special folder called Tickler which you treat as a holding pen for emails you receive but still need to do something about. (If you want to make sure this folder stays near the top of your usually alphabetically sorted list, call it !Tickler.) The cardinal rule: Your inbox stays empty.

If you get a lot of emails this can be time-consuming, so you should set up filters. Filters allow you to tell the computer that any email with a particular word in the subject, sender or recipient field should be sent straight to a particular folder. So, everything from co-workers on a particular team can be sent to one folder just by adding a filter to look for their email addresses. As the emails come in, they automatically feed through to the appropriate folder. Set up as many filters as you need. That way you save time and don't get bored by what is admittedly not one of the most exciting ways to spend your day. Another tip: Make sure the filter works on outgoing messages, too, so that all the emails you write don't clog the sent email folder, but are kept somewhere more relevant.

If you do all this, your email program should look a lot more orderly quite quickly. And there's more you can do. Keeping order in your address book will also make sending emails a lot easier. Some email programs can automatically add any email address on incoming or outgoing emails to your address book, which can be a blessing, but also tends to fill it up with rubbish. Occasionally go through it weeding out addresses you'll never use, and, if the program supports it, make sure the email address has an alias you can easily recognize. An alias is a user-friendly name for the email address: So, instead of having to remember some complicated email address like htgopher56@yahoo.com, you can add an alias like "Harry home." When it comes around to sending a personal email to Harry, just start typing "Harry home" and your email program should recognize what you're trying to do and complete it for you (called auto complete). This can save a lot of time.

Subject fields are a great, but wasted, opportunity to save time and keep order in your inbox. If I send an email to a company, for example, I will start the subject with "press query," then add the company or product name. Chances are they will reply with the subject field intact, meaning that all I have to do is add a filter for "press query" and all those emails, both in and out, will end up in a single folder. Some programs, like the excellent new Barca from Poco Mail (www.pocosystems.com), will let you change the subject field in an email that you've already received, making this process even easier. Cardinal rule: Give emails a subject that is useful, as unique as possible, and one that might include text that could work as a filter.

Indeed, I'd recommend the more adventurous of you to experiment with email programs other than the usual suspects: Outlook, Outlook Express and Eudora have their strengths, but there are other options out there with features that make organizing your email easy.

My favorite remains Courier (www.rosecitysoftware.com), where you can color-code emails (so all Indonesia-related emails, for example, appear purple). But two others are appearing on the horizon with mouth-watering features: A new version of Bloomba released this month offers powerful searches, turning the email program into a sort of database, while the

☞ **brede** (*v, East Sussex*) When you quickly scan a Web page, email or document ahead of a meeting, without bothering to read it more closely. *Have you read the material yet? No, I've just been breding it on the loo.*

newly launched Barca reflects some serious attention to how we use email and how we could do it better.

Bottom line: The more time you spend setting up a system, the less time you'll spend hunting for stuff ahead of vital meetings in muddy English meadows, muttering "Now where did I put the dang Magna Carta?" Good luck.

Of course, with the rise of free services and lots of free online space, email isn't always about using a program, but accessing it through the browser. I've always eschewed it because I always travel with a laptop and because I find it all a bit slow. But as Internet cafés offering connections with decent speeds proliferate, more professionals are using it. Bob Cullinan, a California-based media consultant, travels frequently and finds that "Web-based mail gives me the freedom to access my mail from any point on the planet."

The other attraction with Web mail is the arrival of Gmail (gmail.google.com), with its 2+ gigabytes of free storage. Other email services have had to catch up, to the point where how much email you have online is not going to be an issue. How does this change your email habits? Heinz Tschabitscher, who writes about email for information portal about.com (email.about.com), reckons this is the way to go. With Gmail offering fast searching of emails, and automated linking between emails from the same discussion, or thread, there is no longer any need to set up individual folders, he says. "File early, file often, all in one folder and rely on search to find what you are looking for later," he says.

Another benefit of Web mail: If you lose your computer to a virus, a crash or a thief, you haven't lost all your emails since they're all stored on the Internet. If you're using an email program, there's another way to do this: It's called IMAP (Internet Message Access Protocol). Without boring you with specifics, IMAP lets your email inbox talk more intelligently to the server, or online computer, which stores your emails before you download them. Most folk use the old standard, called POP, which stands for Post Office Protocol, and which does nothing more than find your email account and download whatever is on there to your computer. The emails are really only ever in one place: the server or your computer.

IMAP, meanwhile, creates two copies of your inbox and makes sure that both copies, on the server and your computer, look the same. It does a lot more than that, but that's the basic idea. Why is it a good thing? Well, for one thing you can check your email from anywhere, so long as you have an email program and remember your settings. Secondly, you'll never lose an email again because you've got two copies. The bad news: It's fiddly for programmers to get right, for some reason, so not many programs support IMAP, or at least support it properly. If you're brave, try it.

I write elsewhere in the book about how to combat spam, but the techniques I mention – involving what are called Bayesian filters – can just as easily be applied to sorting the rest of your email. Here's a piece I wrote on the topic in early 2006:

If you want to sort the wheat from the chaff – whether it's separating email from spam, hot stocks from duds, or great movies from bombs, you'll need the help of an 18th-century vicar.

Take, for example, the experience of Matthew Prince, chief executive of Utah-based antispam consultancy Unspam Technologies Inc. Hooked on the annual Sundance Film Festival since 1996, he has had the same problem facing everyone who attends any big cinema festival: Which of the 200 or so films being shown are worth watching? So he and a group of friends began trying to find ways of picking the best ones based on reviews of the films being screened. One day, chatting with a fellow software engineer, they both realized that picking the best films was really the same problem as deciding whether an email message was spam.

What's with that, I hear you say? Let me take a moment to explain why most of the world's spam – and there's a lot of it – doesn't end up in your inbox. It's all because of Thomas Bayes, an 18th-century English vicar, who came up with a theorem to calculate the probability of a future event based on past events. His theorem forms the basis of modern-day

☞ **birling** (*n, Kent*) A reply you get from someone who is clearly using their BlackBerry and therefore a) hasn't really read your email and b) can't type properly on its miniscule keyboard. *I asked her for input but all I got was a birling.*

spam filters used by most Internet Service Providers and email services. Put simply, if a piece of spam you receive contains the word "Viagra," chances are high that subsequent emails you receive containing that word also will be junk email. A Bayesian filter will inspect all the words in an email – including hidden formatting, the headers and other telltale signs of spam, and assign a probability of the email message being junk. All you have to do is to train the filter by showing it a handful of junk and email messages, telling it "this one is spam, this one isn't" and it starts quickly filtering out the rubbish.

Mr. Prince's bright idea was to apply the same filtering technique to film reviews. Would it be possible, he wondered, to throw film reviews of the past few Sundance festivals through a Bayesian filter and see whether it could pick the likely winners? The U.S. Sundance festival, which is a leading showcase for independent cinema, releases a guide to the films being screened every year. Mr. Prince and some colleagues gathered 10 years of guides to more than 360 Sundance films. Based on the individual film's success at the festival and subsequently, each was assigned to one of three categories, or baskets: Below average, average and above average. Their findings gave birth to the website (www.deconstructingsundance.com).

What Mr. Prince and his colleagues found was that, among other things, words were a pretty good indicator of success. But not necessarily the words you might expect in a review: Best. Fascinating. Emotional. Inspired. Great. All are, in the words of the Deconstructing Sundance website, "the kiss of death" for a movie. Riveting, for example, appeared in 46% of reviews for what turned out to be below-average movies, as opposed to 22% of above-average movies. How so? Why would a reviewer call a dud "riveting?" Mr. Prince has his own theory: "Maybe writers, when they struggle with something good to say about something, revert to adjectives like 'riveting' rather than actually describing the movie in a more tangible way?"

Pretty neat. But why stop there? If an 18th-century cleric can help you figure out which movies are going to make it, why not use the technique to predict other things, such as stock market movements, blood clots, or volcanic eruptions? Well, actually, there are people thinking like this. U.S.

shopping search engine Shopzilla.com uses a Bayesian filter to sift customer emails according to topic and, where, relevant, fire back canned responses.

But what can this do for you? Well, if your ISP or office network isn't filtering out your spam, you can set up your own Bayesian filter. I suggest going with POPFile (http://popfile.sourceforge.net) a free, all-platform version of a commercial product called PolyMail developed by John Graham-Cumming. (It was he and POPFile who made the whole Deconstructing Sundance thing possible.) It's relatively easy to set up.

I've used POPFile for a few years and it's kept the spam at bay. Recently I decided to make it work harder. As with Mr. Prince and his crew, I felt that if the software did such a good job with spam, why not let it sort all my email out for me? Email's big problem, you see, isn't just about filtering out spam. It's about sorting everything that comes in, so it doesn't all land (and usually stay) in one big oversize inbox.

My advice is to set up two baskets – say, Personal, and Work – and a Bayesian filter will quickly figure out where your email will go. Instead of having to write a rule for every sender, or for every email with the words "Loan Shark" in the subject field, you can just teach it where a few sample emails go, and then leave it alone. I'm now experimenting with three baskets: 1) what I need to deal with now, 2) stuff I can save for later, and 3) stuff I'll never need. So far it's working pretty well.

Of course, in all honesty, we don't know quite why the Bayesian system works. It just does. Expect the good vicar's theorem to spread beyond spam control to other applications on the Internet.

Oh, and the Deconstructing Sundance project got it right in shortlisting some of the potential winners at this year's Sundance festival, which finished a few weeks ago. They tracked the buzz on two films, for example, that ultimately won the festival's two top awards: "Quinceañera" (dramatic) and "God Grew Tired of Us" (documentary).

☞ **hartsop** (*n, Cumbria*) What you have become when you realize that your being issued a BlackBerry is not a sign of how much the company appreciates you but that it wants to suck the very lifeblood out of you even on vacation.

This is definitely something I still use, and if you've got a serious filtering problem it's a great way of sorting. But email is not just about the stuff coming in. It's also about what's going out. The biggest headache here, I think, is knowing whether what you're sending is ending up where it's supposed to. Is it reaching its destination? Is it being read? This is a topic I've spent some time on, hopping amid what are some thorny issues amid the hedges between privacy and productivity. Here's how I saw it in October 2005:

Sometimes the success or failure of a new product depends on where it registers on The Ick Scale.

Take, for example, the idea of software that checks whether someone has read your email. It sounds like a simple enough function: Send someone an email and then receive word, either via a separate email or program, when they've read it. Is that like sneaking a peek over a colleague's shoulder at work to see whether they've opened your mail yet, or is it no more creepy than sending something registered mail, so you know it arrived safely? And, depending on where you stand on that, how about if the sender could check how long it took the recipient to open the mail after it was sent? Or for how long he or she read it? What if all this was done without the recipient knowing?

This is tricky – if not icky – stuff, and I think it explains why programs that offer these kinds of features remain somewhat fringe. Users of Microsoft Outlook and Outlook Express can request receipts for emails they send, but these don't always work if the recipients use different email programs, or access their mail through websites, such as Google's Gmail or Microsoft's Hotmail. So, in recent years a number of companies have stepped into the gap, releasing products that offer not only some of the options above, but several more that creep further up the Ick Scale.

DidTheyReadIt, for example, lets senders know when, roughly where, and for how long the message was read. The service also will tell the sender

☞ **urlay nook** (*n, County Durham*) An over-the-top sign off signature using lots of different fonts but not the actual email address. *She's nice, but what's with the urlay nook? It looks like a sixth grader designed it.*

whether the recipient reopened the email, whether the person forwarded it to someone else, and, roughly, where those recipients are located. In short, you'll know more about your emails than about your kids. And the recipient won't be aware of any of this unless you want them to know. DidTheyReadIt (www.didtheyreadit.com) is available in several versions, from free to $50 a year, and its creator promises a new version with more features next month.

Then there's ReadNotify (www.readnotify.com), which offers a few more features: a geographic map pinpointing the city where the recipient read the email, whether he or she opened the email from a Web-mail account or an email program, and whether the recipient clicked on any links in the email. That isn't all. You can opt to have your emails self destruct before the recipient has opened it (useful, I suppose, for hastily written "I quit" emails), or to block the recipient from printing or copying an email you sent them. You can also track whether Word, Excel or PowerPoint attachments were opened, whether they were forwarded, how long they were read for, or, in the case of Adobe Acrobat (PDF) files, which pages were read. And again, the sender is blissfully unaware unless you want them to know. The offspring equivalent of this would probably be to tag your kids with tracking beacons.

I think these services go too far. But where is the line? With the launch of a new version of another program in this field, New Zealand's MessageTag, I thought I would try to find out. I have been using MessageTag for a few years now, and feel that on the whole its creators have struck a good balance between providing useful information to the sender and respecting the privacy of recipients. The only information you can retrieve about the fate of your email is when and whether it was opened. And while you can hide what you are doing from the recipient, the default setting is a small line of text at the bottom of each email notifying the user. I've only had a handful of requests to stop doing it, and MessageTag makes that easy enough to do.

☞ **send marsh** (*n, Surrey*) The destination of emails that never get answered, but never get returned either.

But might that change now? The new MessageTag (www.msgtag.com) adds some cool new features, such as allowing you to tag certain emails so you receive alerts about their fate on your mobile phone via Short Message Service. It also works on Google's Gmail service, and lets you tag emails you send to multiple recipients. But this version also lets you track the fate of emails you send to multiple recipients, and an option that bars the user from opening an email until they have acknowledged receipt.

I surveyed 33 friends and readers. Asked how they felt about the idea of knowing whether someone has opened an email they sent, most (20 out of the 33) considered it "helpful but not necessary." Only seven either weren't "crazy about it" or thought it intrusive. How about if someone did it to them? As long, it seems, that the sender made it clear that was what they were doing: 17 felt that it was "a good idea" while only five felt "a bit queasy" or "violated" (it was a scientific survey, but I was allowed to make up the questions). Bar the recipient from reading the email unless they acknowledged receiving it first, and the violated camp swelled to 24. A clear Ick Line was emerging, I felt, when the sender hides what he or she is doing from the recipient. My conclusion: These programs must let recipients know what is going on, and, if they don't like it, let them opt out or make it easy for senders to remove them.

But maybe it's grayer than that. One respondent, Vietnam resident Graham Holliday, says that knowing I used MessageTag had changed his email behavior: "You are the only person I know of who uses it and when I receive an email from you there is a little trigger that goes off consciously or unconsciously: 'Oh, he's the guy who tracks emails. He'll know I got this, won't he? If I don't open it now, he might think I don't care.' That means maybe I respond to your email significantly differently than I would to other mail."

In short: If people know I am monitoring my emails, they may behave differently, a bit like Schrödinger's Cat. It's a good point, and made me feel

☞ **bix** and **assendon** (*n, Oxfordshire*) The state of accidentally deleting a document or email you've been working on for the last 90 minutes; (assendon) the name your coworkers give you when you tell them about it.

a bit guilty about using MessageTag.

Now after some reflection, I'm still using it, but less indiscriminately. Now I only tag crucial messages to colleagues, bill collectors, and, definitely, not Graham. Maybe the Icky Line isn't just about what features you use, but how sparingly you use them.

Email, like everything to do with our computer, is all about getting things done. To me email tagging, whatever you want to call it, has a place alongside other tools that organize your inbox. I've stopped using MessageTag a few times for fear of freaking out those people I correspond with, but the benefits so outweigh the disadvantages – at least for the sender – that I find I can't survive without it. But how do I feel about other people using it on me? That's the tricky one. I don't want people to feel that just because I opened their email I'm going to reply instantly. Or at all. I think the line is here: if you use it, tell people and give them the chance to stop you using it. If you do use it, use it as it would a loaded gun: responsibly.

organizing

One of the most frustrating and yet exciting aspects of computers is the idea that you might be able to organize your data in a better way, not merely mimicking the drawers, folders and intrays of the real world, but leveraging the computer's power and visual potential to create a new method of sifting, searching and organizing your thoughts. Sounds great. How about in practice? Here are some pieces I've written about some of them. First off, outliners:

It's not easy trying to persuade others to try software I've found useful myself. Most just start to nod the more I talk, like those toy dogs on car dashboards, their eyes glazing over as their minds wander into some place where a guy is not going on and on about software.

The truth is, most people stick with the email program their computer was born with, not to mention word processor, spreadsheet, presentation preparer, etc. Really, there is some good software out there that can make things a lot easier for you. But you're in a hurry so I'll tell you about just one kind: Outliners.

An outliner, to coin a phrase, creates outlines: lists of anything – recipes, the constitution of the United States, your CD collection, all the Loose Wire columns ever written – which is stored in the form of a one-sided tree. It's easiest to think in terms of cutting your screen in half, and on the left having a list of items. Click on one of the items and more details about that item will appear in the right-hand window.

You get a view of the overall issue/document/list, and then you get a view of the detail, all at the same time. The left side is usually called a tree, because you can add branches and sub-branches to it, all of which can link to chunks of text (or pictures, or tables, or whatever you want) which appear in the right-hand window. Simple. And not that unusual: If you're a keen word-processing person, you'll know programs like Word have an "outline" feature, which will nest all your headings and subheadings in a tree, so long as you've applied the right styles.

If you'd bumped into someone in the 1980s, when personal computers were beginning to become popular, and asked them about outlining software, they probably would have known what you were talking about. However, after an initial burst of excitement, they never really took off. Nowadays, no big software maker has an outlining program for Windows that I know of.

This is weird, because it's not rocket science. And they really are great places to store large amounts of digital data. They're more flexible for storing your contacts than, say, Outlook, because you don't have to fill in any fields. Just copy and paste in the person's contact details from their email and that's it. They're more flexible than database programs such as Microsoft Access because they allow you to store data in any size or format. Just add a branch somewhere and throw it all in. It's flexible.

The other good news is that despite, or perhaps because of, the lack of interest from software giants, there are a lot of good outlining programs out there. They're mostly made by very small companies consisting of one or two people, which means they care a lot about the product and they listen when a customer has a problem, or offers feedback.

I've long used Jot by King Stairs Software (from www.kingstairs.com) but have recently defected to another product, MyInfo, from Milenix Software (www.milenix.com). There are many such programs on the market but MyInfo wins, in my view, for its simplicity. There are no complicated icons, weird menus or blinding colors. It's just you, two window panes and the beginning of a tree. So who is behind this sophisticated beast?

It turns out to be a 22-year-old Bulgarian called Petko Georgiev. He has been working on MyInfo since he was 18. He was studying business informatics in Sofia when he read about a (now long dead) outlining program called Vault, and decided he could do better. He didn't know anything about writing computer code so he spent a year learning computer-programming language C++.

He released MyInfo in 1999. Things did not go well. "Sales were low and it seemed that there was no future in what I was doing," Georgiev remembers. But he persevered and, after releasing another version the following year, he found he was cultivating a loyal following.

When he got a long, encouraging letter from one user at the end of 2000, he decided he would do it for a living, and make the software as professional as he could. After hiring a Web designer and an assistant developer, he came up with MyInfo 2, which is now a modest success, and is the outliner of choice for online gamers (who have to store and retrieve lots of esoteric data quickly). He's planning another version this year.

Call me sentimental, but I think it's great that an individual can create something so useful and remain so committed to it. Software like Jot and MyInfo has saved me oodles of time that I otherwise would have wasted trying to find a place to save a document, or text, or a Web address, where I could find it again.

I suggest you try it, if you haven't already. If you have, buy me a drink and I'll tell you all about the benefits of some new gadgets I just know would change your life: a USB-powered coffee warmer and a cigarette lighter that plugs into your PC (and can recharge your hand-phone while you nip out for a smoke). Interested?

For Mac fans, I'd recommend OmniOutliner (www.omnigroup.com) as the best bet for outlining. But you could also try NoteTaker (AquaMinds Inc. at www.aquaminds.com) and Tinderbox (from Eastgate Systems Inc. at www.eastgate.com).

I still love my outliners, and use them for dumping any kind of text that I may need to get back in a hurry. Another tool I love, despite its silly name and somewhat geeky status, is the TiddlyWiki. If you're not overly adventurous, you might want to skip this piece, but if not I'd recommend the TiddlyWiki as an alternative to the outliner. And because it's so new, you might also find that by the time you read this it's become more user friendly, and less, well, nerdy. Here's what I wrote about the TiddlyWiki in August 2005:

What I've got to offer this week is a simple piece of software that does stuff many of you might find useful. The tricky bit is explaining how it works and why you probably haven't heard of it. Not least the name of this gem: TiddlyWiki.

First off, I should explain what it does: keeps notes on anything you want, in a familiar format; can be cross referenced, labeled and easily searched; can be stored in one place on your computer; can be published on the Internet or taken with you on a USB key drive; and works on any kind of operating system. Although all these bits and pieces are present in other programs, I know of none that does all of this, and does it for free. Still interested?

OK, the name. Take the Wiki bit first. A Wiki is a document, usually but not always in the form of a Web page on the Internet, which can be edited by anyone who wants to, right there and then. Most Web pages you visit can only be read – a static page, like a newspaper or a book – but a Wiki will have an "edit this" button that allows you to change, remove or add your own words.

Wikis have proved a boon. But some started thinking that Wikis needn't just be about joint documents, and online collaboration. The Wiki is a powerful editing and Web publishing tool in itself, and could be scaled down for personal use – to create your own documents on your own computer, with or without an Internet connection. This kind of Wiki would be a smaller-scale affair: just you and your notes, on your own computer. Hence the term TiddlyWiki.

A TiddlyWiki, simply put, is a collection of individual notes – called tiddlers, naturally enough – that you can create easily, and which can

☞ **hickling** (*v, Nottinghamshire*) Moving around the mouse to try to find the mouse cursor on your screen.

be viewed together or individually, shuffled in lists alphabetically or chronologically. You can search inside them.

So far, this might sound familiar. You may already keep jottings, random notes or To-Do lists via a range of programs. There's no shortage of offerings for this kind of task and some of them are quite good. But the TiddlyWiki offers a glimpse of how things are changing in terms of how people think about software.

First off, a Wiki – big like Wikipedia or small like a TiddlyWiki – is using the same code as a Web page, called HTML. HTML is simple, but not that user-friendly. This is why ordinary folk like us don't do much Web page building, unless it's via a blogging website, which makes it easy by doing much of the formatting and design work for us. Wikis take a similar tack as blogs, hiding all the fiddly bits for you. TiddlyWikis are no different. The beauty of this is, when you've built your TiddlyWiki, you can do with it whatever you might do with an HTML Web page. You could publish it on the Net. You could copy it to a USB key drive and view it on a computer that has a browser. And, if you have the inclination and skill, you can redesign the layout, colors and fonts, as you can with any ordinary Web page.

Alan Hecht, an instructional design specialist at Penn State University, has deployed TiddlyWikis to help his faculty create their own websites without the need for any programming or HTML skills. "TiddlyWiki is an amazing accomplishment in programming and shows the power of Wikis to even the most novice of users," Mr. Hecht says.

That's not all. A killer feature for me is the ability to tag, or label tiddlers – an addition to the TiddlyWiki world from British technology consultant Jonny LeRoy. If you've ever tried tagging websites like del.icio.us, which lets you label and share your favorite Web pages, or online photo collections like Flickr.com, you'll know what I'm talking about. (Think of tagging as another way to search for stuff on the Web, often more efficient than stumbling around looking via keywords or boring old top-down, library-like categories.) With TiddlyWiki, it means you can stick any number of labels you like on each tiddler, or note, which makes finding or ordering them later much easier – whether you're online or offline. Say you're organizing notes on a project. Each tiddler could be assigned a label for the author, for the recipient, for the topic, for the side-issues raised, or whatever.

In sum, what I like about these TiddlyWikis is that they represent a new beginning for simple software. In the same way online websites like Backpackit.com are simplifying online tools, TiddlyWikis don't try to do too much. But they do open our eyes to what software might be capable of, and how restricted we presently are in how we handle and view information. It's early days for the TiddlyWiki pioneers, but I hope they fulfill their promise of simple, flexible software doing powerful things for us.

If you do feel up to it, visit the homepage of its inventor, Jeremy Ruston (www.tiddlywiki.com), and click on the "DownloadSoftware" link on the left. Because TiddlyWikis are Web pages rather than programs, you download it as you would a Web page – by right clicking on the link provided and saving it to your hard drive. From then on it's just a question of feeling your way around: I can't guarantee a 100% smooth ride right now, but I do guarantee whatever effort you put into figuring it out will be worth it.

TiddlyWikis, like outliners, have their limitations. First is that if you're looking for a more visual brainstorming tool, there are better options out there. This takes us into the world of mind maps, another grand obsession of mine. Here's how I saw things in September 2000:

My old economics teacher, the late, great, bow-tie-wearing Sebastian Greenlaw, taught me very little economics. It wasn't his fault; I just didn't quite get it. But he did leave me something I still find useful: spidergrams.

These – more commonly known as mind maps – are diagrams of information that supposedly mimic the layout of the brain. The topic is written at the center of the page and all subtopics are added as branches and subbranches off that first, central word. The result is a spidery-looking map that illustrates graphically the relationships among the subject matter.

It is a great way to organize your thoughts, take notes or work through a brainstorming session. It has its limits; it didn't help me grasp economics, for one thing. But that may have required divine intervention. Its inventor, British-born Tony Buzan, has helped propagate the concept to schools, boardrooms and even the British Olympic rowing team. Since pioneering the concept in the early 1970s, his books have been translated into 20 languages and published in 50 countries. Obviously, for many people, mind maps work. But now, in the Internet age, has mind mapping been superseded? If mind maps map the mind, shouldn't computers do an even better job of giving order to our thoughts and data?

In my view, computers have so far been disappointing. One bright hope: The Brain, from TheBrain Technologies Corp. (www.thebrain.com).

Developed by boy genius Harlan Hugh, The Brain is a snazzy piece of software that links topics, or thoughts, in a graphical environment that moves, depending on what thought you are focusing on. It is very seductive-looking software, and I've been back to it a dozen times since its launch a couple of years ago, hoping the reality of using it would match the promise.

In the end, though, I've ditched it. The moving links end up doing more confusing than enlightening; despite its name, the software leaves my particular gray matter baffled. Indeed, the company has now switched to providing more modest services such as Internet searches and directories through its software, suggesting either that this is an idea ahead of its time or one that doesn't make the grade. Try it yourself and see.

The concept behind The Brain is actually quite similar to Mr. Buzan's mind maps. And there is software that tries, more modestly, to harness computers to help that process. The best is MindManager, from California-based MindJET (www.mindman.com), is a simple enough program that faithfully replicates the mind-mapping process, including offering a database of drawings to add spice to presentations.

It feels sturdy and is highly configurable; it links to other programs and other computers over a network or the Internet. I could imagine a team of brainstormers getting a lot out of it. I use it from time to time, but I have to confess that unless the computer is going to help me think, I still prefer pen and paper.

Indeed, I think the problem with just transporting a concept like mind maps to the computer is that you lose the spatial element. If you are only working in two dimensions, paper is pretty unbeatable. The page can be as large as you like, and you don't have to fiddle with fonts, line-thicknesses and branch titles as you commit your genius to paper.

Hopefully soon The Brain will also be into a new version that sounds as if it might have overcome what I still think are some major limitations. Here's another tool that I took a look at in June 2006:

Ever wonder why, 12 years after Michael Douglas wandered through a virtual filing cabinet and got all steamed up in there with Demi Moore, in the movie *Disclosure*, we still can't do that? (Rummage through virtual filing cabinets, I mean.)

The closest we get to virtualization is when we play around with games such as SimCity, where you build and run your own city. Or online virtual worlds like Second Life. These mimic, visually, the real world, and while they may not exactly resemble our ordinary surroundings, it's a simple idea to grasp.

But visualizing data is a different beast: Instead of trying to make a digital replica, the idea is to use computers to turn data into something easier to see, sort and analyze. Instead of looking at last year's sales data in boring spreadsheets, say, you could view them as a three-dimensional city, which you could walk through using an avatar that resembles your Great Aunt Martha.

Leaving aside whether you would want to look like your Great Aunt Martha, I think we have an answer as to why we're not donning special gloves and pulling drawers, if you'll pardon the expression, like Michael Douglas. There's no real point in turning a real-world filing cabinet into a digital one because it doesn't make handling the data any easier.

But why haven't more imaginative uses of data visualization caught on,

☞ **cublington** (*n, Buckinghamshire*) The little cliques that gather in certain offices, depending on arrangement of cubicles.

either? The answer, says Andrew Vande Moere, a lecturer at the University of Sydney's Centre of Design Computing and Cognition, is simple: Interfaces aren't up to the task. We're fine with "literal" transcriptions of our world into computer worlds, but we're not very good at grasping digital metaphors beyond the occasional folder and desktop. "Most implementations" of data visualization, says Mr. Vande Moere, "seem to confuse people more than help them." The result: The Internet is littered with the corpses of worthy efforts that didn't catch on, from turning your desktop into something approaching your living room, to maps where peaks and valleys represent different data.

There are a few things out there that try to break free of the dull monotony of lists, hierarchies and trees of folders. At the very least, brainstorming applications such as Mind Manager (www.mindjet.com) help you create spidery images of your thoughts called mind maps. While these programs have their fans (myself among them), they start getting cumbersome just at the point you need them most: when you want to step back and survey the data you've gathered, to get a bird's-eye view of what you've got. Which leads me to 3D Topicscape, a Windows-only program that does exactly that.

3D Topicscape, launched by longtime Hong Kong resident Roy Grubb last month, looks like a primitive airplane simulator (it is available for a free 60-day trial from www.topicscape.com). You float below blue skies across endless green terrain, in the middle of which stand cone-shaped mountains of varying sizes. These mountains have labels on them, corresponding to either ideas or folders.

Mountains can be connected to each other as parent and child – terms Topicscape uses – much like a folder and subfolder on your computer, or a topic and subtopic in a mind map. But instead of having to move through folders or thoughts one list or branch at a time, you can use your cursor to fly above these mountains, to search for particular ideas or merely to survey the mass of data you've collected. It's a better way to see and organize large collections of folders and files. No longer do you have to double click on a folder to see all the subfolders contained within it, then reverse engines to look at another folder. In Topicscape, all your folders are laid out like small mountains before you.

But 3D Topicscape works as a mind mapper too – creating a spider web-like image of a topic, where subbranches appear instead as smaller mountains. Each child (topic or folder) can have multiple parents. In other words, it can be linked to several larger folders. Being able to save a file in several different mountains means you're much freer to assemble ideas ("how to build a better igloo"), projects ("purchase of igloo materials"), or themes ("daft projects").

It isn't perfect. I found the linking between mountains a bit confusing, especially when I created loose links or assigned mountains to multiple parents. And although the software was remarkably stable and relatively intuitive, it's still a niche area that requires the user to invest quite a bit of time and effort. That said, it's definitely a liberating experience to be able to fly around your computer. It would also, in all probability, make a better movie than "Disclosure."

All these tools have something in common: They try to reduce the information you have in front of you to some sort of structure, which makes understanding, brain storming and organizing ideas easier. But what happens if you want to take other people's ideas or writing and reduce it to something you can handle as easily? This is where summarizers come in – software that, well, summarizes longer documents into briefs so you don't have to read the originals. As with most of the stuff I write about, they seem to have long promised more than they delivered, and have never gathered the critical mass necessary for commercial success. Here's how I saw them in late 2000:

The rapid growth of the Internet hasn't done much to dent our tendency for verbosity, long-windedness, wordiness, prolixity, call it what you will. But fear not, help is at hand.

First, the size of the problem. Estimates of the scope of the Internet range from a billion or so Web pages to Internet consultant BrightPlanet.com's reckoning of 550 billion online documents. As if to underline their point, and unwittingly add to the problem, BrightPlanet issued a report on how much is out there – 41 pages long.

And that's not counting all the email and other verbiage. It is too much data, and there isn't enough time to read it. Still, you get the nagging feeling you should read it, in case some guy ambushes you by the watercooler and asks your opinion of his 450-page memo on improving intra-office communication.

Now, there is an easy way to have a quick retort ready. It's called the Summarizer, from Quebec-based Copernic Technologies. The program, due to be released today, is simple and small. But don't be fooled, it could save you from an embarrassing watercooler moment.

Summarizer adds a button to your Internet Explorer, Outlook and Microsoft Word toolbars that can magically condense the document you are viewing. At the same time, the left-hand side of the Summarizer window will list the main concepts it can identify in the text. It'll do the same thing for any text you care to paste into the program. In Internet Explorer, right-click with your mouse on any link and Summarizer will sum up the linked Web page.

It does all this remarkably quickly – a second or two at most. It is flexible, too. You can reduce or increase the number of concepts Summarizer identifies, and hence the amount of text in the summary. This gives you some control over the level of detail of the result. You can also export the results to a text or Web page file.

The program summarizes documents in English, French, German or Spanish. Copernic's website (www.copernic.com) promises further additions, including Japanese-language capabilities and integration with its search engine program, Copernic 2000, which would let you simultaneously look for documents while summarizing them.

So how does it shape up? Well, I'm a big fan of Copernic 2000 software, which I've found to be robust, smart and indispensable. But for a few reservations, Summarizer is no exception. It's an excellent product that is

☞ **liss** (*n, Hampshire*) The impatient noise your boss makes through his/her teeth makes when he/she pretends to take in your exciting suggestion about improving a product.

simple but could be a big time-saver.

A lot depends, of course, on the quality of the document you're summarizing. Feed it rubbish and rubbish comes out. By summary we mean extracting the key sentences, not rewriting the text itself. This program isn't going to craft polished executive summaries for you, but it will do a lot of the groundwork. Put it to work on a busy Web page chock full of articles, or a well-structured document that lacks its own summary, and you'll get a quite passable outline.

Copernic's communications manager Benoit Levesque said the product is aimed at "researchers, media, government, technical industry, etc. – anywhere there is a lot of documentation to analyze." Sounds like most of us.

I gave it BrightPlanet's 41-page epic as a tryout. In less than a second, it condensed the Word document into a very commendable summary and list of concepts. In a moment I was transported from a long, graphics-laden document that required scrolling, to a succinct executive synopsis that could be saved, printed, exported or emailed.

Quibbles? It's a great product, but a tad pricey. Existing Copernic users will get a discount, but it's still too much money in my view for a noncore product.

The version I tried wasn't quite as robust as I'd expect from Copernic. Another thing I'd like to see is support for other document formats, such as Adobe Acrobat. A second version with these features built in, Copernic says, is under way.

To summarize: Spare yourself wasted hours dredging through other people's pleonasm and check out Summarizer. It's software that for once may fulfill its promise of saving you time.

Both Coredge and Copernic are still around and offer trial versions of their software. But if you're looking for something more basic, check out Zentext Summarizer Lite from British data management company Corporate Internet Ltd. You can either download the small program itself or just copy the text you want summarized into the Web page at www.zentext.com/Summarizer.

Fun, but not practical, because it won't work with large chunks of text. Even Microsoft Word has an autosummarize function (in the Tools menu), which takes a half-hearted stab at summarizing an open document, although you won't find Microsoft trumpeting the feature on its website: I couldn't find one press release that made mention of it.

Summarizing software isn't the only way to shortcut the hassle of finding what you're looking for. To speed up Internet searches, you might get some joy out of the newly launched Browster (www.browster.com), a browser plug-in that lets you preview websites listed in search results without actually having to visit them. Instead of having to click on each link in the search-results list, you can view condensed snapshots of the Web pages those links go to, judging quickly whether they're what you're looking for or not. It's a tool that I've added to my browser and found it quite useful, assuming you've gotten a decent Internet connection.

search

Search is a topic I love to read about in my old columns because it was actually something I got right. More or less. Here in all their glory are my pieces, stretching back to February 2000:

Why can't my PC be more like the Internet, or at least like my old English teacher Mr. O'Flanagan?

Mr. O'Flanagan was a pipe-smoking genius. He knew intimately the contents and coordinates of every book he possessed but he could never recall minor matters like the whereabouts of his next class (or for that matter, his pipe). His ground-floor flat was given over to books: he had so many they were stacked head-high on every available surface, including the kitchen floor. But ask him to locate a book, quotation, essay or reference and he'd know instantly: With a flourish he would whisk out the required tome from a stack, leaving the rest tottering precariously.

The Web isn't that different from my old teacher's makeshift library. It's a muddle, but finding something is usually almost magically fast: Fire up a search engine like Fast Search (www.alltheweb.com), and chances are you'll get a reply in 15 seconds.

Admittedly, search engines aren't perfect – you are unlikely to hit exactly what you're looking for on the first go – but it's easier than finding a reference to the breeding habits of the Sumatran rhino at your local library. And you don't have to stare at those stern librarians.

Try to track down a file or text on your own computer, however, and you're stuck in the slow lane. Looking for that letter to Aunt Martha you never quite finished? Chances are, you're reduced to using the Windows Find program which moves slower than Bangkok traffic. Given that the Internet grows by tens of thousands of pages a day, and that you might add, say, 10 new pages to your PC daily, you might be forgiven for feeling this is somewhat limiting. It's yet another anomaly that makes computing a less than genial experience.

Well, it needn't be quite so painful. There are fixes to be found in the form of third-party software. But what's surprising is that only a few players have tried to fill this rather large gap. Here are some of them:

My favorite by far, is a program called Tracker Pro, from Enfish Technologies. It does everything you need it to do – and more. Tracker, I'm convinced, should be on everyone's computer. But it isn't. Launched in October 1998 by Enfish (www.enfish.com), it quickly won several awards. It will index your hard drive, even updating itself in real time. The indexing process is much faster than others, and the resulting index takes up much less space.

The program will keep track of whole websites, even your company's network. The results can be seen in a special viewer built into Tracker, meaning you don't have to open separate windows or programs. It will let you set up stored searches (called Trackers), saving a lot of time. In short, it's smooth, sleek and mildly revolutionary. So why didn't it fly off the shelves?

Sadly, Tracker may be a victim of its own genius. It's hard to convince people inured to years of dumb programs with clunky interfaces that there's another way. Enfish's public relations chief Chia Chiang says that's the company's biggest problem. "If we have the opportunity to explain what the product does and, better yet, show people, they get very excited. But it's not an easy product to explain in a single sentence," she says.

There's good news. A year on, I'm not quite sure how I'd live without Tracker. And Enfish promises a new, even sleeker, version soon – Onespace – with vastly expanded capabilities.

Ms. Chia won't say too much about what it will do, except that it "extends the indexing capability found in Tracker Pro." I, for one, can't wait. Now, if only I could find that hard copy of Hamlet…

I may have been spot on about the need for better search, but I wasn't about the product. Enfish almost immediately began to struggle, probably as a result of my being nice about it. But strangely the field remained theirs to lose, as I realized when I took another look in April 2003:

Every time I visit a computer shop I get nostalgic for the dotcom boom. In those days people with money were throwing their cash at people with ideas, however silly, with interesting results. Sure, most of the ideas were so dumb they never saw the harsh light of day – or the harsh light of a business model – but at least some new stuff was appearing.

As I gaze over the software shelves nowadays, empty but for yet another minor update of word processors or system utilities and (admittedly rather cool) games, I wonder: What happened to software innovation? Where are all those great promises of what we could do with our computer beyond using it as a glorified typewriter or calculator?

Sure, folks can now do some interesting stuff with video, pictures and music, but is that what the information revolution was all about? I've got a tonne of stuff on my computer – letters, novels, memos, Chairman Mao-type thoughts, mortgage calculations – but what good is it if it just sits there, hidden behind arcane file names I'll never remember, even under threat of torture? I fear the information revolution – at least on a personal level – has come and gone.

This is all very disappointing. I'd love to see our data made accessible for all sorts of imaginative things that make use of the power of our PCs. A program, say, that goes through all your emails and tells you, based on some fancy algorithm, how many Christmas cards you should send this year and to whom. A program that looks at your finances and, while you're shopping for furniture, works out whether you need a second mortgage and finds the best one for you.

OK, I'm getting ahead of myself here. That we still can find something more easily on the Internet – or in the attic – than we can on our computer is a depressing reminder of how far we have to go. Indeed, in 1999 a small California start-up called Enfish produced the most revolutionary piece of software I'd seen in years – a search program called Tracker that allowed you to search rapidly and easily through everything on your computer. It was magical in its simplicity, elegant in its design, and suddenly made having a hard disk full of all your stuff a sensible idea.

If you could check in a flash what and when you last wrote to Aunt Edith, all the previous litigious letters to your tenants, the last time your country declared war on another country, life really suddenly could get a lot easier. The index would update itself while you were asleep, so you didn't have to do anything beyond installing it. You could save complex searches with simple names, so that you could exclude letters about Aunt Edith from nosy Cousin Connie, or include only those that referred to her pet poodle Alfie but not to Phoebe the cat. It was fab. And as with all things fab, it didn't last (the software, not the cat).

Well, that's not strictly true. Enfish is still going, doing its best to convince a sceptical public that this kind of thing is actually useful. But in the meantime their subsequent software has never approached the quality of Tracker, which sadly won't work with Microsoft's most recent version of Windows XP, and that effectively renders it useless. But at least Enfish is hanging in there: Version six of its software is released this week and to me it's the closest the company has got to its old Tracker.

I can only guess why such a great idea hasn't caught on. There's no great learning curve involved: Once you've explained to users that Enfish is essentially a Google search engine for your computer, there's not much more to say. Sadly Enfish is not yet a household word. But Enfish does have competition, and perhaps they'll be more lucky.

One is the Australian company 80-20 Software, which has this month released version 3.0 of its 80-20 Retriever software (www.80-20.com). While previous versions of 80-20 Retriever will do pretty much what Enfish does – index your documents, emails and whatnot, let you search quickly through them – only this version lets you view the documents without having to launch the program you created them in (say, launching Microsoft Word to view a Word document). This is a vital feature, since you can quickly scroll through documents retrieved by your search, all in one place.

In fact, Retriever does a fine job but falls down, in my view, by trying too hard to integrate itself into Outlook, Microsoft's calendar, contact and email behemoth. My advice to 80-20: You're nearly there, but drop the Outlook interface and just be yourself. It should be a stand-alone program.

Both are worth trying (Enfish Find and 80-20 Retriever can be downloaded and used for a month free). For the heavy lifters, I'd recommend dtSearch Desktop. Although a pricey $200 from dtSearch (www.dtsearch.com), this is a super-fast, super-reliable program that tells you a lot about what's on your computer. By launching your search from a viewable index of words, you can see how many misspelled words you are missing in normal searches. The interface isn't particularly friendly, but it's a workhorse for the serious searcher. Now if only it could help me on my Christmas-card list.

No sooner had I written that when some products started to appear. Such as X1, which I wrote a column about in July 2003:

I have lost count of the number of times I have written about finding text in files on your computer. It's such a basic idea that you would think it would come as a standard function on most operating systems. In fact, if you're a Mac user, it does. For the rest of us, finding stuff is harder than finding something on the Internet. This has to be the dumbest thing that future generations will laugh at us for, except perhaps for considering white plastic garden chairs a charming lawn ornament and acceptable seating option.

But it's not through lack of trying. I remember a program from the late 1980s called askSam (www.asksam.com) which did a very passable job of allowing users to search through large chunks of text quickly and efficiently. But it was quirky and required a lot of patience on the part of the user. In fact, it's still going (and still quirky). In the late 1990s, Enfish Corp (www.enfish.com) launched a great product called Tracker Pro. Tracker Pro was ahead of its time, and like all things ahead of its time now is sitting in the corner mumbling to itself, ignored, dribbling out of the corner of one toolbar menu. Enfish continues to push something called Find that it is a shadow of its former self, and seems aimed more at the commercial customer than the individual. There's also dtSearch (www.dtsearch.com) that does text searches quite well. But now, the Holy Grail may have arrived.

It's called X1 and is simply a fast way of searching for stuff on your hard drive or network. (Trial versions are available free from www.x1.com.)

It's a bit like Googling your own computer. The program appears as a rather suave-looking toolbar on the top of your screen. Enter the text you're looking for and it will immediately start displaying files that include those words. X1 is similar in look and feel to Enfish Find (indeed until a week ago it, too, was called Find), but where I think it may succeed is that the folks behind it, U.S.-based Idealab, seem to have learned their lessons well. "Our approach isn't that much different than others, but we are staying focused on simplicity and speed," says Mark Goodstein, chief cook and bottle washer (*sic*) of the project. Goodstein believes that the program's interface is sufficiently intuitive and innovative to allow users to narrow their searches down instantly from all to just a few, as opposed to today's search engines and desktop dtSearch utilities, which take for ever. Using X1, it takes about 10 seconds to find an exact match. Part of the problem with previous programs, I think, is that people have just grown used to not being able to find stuff. So we have forced ourselves to create complicated filenames and separate folders for everything we do.

The result is we sit around twiddling our thumbs as we search through mountains of emails or documents. The folks at Enfish, despite their heroic efforts, never succeeded in persuading us that this was something we really needed. I, however, at least tried. I used Enfish products since they were first launched and only stopped this year when I couldn't get them to work properly with Windows XP. During all that time I tried to persuade my friends, colleagues and passers-by to use Enfish; in most cases without success.

So what will X1 do that the others failed to do? It's early days: The software was only released last week, but if my discussions with Goodstein are anything to go by, these guys are serious. For one thing, they seem to have taken the suggestions of beta testers (suckers like myself who enjoy testing unfinished software, and then reporting problems and offering input) seriously. The team works from the long list of suggestions and bugs and appears to have incorporated nearly all of them in the final version. That's pretty impressive, especially when you see that the program remains sleek and uncluttered, without lots of unnecessary buttons and options.

Not that X1 is perfect. I had some problems viewing the contents of Word documents. I also found some of the option boxes a little confusing. But these are minor gripes. Goodstein promises that the program will "get richer over the coming weeks and months, as we add more consumer features." These include easier searches for files that are not just text, such as pictures and music and also support for indexing attachments, contacts, events and Adobe Acrobat files.

It's early days. Tracker Pro looked like a winner when it appeared four years ago; now its descendants seem to be happy jostling for space in a small corner of the corporate world. If X1 is going to survive and prosper, it's going to need to persuade ordinary users that it's not the inevitable order of things that their computer files are about as accessible as last year's tax receipts.

A year on, and more players were entering the field. This from August 2004:

Consider this: Your hard drive probably contains more info than you could ever imagine. Say you've got a modest hard drive of 20 gigabytes. That's the equivalent of about 20 copies of the Encyclopedia Britannica. Or 20,000 floppy disks. That's a lot of stuff, and, chances are, you have little or no idea what's actually on there or, if you do, how to find it. Be ignorant no more: Help is at hand.

Now, I know we've been here before. One of my bugbears has been the lack of a decent program to find files on your computer. By this I don't mean looking for anything particularly obscure, just your last letter home, or the email you got from the accounts department demanding your expense report from covering the Burma Campaign. Simple stuff, and it's always annoyed me that Internet search engines do this so much better on the world wide Web than they do on our own Word files or emails. (Mac fans will chime in at this point and say they've always had this feature; Windows fans will say XP has its own search-and-index function. But, with respect to both groups, I'd say neither is particularly useful and, in the case of XP's, practical. It's clunky, hard to figure out, and slows your computer down to a snail's pace.) But now sharp new programs promise to do something about this, and they are aimed directly at the casual user who just wants to find stuff, without a lot of fuss.

First, check out blinkx (www.blinkx.com), launched late last month. It's a half-screen size window that lets you enter search terms and look for matches both on your hard drive and the Internet. Results are neatly laid out, and you can choose whether to look for only a certain type of file (Microsoft Word, Adobe Acrobat, email) or everything. Move your mouse over one of the matching files in the list and a little pop-up window will appear giving the matching word in its context. It does all this super, super-fast, and it's free. There are myriad other little features in there, but they're there to be discovered, rather than overwhelming you. As blinkx co-founder Suranga Chandratillake says, "Our focus is heavily on the random home user who downloads it for personal use and gives it just five minutes before deciding whether to keep or un-install." That sounds like most folk.

Another option is FILEhand (www.filehand.com). This has a more "no-nonsense, find-it-before-lunch" feel to it, but gives you a bit more control over, for example, how much of the matching documents you want to see. There's no Internet search involved but it's also super fast.

Copernic, the Canadian search company, will launch its own Desktop

Search this month, which automatically adds new files and updates old ones without overloading your computer's processing power. From what I've seen, it looks impressive. Another desktop-cum-Internet search tool, Tukaroo, was recently bought by search engine Ask Jeeves before its official launch, so expect to see something from there soon. Google and Microsoft are both reportedly planning their own challengers.

Finally, there's X1 (www.x1.com), which I've looked at here before. A new version released last week resolves most of the quibbles I had with previous versions, and probably puts it at the head of the pack. The program looks nice, feels sleek and, importantly for me, lets you see all the matches in a preview of the entire document – so you don't have to open the original program.

In the new version you can do more advanced searches involving phrases, Boolean strings (not the garters that hold up Amish dancers' leggings, but more complex searches including ANDs and ORs). It also has the ability to save searches so you can run them again quickly. The price: $100, which is a tad steep, but it's selling for $75 until September 15.

A small price to pay for all that wisdom hidden on your hard drive.

Actually, money wasn't the issue. Google and Microsoft were indeed entering the field. By 2005 I was able to write, in a piece called "Getting Organized for the New Year", that finding stuff on your computer was now as easy, and cheap, as finding it on the Internet. My five year old dream had come true:

Google has Desktop Search (free from www.tinyurl.com/68btb) which does an excellent job of trawling your hard drive, much as Google trawls the Internet, so you can find what you're looking for quickly and easily but there are others. Check out a list of them on my blog (www.tinyurl.com/4n9sy). My favorite? X1 (www.x1.com), which gets better with each release, but also costs a fair bundle: $75 unless you can wangle a discount. If you aren't a fanatic, I'd go for a freebie toolbar, such as Google's.

Since writing that, X1 now has a free edition, and Copernic's Desktop Search is about to come out in a new version. While Google remains the most popular, I'd suggest both are worth a shot. Me? I still use dtSearch for the heavy stuff, simply because I can find and see more on my screen. But for ordinary users, the others work fine. Happy hunting, and consider yourself blessed the past few years brought to an end the fruitless hunt for a missing file.

file managers

Search is great for finding stuff. And I hear a lot of folk, including my friends Jim and Colin, say they don't bother about giving their files consistent names, or putting them in orderly folders, because they can find the files using a search program anyway. But to me that's not the point. Keeping your files in some semblance of order is good practice for any number of reasons: one day you might want to know what you have and what you don't have, you can't find a file using a keyword because you can't think of what keyword is in the file, or simply you don't want to have lots of duplicate files sitting around. So here's the message I preach, going right back to May 2000:

My computer crashed the other day. It was on the fritz – blinking the c:> prompt at me for nearly 24 hours – which led me to do what anyone would do under such circumstances: I typed in "cd c:/windows/options/cabs," then "setup," reinstalled Microsoft Windows and everything worked fine.

Of course, I'm kidding. I tried doing that and everything got steadily worse. The lads at International Business Machines Corp. offered to restore everything by erasing my data, so I politely declined, reinstalled Windows a couple more times myself, uttered a little prayer, and held my breath as I rebooted the computer for the umpteenth time. Miraculously, it worked!

Now, as long as I don't hit the keys too hard, and try not to be rude to it, the computer's fine.

Why can Windows still be such an unfriendly beast? Luckily I remembered enough about DOS, and where that setup file was, to get Windows running again. But it's a worrying reminder that for all the sophistication and alleged user-friendliness of computers, finding your way around on your own is still an unpleasant experience, even in Windows. With a little patience, and the help of a program called PowerDesk, things needn't be so bad. It won't necessarily save you from the c:/ prompt, but you might feel more in control of things.

PowerDesk is what's called a file manager. It replaces the Windows Explorer filing system and is designed to make searching for files, organizing folders (which used to be called "directories" in DOS days) and moving stuff around a lot less painful – especially if you're working on a network.

For me, it's a vital part of life, and I'm not sure what I'd do without it. Yes, I know it's not a sexy corner of the computing world, which may explain why there aren't that many players out there. Indeed, the king of file management, Symantec, says it hasn't upgraded its own offering, Norton Commander, since late 1998.

Which leaves the field open to programs such as PowerDesk. It uses the familiar format of a list of folders on the left of your screen, their contents in a second pane on the right. The program's been around for a couple of years, but the latest version, released last month, has lifted the bar. Basically, it'll save you a lot of time by offering you a host of features you wouldn't realize you desperately needed.

Consider this, for example: You're typing away in, say, Microsoft Word and you decide it's time to save the file before it disappears into the ether. You click on "save" and a dialog box pops up offering you a directory. It's never the right one. Which means you either go ahead and save, foolishly confident you'll remember the folder name, or you start clicking your way through other folders, until you find the one you want or it's time to go home.

With PowerDesk, all that's history. A widget called Dialog Helper will add two extra buttons to the corner of your Save dialog box – one a folder and one a blank piece of paper. The first one will remember the last dozen or so folders you accessed, while the second will remember recent file names. This feature isn't unique to PowerDesk, but it's a great start. It saves me hours, especially on networks.

Use some folders regularly? PowerDesk allows you to record your favorites in a special pull-down menu – much as you would bookmark a website, making getting back there a breeze. If you buy the pro version for about $20, you get some more cool features, such as built-in viewers, which let you read the contents of many types of files without having to open them.

Downsides? Well, if you never go near your Windows Explorer this may not be the terrain you feel comfortable in. And, while the program is well designed and well supported by its new owners, it does occasionally crash. But, on balance, it's the kind of software the big players don't seem to be interested in making anymore, and it's the kind of software that really does make your life easier. It won't save you when your computer crashes, but using it might give you a greater understanding of how your computer is organized, so that you know your way around when it does.

PowerDesk has gone through a few different incarnations since then. But it's still the best place to start (v-com.com/product/PowerDesk_Pro_Home.html). Here's what I had to say five years later, in August 2005:

If you're anything like me, you'll have been impressed at some point with how you can just plug your digital camera (or MP3 player) into your computer and the latter will seemingly know what you want it to do. With nary a beep, your photos or music, or videos, will be uploaded to the computer and you'll sit there wondering why you didn't ditch the old film camera/Walkman/portable gramophone years ago. You'll still be thinking this right up to the point you realize that, while you're reasonably confident all your photos, videos and music have been stored away on your comput-

☞ **stoke poges** (*n, Buckinghamshire*) A file that took ages to download but now won't open because the associated program is not installed or the file is corrupt, They sent me a stoke poges so I have no idea what all the excitement is about.

er, you have little idea exactly where. Congratulations. You've just replaced one type of pain – drawers full of family snaps, nothing to indicate where they were taken and only the embarrassing hairstyles and jackets to guide you as to the year – with another kind of pain: Digital Disorientation.

Digital Disorientation needn't be a problem. But overcoming it does require adopting some sound practices about what to do with your music, photos and videos. And no, I'm not going to try to pitch you some magic cure-all. Here's what I suggest you do.

First, don't blindly accept what your computer and software tell you – those dialog boxes, for example, that say, "Your computer has spotted that you've connected a camera or storage device. Would you like to transfer the photos to the following location?" It sounds great. It sounds as if your computer knows where you keep your photos. But every piece of software is different. And your computer, bless it, isn't smart enough to figure that out. So, if you blithely click "yes" on a dialog box like this, you may be committing your photographs to some subfolder from nomenclature hell that you will never find again. Not just that: The software may add a subfolder to that subfolder and give a weird name to it and to the files it transfers.

This may be fine if you're going to use the same camera and same photo software for the rest of your life. But chances are you won't be and that you'll be a two-camera or even a three-camera family, in which case your photos will end up in differently named folders with different file names. Remember: Control your computer. Don't let your computer control you. That's the golden rule. Here are the silver rules that follow on from it:

1. It's Your Folder, And You Can Rename It If You Want To

Decide where on your personal computer you're going to store your photos (this also applies to other files that you keep a lot of – video or music files, for example). You have quite a few options here: Windows and Macs tend to offer a single folder (My Photos, or some such), which isn't a bad place to start. But then you need to think about how to organize files inside that folder. Do you keep them all in the one subfolder, or do you create subfolders for each batch? If the latter, how are you going to label them?

Most photo transfer software will try to create subfolders for you, and there will be limited options for influencing how they are named. The best you can hope for is something that is a recognizable date, but there's nothing stopping you from renaming the folder later – "2005 June, Joe's Wedding." Another tip: Some photo transfer software will try to start a new subfolder with the product name. Explore the program's options menu until you can change this. There's nothing worse than having your firstborn's baby steps buried in a folder called "WhizSnaps Pro 2.0."

2. Trust No One

Some people will suggest you use photo organizing software (such as Adobe's Photoshop Album or Picasa) to organize your photos. There's nothing wrong with this sort of thing but don't mistake organizing stuff with storing stuff. These programs will dig around your hard disk and CD-ROMs and find all your pictures for you, but if your photo storage methods are lousy, they won't be much help. All you'll get are lots of duplicates and missing links, should you ever move your files around or lose a CD-ROM. Much better to give some order to your photos before you fire up one of these babies. (Needless to say, should one of these programs stop working or the company go bust, you're back to square one.)

3. Think Outside The Box

A few years ago we thought one gigabyte was a lot. Now 80 gigabytes can barely contain an average MP3 collection. So, chances are, your hard drive is already becoming not only messy but cluttered. My antidote for this is an external USB drive. They're as simple to attach as a camera, they're cheap (less than $150 for 80 gigabytes), they're portable and they'll keep working even if your computer doesn't. I now have four or five of these things and I spent a recent weekend splitting up my documents, music files and photos/videos and putting them on separate drives.

☞ **siston** (*n, South Gloucestershire*) The maze of network folders in your office that have long been abandoned.

You may not need to go so far as a weekend of unparalleled excitement, but I'd certainly recommend keeping these big image files off the main computer. At some point – when you upgrade, or when there are just too many files competing for space – you'll have to move them anyway, so it pays to think ahead. The other great thing about this is that you have your photos (or videos or music files) in a form you can put in your pocket.

Don't want to splash out on more hardware? Assign an old computer or laptop you no longer use to just storing your photos and music. If you have a home network other members of the family can also access these files.

4. Folder Management

Staying on top of your file folders pays off big time later. Take the time every so often to wander through your photo (or MP3) folders to check everything looks hunky dory, weed out duplicates and rename folders to make them more intelligible. I cut my photo folder nearly in half by getting rid of duplicates or pictures I knew I would never need. (In Windows Explorer select the View option "Thumbnail" so you can easily see what the photos are, rather than just their file name.)

Doing a spot of housekeeping on your files – whether they're photos, music or other kinds like Word documents or PowerPoint presentations – isn't something that Microsoft seems to encourage. The Windows Explorer program, which shows you what is stored in all the folders on your computer, is buried in the Accessories menu in Windows XP.

This has always struck me as a little silly. It's a bit like hiding your in-tray in the basement to make your office look cleaner. I'd recommend spending quite a bit of time looking not just in your My Documents folder but in other folders dotted around your hard disk, so you can see what's being stored where.

Windows Explorer and PowerDesk are fine for this, but there are other programs that offer some extra bells and whistles. A popular and free file manager (as they're usually called) is ExplorerXP (www.explorerxp.com), which lets you look in lots of different folders at once. More fancy ones, such as ExplorerPlus (www.sendphotos.com/Products/ExplorerPlus), also let you simultaneously view the contents of files, which makes housekeeping a lot easier.

For a more extensive list check out this page on my Loose Wire blog, which is regularly added to by readers: www.tinyurl.com/ccsxm. File management isn't for everyone, but if you're serious about keeping your memories on your computer, I'd recommend giving it a try.

productivity tools

We all talk about computers, but actually it's inside software where we spend most of our day. Which is why I spend a lot of time looking at programs, testing them, getting excited about them, cursing at them, and, ultimately, getting a bit disappointed with them. My rule of thumb is that software has to be well designed, nice to look at, intuitive, and serious about saving me time and making me more productive. A tall order, which is why most programs I try out I rarely recommend to readers. But here are some I think do at least some of the above, and which is why I've included them here (see also the chapter on organizing stuff). First off, a program called ActiveWords, which I first wrote about in early 2004:

I'm about to tell you about one of those software programs that could save you some serious slogging. So if you're a lawyer or someone else who bills for your time, then you may want to skip this week's column. But if you're interested in getting more out of your computer by doing less, then you should buckle up and read on.

This is the deal: Right now, when you use your computer (I'm talking about Windows here, but it's also true for Apple users) you're working with what the boffins call a Graphical User Interface, or GUI, for the windows, the buttons, the icons, the toolbars, all that hoopla. You use a mouse or a track point to navigate it.

This is what the scientists call a Major Advance On The Old Days, when your screen was monochrome, you had to launch your word-processing program by typing "wordperfect" into a blinking spot on the screen called a c:> prompt, and you could only attach cute pictures of your nephew to your desktop using sticky tape. Icons? Windows you could move around? Opening more than one program at a time? Forget it.

Now think about all this for a second. The whole idea of the GUI thing was to make life easier for us. But is it? How do you launch your word processor? Remember the program name (Microsoft Word), remember what the icon looks like (a blue "W" shape), remember where it's located (somewhere in that menu thingy on the left, right?), move the mouse there and click. Bingo, you're in. How about if you need to open a particular folder – say, your customers' invoices – which are stored, because you're an organized person, in c:\MyDocuments\Customers\Invoices. You would do all the same things you did to open Microsoft Word, except click on the Windows Explorer icon instead, then navigate through all the subfolders until you got to the Invoices folder. Bingo again.

But why is it so convoluted? Sure, it may be easier than the old ways of doing things (which most of you will be too young to remember), but is it really necessary to do all those clicks? Answer: No. Not if you use something called ActiveWords.

ActiveWords (www.activewords.com) is a very simple program that requires a bit of prior explanation, which is why I've blathered on a bit. Now imagine you're doing all the stuff mentioned above, only this time using ActiveWords. To open Microsoft Word, for example, type "word" anywhere, in any Window. Then hit the F8 function key. Hey presto, Word launches. Open the invoices folder? Type "invoices," hit F8 and off it goes. Your hands never leave the keyboard to grab the mouse, or scratch your head trying to remember what the Word icon looks like and which submenu it's in. You just have to remember "word" or "invoices." In the words of one of the creators of ActiveWords, a friendly, loquacious Minnesotan lawyer called Buzz Bruggeman, it's all about "getting the machinery out of people's faces."

Put simply, Windows is too graphical. We recognize pictures more easily, but some things are easier to remember as names. If you called a folder "photos," it's going to be much easier to find if all you have to do is type "photos" instead of remembering which subfolder it's in. But ActiveWords doesn't stop there. Say you do a lot of typing of the same old stuff, day in, day out: boiler-plate phrases, from your name to the company's name, to letters along the lines of "thanks for your offer of a mildly masochistic relationship but I'm rather tied up at the moment." All this can be assigned to short memorable words, or initials, or just single letters. If you're tired of typing your name, just instruct ActiveWords to replace JW with Jeremy Wagstaff and, if your name happens to be the same as mine, you should be extremely happy.

ActiveWords is unobtrusive: It's a small bar that sits at the top or bottom of your screen and waits for you to do stuff. It requires some setting up, and a bit of getting used to, not so much because it's difficult (it's not), but because it involves you thinking a bit differently about how you work. At about $50 it's not dirt cheap, but it's well worth it for the time it saves. Try it. Just don't blame me if you get so productive you run out of ways to fill your day.

Another lesson I've learned over nearly two decades fiddling with software and six years writing about it: While software should look nice, don't be fooled by the size of the box it comes in, or the fancy graphics on the company's website. In fact, a lot of software is homegrown, some individual's labor of love. This is called shareware, a kind of product I paid tribute to in October 2000:

There used to be a little tumbledown house not far from the Tower of London where two craftsmen sweated in front of a furnace making the typeset for a bus conductor's ticket machine. When the part-English, part-Irish poet and writer P.J. Kavanagh stumbled across them in the late 1950s, he found two men in pastry-chef hats depressed that their hot, soot-soaked work was destined for oblivion: "You never really look at your ticket, do

☞ **brasted chart** (*n, Kent*) A PowerPoint presentation that is heavy on graphics and low on information. *The seminar was a washout. Lots of brasted charts and monologues.*

you – read it, I mean?" he quoted one of them as saying in his memoir, "A Perfect Stranger."

Those typesetters, like many artisans the world over, are long gone. But it doesn't mean the Internet age has deprived us of individuals who, in the words of Mr. Kavanagh, "work alone, with a high degree of pride and skill, seeking nobody's praise." Indeed, the Net has been a boon to such people, providing them with easy access to a market and an easy way to interact with their customers. Chief among these new artisans: software writers.

Take, for example, Robert Galle, a 28-year old Slovenian whose archiving program Where Is It? boasts 23,000 registered users (www.whereisit-soft.com). I'm one of them, and having used it for a couple of years, I can testify to its excellence. The program will quickly index all the files on CD-ROMs, Zip drives, floppies, or any other media, allowing you to quickly find errant programs or document files among your stacks of disks. It's small – about 2.5 megabytes – yet loaded with features and configurability.

Mr. Galle is clearly someone who takes pride in his work. A former high-school teacher who started learning his craft at the age of 10, he can be spotted scouting for Internet connections on holiday so he can field as many as 80 customer emails a day. "I believe that delivering functionality through well-thought- out design and user interaction is the basic key," he wrote in a recent email. The fact that he writes all the software by himself probably helps. "I always try to write software the way I would want to have it as a user, even though this often complicates my life as a programmer."

In a world of increasingly bloated programs written by committee, it's a refreshing attitude. It's similar to the point of view taken by Michael Marshall, 33-year-old author of another killer application, Jot Plus (www.kingstairs.com/jot). An American resident in Britain, Mr. Marshall has built up a loyal following of 3,000 customers in 42 countries. Jot Plus is a simple, elegantly written text database program that stores information in tree-and-branch style: Headings and subheadings appear in a pane on the left, the main text on the right. It's a great way to overcome a key obstacle

☞ **blatherwycke** (*n, Northamptonshire*) The person who comes into your cubicle and won't leave, and yet somehow manages to get their work done and go home long before you do.

in computing – storing chunks of information, and giving them some semblance of order without creating elaborate databases. And it's small. You could fit the downloaded program on a floppy disk.

Discipline is key to crafting such programs. Mr. Marshall says that while he stays in close touch with users, he's politely declined suggested enhancements that might increase the software size and take it away from its core task. "The software needs to be focused, developed with a specific market or intention," he says.

But aren't such artisans a dying breed, likely trampled by the behemoths of the computing world? I reckon not. I, for one, rely on several of them to get my work done. Mr. Marshall's King Stairs Software has been profitable since 1996, which, while not enough to live off, has helped him win clients in his computer contracting business. "Prospective clients can be quite impressed when you tell them that your 'hobby' is a profitable professional business," he says. For Mr. Galle, Where Is It? generates income about 10 times the Slovenian average. Not bad – and no blazing furnaces or soot-filled air for either of them.

Both of these programs and their makers are still going strong, I'm pleased to announce. And I still use both programs. Shareware is by definition not going to make their masters rich, but that doesn't stop people from building programs. Indeed, for a columnist it's an uphill battle trying to sift through all the programs available to find stuff that's worth passing on. That most of the companies behind them are one person, without a PR department to spread the word, it's mostly a case of hit and miss. Despite that, shareware has its own history, and its own hero, whose passing in November 2002 I felt merited noting:

Bob Wallace, one of Microsoft's first employees and yet as unlike Microsoft as you could get, died last month aged 53. In a position to make millions – his original Microsoft stock was worth $15 million at one point – he showed little interest in money, preferring to pursue his interest in the therapeutic use of drugs like ecstasy. "My philosophy is that I want to make a living, not a killing," he was given to saying. By all accounts a gentle and decent man, his attitude was a significant contribution to one corner of the computer revolution that remains largely untainted by dot-com greed. It's called shareware.

Shareware is 20 years old this month, give or take a week or two, and its durability is a reminder that underneath all the faddishness of technology there are enduring currents that keep the revolution going. In the early 1980s very few folk had a computer, and even if they did, there wasn't much they could do with it – a bit like buying a sports car with only your backyard to race around in. The shortage of software drove enthusiasts like Jim Knopf, from Washington, and Andrew Fluegelman, from California, to write their own, which they did: Knopf a labelling program called Easy-File, Fluegelman a program which allowed a computer to dial up, using a modem, to another computer. Not revolutionary, but both filled a hole. Neither man was particularly interested in making a pile of money out of his work, but handing out the programs on diskette started getting expensive, particularly for the growing number of folk who wanted updated versions when they became available. Both, working independently and unaware of each other's existence, came up with the same idea: Add a little pop-up message to the program that invites satisfied users to make a donation. To their astonishment, money started coming in. And when Knopf found out about Fluegelman's approach, they got together and a new industry was born.

Only they didn't call it shareware. Fluegelman called it "freeware" and then, perhaps a tad foolishly, and not quite in keeping with the touchy-feely nature of the enterprise, went off and trademarked the name. All that did was to ensure no one else wanting to distribute their software in the same way called their product freeware, and the label ended up being used only for products for which no payment was expected. Knopf, who went by the daring nom de guerre of Jim Button, preferred "user-supported software" which quietly died for a different reason: It wasn't memorable, and while strictly speaking accurate, sounded more like a middle-aged

☞ **fonthill gifford** (*n, Wiltshire*) The confusion that arises from having too many typefaces to choose from.

woman's undergarment. It was only when Bob Wallace, who at that time had quit Microsoft to produce a small editing program called PC-Write, started using the term "shareware" that it started catching on.

Shareware was all very homespun in those days, and still is for many of the thousands of folk who write and sell software this way. But for many it's also been a lucrative business: Wallace's company, QuickSoft, was employing 30 people and turning over $2 million a year at its height; 45,000 people had registered to use the software. Jim Knopf quickly found his editing software was making him 10 times what he was earning at IBM so he quit his day job: His software had 700,000 users at its peak. At shareware's heart was a simple concept: Try the product first and if you like it, pay for it. That payment will also ensure you get upgrades of the product.

Brilliant in its simplicity and addictive in its appeal, shareware evolved as technology changed. Originally focusing on mainstream programs like word processing and spreadsheets, shareware developers were unable to keep up with the big companies producing sophisticated Office-type suites, and so they moved into more niche markets, like utilities to fix computer problems, or managing CD collections or keeping a record of your dwindling gym visits.

As the Internet has expanded, and access has grown faster, so has the world of shareware. There are now thousands of sites devoted to shareware, most of very high quality. The model is that devised by Bob Wallace and the others: Users can check out the software for a month and then either be nagged by pop-up windows into paying to keep using it, or find that certain features stop functioning. In some cases software developers have found such restrictions unnecessary: Karen Kenworthy, who has developed several tools I couldn't live without, allows users to download any or all of her software for free (www.karenware.com), but finds that enough people pay for the whole set of programs on one CD-ROM to offer her a decent living.

Of the three founding fathers of shareware, only Knopf is left (although I didn't manage to track him down for this article). After a heart attack in 1992, he retired to the peace and solitude of the Pacific Northwest. But their dream lives on: Shareware is an engine of the PC revolution as writers come up with new ideas – that sometimes get taken up by the industry big boys. Spam blockers? Virus checkers? MP3 players? All of them started out as shareware (or freeware). Indeed, with the exception of the likes of Microsoft, or of programs that are too big to download, most software is now available on a try-before-you-buy basis. There's no better testament to the gentle Bob Wallace.

While shareware marches on, another kind of software has ridden the wave of better Internet connections and a newfound passion for simplicity and stripped down functionality: The web application. Here's how I saw it in late 2005:

Why do they make software so complicated, when it was software that was supposed to make our lives easier? Take Microsoft Word, for example. We all use it. But do we have any idea what most of the program's buttons and menu items actually do?

I had a slow morning recently, so I started counting the number of functions in the latest edition of Microsoft Word. In default mode, there are nine columns of menus, each with between 10 and 27 submenu items. That's between 90 and 243 functions, or almost one function for every day of the year. And then there are all the little dialog boxes and pull-down lists you can tick, untick or whatever: I counted more than 150 different tick boxes in the Options tab alone. Does anyone have any idea what all these little buttons do, and, more importantly, how they should be used? I've been using Microsoft Word for more than 15 years and I still don't know. And those I do know about I've never completely mastered. Stylesheets leave me baffled. I still can't quite grasp the tracking changes function.

This is known in the industry as "feature bloat." But is there a cure? Sort of. There is a growing movement away from big programs in favor of smaller ones – users don't want a lot of features in a program. These applications – called "Web apps" – are usually stored on the Internet and accessed via a Web browser, rather than saved on the user's own computer. Because accessing software over the Internet is going to be slower than accessing something on your own computer, these programs are by necessity smaller and simpler. I think of it as software getting out of the way of the user.

Consider this column, for instance. I'm writing it in a browser on a website called Writely (www.writely.com). The page actually looks a bit like Microsoft Word, and it feels like Microsoft Word. There are some pull-down menus to change the font and size of the letters, as well as bold, italic and underline buttons – the usual basic editing palaver. But not much else. No complex menus, no endless rows of indecipherable buttons. In fact, little to get in the way of writing this piece. And the file itself is stored on the website rather than in my computer, meaning I could easily finish it more or less anywhere I happened to have access to a computer. Oh, and it's free.

There's another aspect at work here. Because these programs are Internet-based, they are great for collaboration. Usually "collaboration" doesn't mean much more than editing a Word document, emailing it to a colleague who then changes stuff, adds stuff, deletes stuff and introduces a few more errors before sending it back. Sure, Word will let you track those changes, but that function is ugly, slow and often more than you need. Writely isn't only simpler, but it lets you collaborate with other users at the same time: A little message in the bottom of the browser will alert you when someone else is editing the document you are working on, and your changes will be synced with theirs in real time.

You might think that a Web-based application would be clumsy and slow. What helps these applications work is a newfound technique for making Web pages work faster. Sometimes called Ajax, this technique is really a bundle of existing technologies that, simply put, speeds up the interaction between your browser and the computer that the Web page (or application) is sitting on. Usually when you click on a link in a Web page, that instruction goes back to the host computer, which in turn refreshes the whole page. That can take a while, and is especially annoying if only part of the Web page comes back updated. Ajax (and similar approaches that aren't, strictly speaking, techniques that fall under the Ajax umbrella)

☞ **okeford fitzpane** (*n, Dorset*) A program that always crowds out other programs from your screen, wherever you move it. *I can't get any work done. The program is an okeford fitzpane.*

either sends back instructions to update only that part of the page that needs it, or else handles the instruction on your computer. The result: Your browser starts responding as efficiently and quickly as a program sitting on your computer.

Enough mechanics. The bottom line here is that a lot of people are building more simple, task-focused applications that make use of these new approaches without bogging it down with new features. A new player on the block this month: Writeboard, which allows individuals and groups to edit a piece of text online, all the while seeing what has been removed, edited or otherwise changed from previous versions. Once again, this is possible with Microsoft Word, but I've never really figured out how to do it, whereas with Writeboard (www.writeboard.com) I figured it out in a couple of seconds.

Now, it isn't that the guys writing these simpler programs couldn't add more features. They are just following a different approach to their forebears. Whereas in the past, software would be developed in secret and then released in its entirety on a gasping and impressed world, a lot of software developers prefer to release a basic working model and then add features depending on how customers use the application and what extra bits they request. While this sounds like the tired old story of companies releasing products before they are ready, it isn't like that. For a start, these Web applications are simple, so the chances of big bugs are small. Secondly, because the application is stored on the company's own server, the software itself can be fixed quickly and easily. No patches and updates that need to be downloaded.

Downsides? Not everyone has a reliable Internet connection, meaning sometimes you mightn't be able to access the application you need or, if your files are not stored on your own computer, your data. And while some services say they take snapshots of your data, if your Internet connection goes down half way through editing a document, the risks are higher that you'll lose stuff. There are also privacy issues: The Web pages your collaborations are stored on are password protected but of course they are vulnerable to a skillful and malicious hacker or someone who really, really wants to know what you are doing. Then again, that's true of pretty much anything you do online. And a minor quibble: I've noticed that typing a document into, say, Writely, inserts different apostrophes to the ones that I (and, more importantly, my editors) use. But these are minor quibbles and are eclipsed by the benefits of being able to do what you need without lots of fuss, digging around in menus, or expensive software. Computers, helped along by the Internet, may yet make our lives easier.

There are plenty of other examples of this kind of simple software out there – in fact the market has become saturated in the months since I wrote that piece. Microsoft, Yahoo!, AOL and Google are all entering this field in force, either buying up or trampling on smaller startups (Google bought up Writely, for example). Anything I recommend here might not be around by the time you read this, but here's a mention of a few: Online editors and collaboration tools include JotSpot Live (www.jotlive.com), which lets you add pages and edit them in real time with others. There's Zoho Writer (www.zohowriter.com), another online editor, and its close kin Zoho Planner (www.zohoplanner.com), which like BackPack (www.backpackit.com) lets you organize to-do lists, keep appointments and collaborate with others. Another editor is SynchroEdit (www.synchroedit.com), which takes a somewhat different tack, developing an online editor, that is free to be developed by others and incorporated into their respective Web applications.

Looking for a simple online spreadsheet? Check out Num Sum (www.numsum.com). A more personal kind of spreadsheet-cum-database can be found at TracksLife (www.trackslife.com), which lets you keep track of your diet, your budget or your exercise program, online. For those familiar with the Wiki concept a great example is Schtuff (www.schtuff.com), which simplifies the Wiki approach to let users quickly collaborate online. Lastly, for those mind mappers out there, check out Mayomi (www.mayomi.com), which lets you build impressive looking mind maps – quickfire drawings that link ideas to a central topic – online in seconds. All of these applications are either entirely free, or offer a free version with some limitations. All are worth checking out.

scanning

Here's another lost cause I've been espousing: the paperless office. Here's how I saw it in an early piece in 2000 about a company called ScanSoft, which had recently snapped up most of the available scanning and paper management software:

What exactly is document scanning/management? Well, in brief, it's about that long-predicted nonevent, the paperless office. Don't laugh. It still could happen, despite the fact that today people use more paper than ever, according to Wayne Crandall, senior vice president at ScanSoft.

I, for one, have to 'fess up: I'm a scanning nut. I figure if you can't scan it, it's not worth hanging on to. Business cards, bank statements, letters from Mom; you name it, I've scanned it into my hard drive.

So now my entire life is no longer hard copy. Last year I threw out a four-drawer filing cabinet. And no regrets: Now I can find my Visa card statement from 1992 faster than my bank can. That layoff letter from the BBC? Got it to hand, virtually. A letter Aunt Margie sent me in 1992? It's there on my hard disk. Wherever I go. And retrievable in seconds.

It's a simple enough process. Buy a scanner – more or less any one will do. Run it over whatever you want to store. Give it a name. Save it. Want to convert a letter to text you can edit? Fire up the Optical Character Recognition, or OCR, program. It's there in Microsoft Word ready for you to edit. Want to touch up a photo? The software is there to handle it.

Then you can store it, fax it, copy it, alter it – and throw out the original. That's it.

It's not that this stuff is particularly new. OCR software was boasting high success rates in the early 1990s. But only now is that claim halfway true. Other changes make scanning and document storage something worth considering. Hard drive sizes are growing and prices shrinking: And these scanned files do suck up room. Scanners are cheaper, too: They're about $100 these days, if not less. And they come bundled with basic scanning software. Processors are faster, meaning the entire scanning and OCR process isn't too tedious. And finding stuff you need later is, in theory, easy.

If you want to take the plunge now, where should you start? Well, scanners are all pretty much the same. You have a choice between flat-bed (they look like a photocopy top, without all the paper trays), and sheet-fed ones, which vary in design: An old favorite of mine is Logitech's PageScan Color Pro, which takes about 10 sheets in a feeder and can be removed from its base to scan books and other bound documents you're queasy about ripping to bits.

It's the software that's key. For all this to work, you've got to have software that helps you scan things quickly, and helps you slot things away somewhere safe, allowing you to get them back quickly and easily. Which brings us back to ScanSoft. With the purchase of Caere, ScanSoft now owns three of the four main players in the field: Pagis Pro, PageKeeper Pro and PaperPort. Lurking in the background is one of the first document-management products, PaperMaster, owned by Documagix before it too was bought out, this time by eFax.com.

So how do they shape up? I tried out version 3.0 of PageKeeper, which was launched when Caere was still an independent company. I had trouble installing the program, which wasn't a good sign. And it comes bundled with a software version of Post-It Notes, which loaded itself without asking me. But once it was running, everything worked well. As with most of these products, the software is built around an Explorer-style interface, with drives and folders listed on the left, the contents of your files – pictures, documents, clippings – on the right. Scan in whatever you need, and you can see a thumbnail on your screen. PageKeeper works hard to automate as much of this as it can, while adding two important features: Scanned files are left in their original format – meaning other programs can read them – and also will work as the main repository of other files on your hard drive, scanned or not. The result: a one-stop shop for keeping and finding stuff.

That said, there are shortcomings. I put mom's letter into the default directory offered, and I had trouble finding it again. Not something she'd be happy to hear about. Another gripe: The software doesn't feel particularly professional, despite its name. It's as if Caere isn't really visualizing that users will be serious about storing stuff.

Pagis Pro has a better feel to it. Bundled with high-grade Textbridge OCR software and programs that help you to fill out scanned forms (a real timesaver), copy documents and alter photographs, Pagis Pro takes compatibility with Explorer a stage further by adding easy-to-spot folders in your hard drive's hierarchical structure. It's both more intuitive and more functional: You now can view any file on your hard drive from Pagis Pro's souped-up Explorer interface. Want to OCR a document? Just drag it onto the OCR icon at the bottom of the screen.

Like PageKeeper, you can let the software keep a track of your hard disk, indexing new stuff as it's added to ensure you can find documents quickly. This is a good feature but uses up memory and slows things down.

Paperport, meanwhile, now on version 6.5, hasn't improved much since I first tried it as the bundled software with a Visioneer scanner in 1996. (I ended up chucking both.) Documents are stored as piles that manage to appear unsightly and hard to read at the same time. And there's not much you can alter in the interface to suit your preferences.

But for disappointments, eFax.com's PaperMaster takes the cake. It's a once-great product that has failed to move with the times. Eschewing the Explorer style interface for a filing cabinet metaphor (pull-out drawers and

☞ **snaisgill** (*n, County Durham*) The person who last used the communal printer but didn't replenish the paper.

folders, gray metal-looking cabinet), PaperMaster 98 does have its pluses. It does a good job of letting you view documents: Thumbnails appear in the top of the window with the selected page below (an improvement on the other products reviewed here). Scan a document and it'll try to work out what folder it fits best in. But the filing cabinet thing looks cheesy these days, and with no room for the user to control folder and file names, things can and do go missing. I have no idea what eFax intends to do with the program since my emailed requests for information went unanswered. eFax doesn't even refer to the product on its homepage but has acknowledged in security filings difficulties in absorbing Documagix into its primary business, namely Internet faxing.

This raises one of several warning flags if you're considering a shift to the paperless-ish office: Don't get stuck with a product that saves scanned documents in its own file format. If the company goes bust, or disappears into the ether like PaperMaster, you're stuck. (Following this advice, PageKeeper wins, with Pagis Pro a near second. And ScanSoft's Mr. Crandall confirms the company intends to keep supporting all products.)

Another word to the wise: Back up your computer regularly. Losing a hard-disk worth of filing cabinets could be a problem. Especially if Aunt Margie finds out you trashed the hard copies of her letters.

Scanning isn't just about documents. Another beautiful idea which is still struggling to take hold is that little pocket scanners can convert piles of business cards into a digital database. A year later, in July 2001, I took a look at what was available:

I'm not sure which relative offered me this pearl of wisdom: Never trust anyone whose eyes are too close together, whose feet are smaller than his hat size, or who has a moustache. Now, of course, I have no truck with this kind of offensive, prejudiced talk, but I have to confess my own little bias – business cards that have to be read vertically, and not horizontally.

What is it with the people who design these things? Have they never figured out that these cards have to go somewhere, and that's usually in a horizontal card box? Most importantly: have they never tried to feed these things through a business card scanner?

They have no excuse in my view; business card scanners have been around for a while. Basically, they are small desktop gadgets that plug into your computer, read a business card and then try to map the contents to a database – name in the name field, company name in the company field – you get the picture. The user, then, can find a number easily and dump the cards. Not exactly rocket science, but a useful tool, until the day we can do away with business cards altogether.

So why hasn't that day dawned? In our new digital world we were all supposed to be walking around with virtual business cards – vcards – that stored all our important contact information and could be moved effortlessly between computers, mobile phones and personal organizers.

Well, it isn't that nothing has changed, just that it is changing very slowly. Palm-sized digital assistants, or PDAs, have helped create a standard of sorts for managing contacts. Users of the Palm brand of PDAs, for example, are famous for beaming their contact details to one another. vcards aren't completely dead, either. And online databases allow users to automatically update their details with other users. In theory all this is great. In practice, very few people are using such things, which means it is some way from reaching critical mass.

In other words, we are still stuck with business cards – and scanners. My advice: If you have a stack of business cards on your desk and don't already have a scanner, buy one, but don't expect miracles.

This is because they haven't really improved much since the last time I took a serious look. True, most now work off the USB – or universal serial bus – port of your computer, meaning they are a bit faster, usually don't need an external power source, and are easier to install. But they could be better.

The IRIS Business Card Reader from Image Recognition Integrated Systems SA (www.irislink.com), stands upright and the cards are fed from the top, dropping into a trough. A nice touch. The CardScan 600c from Corex Technologies Inc. (www.cardscan.com) follows the more usual practice where the cards are fed in horizontally. BizCardReader 600c, made by CardReader Inc. (www.bizcardreader.com), is more compact but doesn't have a tray for the cards, which is messier.

Scanning itself isn't the problem; all these products do a good job. It is what happens to the contents that counts, and here it starts to get ugly. Each product has its own scanning and field-mapping program, and they aren't great. For one thing they're clunky and look as if they were written in the mid-1990s, when it was acceptable to have weird menu configurations and little guys twiddling with their moustaches instead of buttons. IRIS's Cardiris, for example, loads a separate, unexplained program which doesn't inspire confidence, and while it has a neat option for switching scanning language (from Belgian Dutch to Taiwanese English, whatever they are) it also crashed my computer.

BizCardReader's software didn't look to be much of an improvement – the icons look as if they were designed by a four-year-old – but at least it didn't crash. CardScan's software is a lot better: It even reads vertically aligned cards automatically. All the programs do a pretty good job of reading the card – with about 90% accuracy – and assigning the data to the right fields. CardScan is the most flexible in allowing you to fiddle with the results by dragging text around.

In the end, though, these gadgets appeal to people who already have contact software such as Microsoft Outlook, and who most probably have a Palm or other PDA device. So they only make sense if they hook up well with these things. And do they? Well, they try. Most allow exporting (moving the data to another program), or synchronizing (checking if the data matches that in, say, Outlook). CardScan, however, wins out, since it can, at the click of a button, move data to Palm software, Outlook, a Windows CE or even a Psion.

In short, they could be great time savers. But the manufacturers have yet to figure out that the scanners are only as good as the software that comes with them. And that doesn't mean building lots of cutesy features

☞ **blockley** (*n, Gloucestershire*) Error messages that won't go away,

into the program, but in making it a simple and fast interface between the scanning unit and the user's contact-database program. In a perfect world the software would be no more than a button in Outlook that does the whole scanning, interpreting and mapping thing seamlessly. And please, no little guys twiddling their moustache on the button.

I felt the paperless office was worth another look three years later, although I remained suitably cautious:

If you have read any book or article on the paperless office in the past 10 years, you'll almost certainly have also seen the words "myth," "non-existent," "failure" or "disaster" somewhere in there. Trees have been felled to write reams on how our hopes for a paperless work environment have not been realized, and that it's never going to happen. Well, I'm here to tell you that is all hogwash, and we've just been asking the wrong questions. It's quite possible to be paperless. I'll tell you how.

The first Loose Wire rule of paper management is: Forget about printouts for the moment. The question of making an environment paperless is not "How much are you printing out?" but "How much are you storing on your computer?" The paperless office, to cite Abigail Sellen and Richard Harper, authors of *The Myth of the Paperless Office*, is not about using less paper, but about keeping less paper.

Think about: How can I move stuff that is in piles, cupboards, folders, box files and under my desk into my computer? To do this, you need to make a distinction between documents that I would call "live" and those that I would call "filing fodder." A bank statement, for example, is fodder. You may need it at some point but you don't need it now. A mind-map you've drawn on how to make your home-office paperless, however, is live: It's not just a piece of paper, or a printout, but a receptacle of your ideas, doodlings and several phone messages you took while you were drawing it up.

☞ **bilbrough** (*n, North Yorkshire*) The place where all your bills go so you can't find them.

More than that, it's a trigger to more ideas in your head that you didn't get to commit to paper, so it's still living, still useful, and best kept close by. It reflects the best of paper: flexible, tangible, multi-colored, something you can carry with you to the rest-room or lunch. Clearing it away won't help you, but getting the bank statement out of the way might.

Now, there's a very good reason why we don't like going paperless, and that's because we carry around very good mental maps of where physical objects are. (It must date back to our ancestors, who could find anything in their cave even when the fire had gone out.) So even – perhaps, especially – folk with messy desks can find stuff in a blink. Paperless means letting go of that, by scanning documents into your computer. That means entrusting stuff to the likes of Mr. Gates or Mr. Jobs (or Mr. Torvalds, if you're a Linux devotee) and if you've learned anything from me it's that that is not a great idea. How are you going to find something if you scan it into your computer? The answer: planning. Hence the second rule: Have a system.

What you need: a scanner to feed your paper through, some software to convert it into a digital format that you can store on your computer, and then some way of finding the document quickly and viewing it on your computer. Choosing the right scanner is important: If you've got a ton of A4 sheets to scan, there's not much point in buying a flatbed scanner (one of those lie-down ones that look like a photocopier without the body) because you'll still be scanning on Doomsday. Neither does it make much sense to buy a sheet-feed scanner (one which looks like a wringer where you feed the paper through one side and it comes out the other) if all the stuff you want to scan is bound into books, magazines or the Dead Sea Scrolls. Here is a basic principle: Don't buy anything that scans slowly. Nowadays you should be able to scan a stack of 20 pages in about five minutes – both sides. Anything less and the whole paperless office gets boring pretty quickly.

But scanning is only half the trick in Paperless Land. You want to make sure that what you scan is in a format that you can fiddle with and move around easily, and that you can find it again without employing forensic auditors. Sadly, there is no single program I'd recommend here.

PaperPort from Scansoft is not a bad piece of software which helps you to tweak and organize your scanned documents but it's not perfect. Papermaster, now owned by J2 Global Communications, used to be a great scan-and-file program, and does some things better than PaperPort, but has lost fans with its new interface, which takes away as many features as it adds. My advice: Use one of these programs, but spend some time thinking about how you want to organize your scans, and be consistent in labeling them.

In the end, whether the system works for you and you stick to it will depend on whether you can recover the documents again quickly. As Barbara Hemphill, author of *Taming the Paper Tiger at Work*, puts it: "The issue, based on my 20+ years of experience is not whether it's paper or whether it's electronic, it's 'Can you find it when you need it?'" Exactly. And now, dear reader, for future reference, and as your first task, please scan this article.

One of the devices that changed my mind about scanning was Fujitsu's ScanSnap 5110EOX (selling for between $300 and $650) which is small, sleek and fast. It moves through pages – both sides – in seconds and works with the push of a button, scanning everything into Adobe Acrobat format (a very common kind of file format). I still use mine, and find it prevents one of the biggest bottlenecks in trying to go paperless: the mound of unscanned documents that sit in a tray waiting for someone to scan and annotate. With the ScanSnap you only need a minute or two to scan in several pages, especially if you couple the device with software like PaperPort. If you want to scan, I'd recommend it. If you're not inclined to scan, I'd not recommend you start now. (Although I'd love to know just how you do cope with paper overload!) If you're looking for a compromise, you might want to consider just scanning those things that really need scanning, such as receipts. I took a look at this corner of the market in a piece in May 2006:

Receipts. We hate them and we love them. We hate them when cashiers hand them to us along with our change, or wrapped around our credit cards like little blankets. Then the receipt has no meaning or value; it's just an annoying piece of trash that gets stuffed into a pocket, a shopping bag or down the back of your partner's jacket as you leave the shop or restaurant or wedding parlor. Then, come tax- or expense-filing time, it becomes the most sought-after scrap of papyrus since the Gospel of Judas, sought throughout the house, trash and nearby landfill and then painstakingly restored by a team of archeologists, poring over its faded ink in a desperate bid to extract meaning. ("Yes, it's definitely evidence of a pen-buying spree. I'd say ballpoints.") By then it feels like the receipt is worth more than the thing it records payment for.

Doesn't it strike you, in the early years of the 21st century, as a bit weird that we still use pretty much the same process of recording transactions as early Mesopotamian barley sellers? In fact, they had it slightly better: Their receipts were carved on stone tablets, reducing the chances of losing one behind the sofa, or of the writing being rendered almost immediately unreadable because it was printed on rapidly fading thermal paper.

It isn't much better on the Internet. True, there are e-receipts, where you buy something online and are either sent an email or asked to save a Web page. Great, except that now your receipt is even easier to lose than a physical one, simply by hitting delete, forgetting what folder you saved it to or losing it in your email inbox. So most people print it out and lose it in the traditional way.

There are plans for digital receipts, to replace the old paper ones. Some involve smartcards that store all your receipts, allowing you to load them onto and sort them on your computer. If you have to return something to a store, the retailer can view your receipt by swiping the smartcard through a terminal.

Another option comes from Philadelphia-based company NeatReceipts Inc., which recently released a new version of its Scanalizer, a combination of scanner and software that, in theory, should ease the pain of the whole receipt-storing and retrieving process. The scanner is thin and portable:

☞ **bream** (*n, Gloucestershire*) The pile of unclaimed printouts in the communal printer.

about the same shape, weight and size as a packet of spaghetti. The software itself not only lets you scan in the receipt; it also reads the scanned text and extracts details, such as the value and date of the transaction, putting them into a database. It will even try to figure out what kind of transaction it was – restaurant, hotel, or whatever.

The software also tries to cater for people filing tax returns; it includes several tax-related fields and a way to create reports according to client, payment type, project and vendor. Such reports are acceptable to the U.S. Internal Revenue Service, as the receipts can't be altered once they've been scanned.

The guys behind the Scanalizer seem to have done their homework, and have forged an interesting niche that's halfway between "scan and forget" products like Nuance Communication Inc.'s PaperPort, that allow you to scan any document into your computer, and general financial organizer products like Intuit Inc.'s Quicken and Microsoft Corp.'s Money. The result is a product that is gradually finding a sizable market of its own, says Jeff Vogel, marketing director of NeatReceipts. "Our original customers were business travelers doing expense reports," he says. "We have since moved primarily to small business...owners, and even the home market, for people who want to keep organized budgets and so forth."

I'd recommend NeatReceipts if you're getting buried under cash register rolls. With a bit of discipline you could really organize yourself, even if you're on the road. (The scanner comes with its own cute little bag, and runs off its USB port connection to your computer, so you don't have to carry any extra power adapters.) And the scanner can just as easily scan photos or documents into other programs. At about $220, it isn't a bad deal.

Of course, it isn't a perfect solution. A perfect solution would be: all receipts, whether they're issued by Big Bad Corp. or Smelly Joe's Roadside Diner, the same size, with all the necessary information printed in a legible font on proper paper with real ink that lasts longer than it takes you to leave the establishment that issued it. This receipt would also be beamed to your smartphone, which would synchronize with your computer's database of receipts, expenses and tax deductibles, arranged neatly for your accounting department or the taxman.

That's not about to happen any time soon. But expect to soon be able to store your receipts digitally on the fly by snapping them with your camera phone, which would be a start. For now, the Scanalizer is a useful bridge between the old world and the new. Just don't lend it to your Mesopotamian neighbors. Those stone tablets really chew up the scanner's mechanism.

keyboards

Most of us use keyboards to enter text, despite my best efforts to persuade you otherwise. But even if you only use keyboards, there are some things to take into account. Like what kind, keeping it clean, and learning when to walk away. Here is a column I wrote about about living with the humble keyboard in February 2005:

In the future, I'm told, we won't use keyboards. We'll just talk to our machines, and using a wedge of plastic with lettered buttons on it will seem quaint. But for now we're stuck with keyboards, so why do we pay them so little attention?

In offices all over the world, companies spend millions of dollars on new computers, servers, monitors and ergonomic chairs, but then connect a $10 keyboard and think they've done a good job. Laptops and notebook computers can cost thousands of dollars, but ask a sales assistant to let you tap away on the keyboard to see if it suits you and you'll often get a frosty stare.

This is daft. I bought an Acer laptop a few years back whose keyboard felt beautiful, but had oddly positioned keys and a sluggish response that wore me out after a while. I was reduced to buying plug-in keyboards wherever I traveled and leaving them behind. Bottom line: Unless you're using voice recognition, the keyboard is the part of the computer you're going to use the most, so it pays to find one you're comfortable with.

For laptops, I favor the IBM ThinkPad keyboards, not least because they're rugged and full-size, and the important but oft-ignored keys such as Tab and Enter are given their proper location. But even then, when I'm not traveling I'll plug in an external keyboard. Not having your fingers so close to the screen feels more comfortable. You can also use external monitors, either alongside the laptop screen or replacing it. Or, if you prefer, buy a laptop stand that lifts the screen closer to eye level. Check out Griffin Technology's iCurve (www.griffintechnology.com) or Contour Design's NoteRiser (www.contourdesign.com).

If you're concerned about possible injuries to your wrists, fingers, arms and shoulders, then there are some serious options. I counted at least 20 different kinds of ergonomic keyboards, ranging from the straightforward – molding the layout so it fits more closely the natural angle of our arms – to the relatively odd, such as keyboards that stand upright.

I tried out a couple. One was EZ-Reach (www.typematrix.com), which boasts it can save your fingers from having to reach out for the Enter, Backspace and Shift keys, but is also compact enough to fit in your laptop case. The other one is the abKey, designed and developed by Singaporean Bob Teo, who took time out over the Lunar New Year to walk me through his device, which will hit stores in Asia in March. The keyboard is imaginatively designed, hinged at the upper rim so you can swing the two halves of the keyboard apart to suit the angle of your arms, while the keys are laid out in a pattern that Mr. Teo says is more logical, and takes only half an hour to learn.

Any keyboard you like should be small enough to carry with you. Some keyboards designed for personal digital assistants, or PDAs, and smartphones might fit the bill. I've been a fan of keyboards by California-based Think Outside Inc. since I first unfolded its PDA-size Stowaway into a full-size keyboard and felt it more comfortable to use than many top-end keyboards. The Stowaway XT (www.thinkoutside.com) now works with any Windows XP computer with a USB port, and while it is primarily designed for tablet PCs, there's no reason you can't use it with a desktop PC or a laptop.

If you do this, of course, you might want to consider ditching the laptop altogether. Pocket PCs and Palm devices now do many of the tasks your laptop can do, and, if they have a phone built in, sometimes more. Think Outside provides keyboards for most handheld devices, and one or two phone manufacturers are following suit: Nokia, for example, is now selling its own foldable keyboard, the SU-8W.

Most of the devices coming from the major players still work with only a single type or make of product. If you want a keyboard for a broader range of gadgets, then try some of the offerings made by Asian companies that are so small they don't even put their name on the box.

Take the Smart Keyboard which works, via Bluetooth, with most moderately smart phones, and nearly all PDAs. Or the IR-503 IR Keyboard which uses infrared to connect to more or less the same range of devices. Neither keyboard will win any design awards – the keys on both have nothing of the action and response of a Think Outside device – although their fold-out stands are each quite ingenious. Both are Chinese made and, while carrying instructions in English, give no clue to what company manufactures them. You should, however, be able to find them in most Asian computer malls, or online. With a bit of tweaking, I got both to work with my four-year-old Nokia 7650 Symbian phone.

These offerings illustrate that it's quite possible to develop a keyboard that works with most devices. But for a sign of the future, check out the Virtual Keyboard, which doesn't use actual keys at all (www.virtual-laser-keyboard.com). Instead the device, about the size of a salt shaker, projects a laser image of a keyboard onto any flat surface, connecting with your computer, smartphone or PDA via cable, Bluetooth or infrared. The user types on the projected image, as if it were a normal keyboard.

Keyboard-makers, and users, it's time to be a bit more adventurous.

☞ **fingringhoe** (*n, Essex*) The extra keys that manufacturers put on their keyboards that look great and do things like play music and alter volume but never really work properly after the first couple of days.

Keyboard makers didn't exactly rush to heed that request. But some of them did notice that we were spending so much time with our keybaords they might actually be making us sick, as I observed in this September 2005 piece called "Bacteria at Your Fingertips":

The gunk in your keyboard could kill you. Really.

An exhaustive poll of my friends reveals that all sorts of stuff is being spilled over the average keyboard: biscuit crumbs, mango, fizzy beverage, the odd stray cornflake, nail varnish, rice, soy sauce, coffee, wine (red and white) and hand cream. Under your keys lie a faithful record of every snack, lunch and beverage break you've had at your desk since you joined the company. It's like typing on a pile of week-old dirty dishes.

This isn't only somewhat gross (and likely to lead to the keyboard's demise at some point) but it also makes your main data input device a Petri dish of bacteria and other microorganisms that could kill you before the job does. A study conducted by Charles Gerba, a professor of environmental microbiology at the University of Arizona, concluded that the computer keyboard was the fifth most germ-contaminated spot in an office. (Topped only by your phone, your desktop – home to an impressive 10 million bacteria – and the handles on the office water fountain and microwave door.) Out of 12 surfaces studied the toilet seat came in cleanest, in case you're wondering where to have your next lunch break.

On top of that, a study by Chicago's Northwestern Memorial Hospital earlier this year found that hospital keyboards harbored bacteria for more than 24 hours, during which time it easily spreads to bare, and sometimes gloved, hands. These are bacteria that could cause pneumonia and infections of the abdomen, skin, urinary tract and blood stream. Not the kind of thing you want nearby. The study's advice to users: Wash your hands every time you use a computer. I assume that's now a sign on every hospital PC.

OK, so you probably don't work in a hospital. But think about your

☞ **curry rivel** (*n, Somerset*) The leftovers of an Indian takeaway, including strands of pillau rice, that find their way onto your computer desktop and into your keyboard.

workplace. Think about how much time you spend there eating, thinking, napping, typing, talking on the phone, drinking. Now wipe down your desktop, your phone, your mouse with disinfected cloths. But what about the keyboard, where your fingers spend much of the day? Not quite so easy, with all those nooks and crannies.

It's not impossible, however. There are things you can do with an external keyboard. For a start, clean beneath the keys. Remove the screws on the keyboard's underside, separate the two parts and remove all detritus with a brush. Wipe the keys with a disinfected (but relatively dry) cloth. Alternatively, you could throw the whole keyboard in the dish washer. No really: People do do it, and for some it works. Scott Moschella of website Plastic Bugs (www.plasticbugs.com) did it (his tip: don't use the "heated dry" cycle) and enjoyed a torrent of responses from people who have tried similar approaches. One person said she and her husband had "done this for years" and the keyboards "look and work like brand new afterward." Another user successfully sped up the five-day dry out period by putting his in the oven on a low heat. Not everyone claims success: Some report a Coca-Cola spill is a keyboard killer, while Pepsi isn't.

This doesn't really get to the germ bit of the problem. In which case you could regularly replace your keyboard (not a bad choice as they cost as little as $10 these days). Or you could turn to a company called Unotron Inc., which sounds like it should be making washing machines, but actually makes "SpillSeal" keyboards that seal the contacts beneath each key preventing any "liquid or airborne penetration." In short, the company says, you can pretty much throw any liquid at your SpillSeal keyboard and it will keep working. Not only that, you can then rid it of germs with any commercial or hospital-grade cleanser without frying its innards.

So how well do these claims stand up? Being a technology professional I put the SpillSeal through rigorous testing, first of the keyboard's functions (nice layout; key response a little stiff but solid), then by dumping it in the sink and throwing every liquid I could find over it. Here is a list (and I am by no means promoting, or seeking sponsorship from the manufacturers, although donations to restock my kitchen would be welcome):

- Coca-Cola – 0.3 liters
- Spice Islands Gourmet Premium Red Wine Vinegar – 3 tablespoons
- Salad Magic Italian Dressing – 2 teaspoons
- Heinz Worcestershire Sauce – 15 ml
- Royal Gold Fish Sauce – 15 ml
- Del Monte Ketchup ("More Tomatoes") – 3 dollops
- MasterFoods Barbecue Sauce ("Deliciously Rich and Tasty") – three generous squirts
- Half a tankard of two-day old café latte – poured evenly over keyboard
- Some brown-looking liquid with unusual bouquet and rust-like deposits found at back of cupboard – two sloshes

I left the mélange in the sink for a reasonable period and then followed the cleaning instructions: Wash under running water using soap, dish washing liquid, or disinfectant, and the like; shake; and then dry with hair dryer. Add mousse to style and then reconnect to computer. Voila. (I made up the bit about the mousse.) You won't be surprised to hear the keyboard worked fine, although it does give off an interesting smell, half way between a morgue and my fridge. The guys at Unotron are definitely onto something, although they don't seem interested in taking the differently scented unit back.

So, should you run out and buy a SpillSeal? In this age of bird flu, severe acute respiratory syndrome and what-have-you, it isn't a bad idea. Other options are limited: One is to buy a keyboard protector – a piece of plastic, basically, that covers the keyboard. I found one (www.teknomaster.com) that fits all ordinary keyboards but which sounded, from its packing, more like a condom ("Super thin for best feeling"). When I put it on the keyboard I felt like I was typing through a badly fitting surgical mask.

Bottom line: Treat your keyboard with respect. Sanitize it regularly. You never know, it may one day be as clean as the office toilet seat.

Now there's a thought. It's not just the germs in the keyboard that could hurt you, though. We're using our keyboards so much that our fingers, wrists, arms and shoulders are rebelling. Here's how I first looked at the issue of RSI in September 2001:

It hits people in different ways, but these days no one who uses a computer keyboard and mouse intensively seems to be free from repetitive strain injury, or RSI.

It's no laughing matter, and it isn't for me to advise on how to treat the condition – which is an umbrella term to include a range of afflictions caused by repetitive actions – except to say that if your hands, elbow, wrist or shoulder start to hurt or tingle after using a mouse or computer keyboard you should see your doctor.

Still, there is software that can help you either stave off RSI, or reduce its impact.

First, stretch before you work and take a break regularly. RSIGuard from GoldTouch Technologies is a useful program that not only will nag you to take those breaks, but show you how best to use them. Its unobtrusive interface can be configured to your condition, determining how frequently you should take breaks and how long those breaks should be. The program is a tough taskmaster: During breaks the keyboard and mouse won't respond to most commands. Instead a window will guide you through exercises to help your hands and arms, illustrated by some rather odd-looking characters. You will quickly grow to hate the nagging but in the long run you will be grateful. You can download a trial version of RSIGuard from www.rsiguard.com; the program costs $40. A similar program, WorkPace, is available from www.workpace.com for $49. A somewhat simpler, and cheaper, alternative is No-RSI, from www.rsitools.net, which will do the nagging bit for $15. Broke? Set a timer on your desk or download RSI Break from Carter Computer Solutions at www.niagara.com/~mcarter/rsibreak.htm. It is free for personal use.

Overuse of the mouse seems to be a major source of aggravation. There are ways to minimize use of this innocent-looking tyrant, however. RSIGuard has a useful feature that removes the need to click: Move the pointer over a window, button or whatever, and after a second or two the program will assume you want to click and do it for you. Neat.

For those who want to do away with reaching and gripping the mouse altogether, there are other options. One is to use keyboard shortcuts when possible. In most cases programs have at least two ways of doing something: Selecting text, for example, can be done either with the mouse or by holding down the Shift key and moving the arrow key over the text (hold the Control key down at the same time to select a word at a time). Most programs use the same key combinations, so you only need to memorize them once. Pressing the Control key and the F key, for example, nearly always launches a box for finding text in the document you're viewing, whether it's a Web page or a Microsoft Word document; Control and X for cutting text; Control and V for pasting, etc. These keystroke alternatives usually are listed alongside the menu commands.

This is fine for working within programs, but what about launching or moving between them? This kind of task usually is done by mouse but, once again, there are alternatives. If the program already is open you can switch to it by holding down the Alt key and pressing Tab. Launching programs also can be done by keyboard using free software such as WinKey, which can be found at www.copernic.com/winkey. This allows you to configure the otherwise underused Windows key (on the left of the spacebar on most keyboards) to use in combination with other keys. Hitting the Windows and W key, for example, could launch Microsoft Word, saving you a trip to the start menu. This combination of keys is called a macro.

If your keyboard doesn't have a Windows key, try other macro programs such as Macro Express (www.macros.com) which can store whole sequences of often-used commands – say, opening a dial-up program to call into the office, then loading your email program and receiving unread messages – in one keystroke combination. Another way to give your fingers a break is to store blocks of text you use a lot – addresses, say, or the name of your company – and assign them to macros. Many word-processing programs allow you to do this – in Microsoft Word, for example, check out AutoText in the Insert menu – but these won't work automatically in, say, your email program. To get around this, download ShortKeys from www.shortkeys.

com($20; a stripped-down version is available free), which will do the same trick but work in whatever text-editing program you are using.

I am still a bit amazed at how many folk have RSI, or symptoms of it, and how many other folk think it's a huge joke. As a mild sufferer, I've got a lot of sympathy for those who are thoroughly debilitated by the disease. One solution: voice recognition. In fact, it's worth mastering just to take some of the pressure off your hands even if they aren't hurting. I first took a look at the technology in 2000 and concluded:

Speech recognition for dictation is still bumbling along too slowly for my liking. I've been trying out International Business Machines Corp.'s Via-Voice software for some time now, and it isn't any closer to understanding me than it was when I removed it from its shrink-wrap before Christmas. That's after an hour of "educating" the software to the vagaries of my voice by reading out long passages from "Alice in Wonderland." Lernout & Hauspie's Voice-Xpress works slightly better in my view, but they all have downsides: You have to speak pretty slowly, very clearly, and shoo everyone noisy out of the room. Which pretty much rules out dictating copy direct from a football game.

Of course, it was easy to take a cheap shot at software that may probably not have been quite ready for prime time. But I was surprised by how many people I spoke to felt that programs like Dragon NaturallySpeaking (one of the few players in the field left after a few years) had made their lives easier, and so when I took another look in mid 2005, I was impressed by how things had definitely gotten better:

Are we ever going to get to the point where we can chat comfortably with our computers? For years now, decades even, we've been told that the keyboard is on the way out, that it's a dumb way to interact with such a sophisticated device. Instead, by now we should all be barking commands at our computer or dictating long emails without once using our hands. So why are developments in speech recognition so bad that we still have to tap away on keyboards and fiddle with mice?

Well, actually they're not. Speech recognition software is actually quite good. The problem isn't the speech recognition software. It's us.

The image of a guy sitting at a computer using a speech recognition program, s p e a k i n g r e a l l y s l o w l y into the computer, enunciating every word and inserting every punctuation mark as if his life depended on it, is an outdated one. Nowadays, speech recognition is much smarter. In fact, it works better when you speak in a normal conversational voice because then it can figure out what word you're speaking not just by how it sounds but by its context.

In other words, speech recognition can be just as fast as dictating, if not faster. The latest version of ScanSoft's Dragon NaturallySpeaking, for example, takes about five minutes to train before it understands you when you talk normally. Mistakes average about one a paragraph. The software guesses where you want periods, and it usually guesses right. It's also quite intuitive in terms of correcting text or inserting formatting. Want to start a new line? Say "new line." Want to delete the last phrase? Say "scratch that."

This is not the difficult bit. When people try out these products they tend to be impressed. There's definitely a "wow" moment when you first see your words appear on the screen, magically punctuated and capitalized. And you may even be inspired enough to read the manual and try it out for a week or two. But then things quickly run aground.

First off, there are inevitable mistakes, and the chances are that those errors will come when you least need them (we tend to talk faster and less coherently when we're stressed). Sadaoki Furui, an expert in speech recognition at the Tokyo Institute of Technology, has found that even though many cars now contain speech recognition technology, it goes largely unused. "Speech recognition technology makes errors, so humans like to use buttons, even in cars," he says.

☞ **finghall** (*n, North Yorkshire*) The keys on a keyboard where the letters have been worn away from overuse. *Which is the A key? This keyboard's so old it's covered in finghalls.*

But there's another, bigger problem. We do a lot of things on our computers, and not all of which lend themselves to dictation. Surfing the Web. Reading email and moving emails between folders, or forwarding them, or copying little bits of text, links or images in them to other emails. We listen to music. We edit photos. Even when we're writing stuff – an obvious area for dictation – the way that we compose and manipulate text or data isn't something that always works well with dictation. I could quite happily dictate a letter to my mother, for example, but how about a complex proposal for funding that requires revising the text until it shines? Frustration will build quickly.

You see, it turns out that the problem with speech recognition isn't recognizing what you're saying. The problem is interpreting what you want the computer to do beyond that. As Scott Weinstein, who runs a website dedicated to speech recognition (www.speechwiki.org) puts it: Using speech recognition is "like co-editing a document with someone else at the computer." If you've ever done this, you'll know the frustration: Asking that person to change the word "him" to "her" by either pointing at the screen or counting the number of lines from the top of the page, or explaining how to find a command that you know you could find more quickly if only you could just grab the mouse (and "accidentally" tip the person out of their chair and off the team). That's what speech recognition can be like.

In short, it's not about the text, but about the interaction. Your computer can do a great job of reading your lips, so to speak, but it can't read your mind. It turns out that we're just not very good at giving instructions to other people, a fact that won't surprise a parent, a teacher, or anyone who has tried to help someone fix a computer problem over the phone. But this doesn't mean speech recognition is useless. It's just that we need to understand where it fits into our world.

Speech recognition, in fact, has already found its way into niche areas, such as switchboard telephone directories. Mobile phones are great for this kind of thing, and companies are sprouting up to let you search for songs or ring tones by speech.

One company, V-Enable, is working with Amazon to let you search for books via speech ("Martin Cruz Smith's latest" or somesuch.) Expect this kind of thing to expand into local search – tracking down a pizza restaurant in your neighborhood, say – as people get more used to the technology. Indeed, V-Enable CEO Sam Poole says the biggest problem is the stigma, which is why he prefers to call his service "speech search." "Unfortunately speech recognition has gotten a bad rap in the past, and maybe it was too early," he says.

So, is there any point in trying to chat to your computer? If you are worried about injuring your hands through repetitive typing, I'd suggest giving it a try. You may never feel like you're on first name terms with your computer, but at least it understands you a little better.

I still use the software from time to time, and would heartily recommend it, especially if you're working in a quiet environment – your own office, home, or on a mountaintop. And of course the more you use it, the better you'll be at it.

looking after your computer

Looking after your computer isn't just about polishing it and stroking it occasionally. It's probably the most ignored part of preventing serious loss of data, or, at least, of loss of speed. Your computer is like a car: If it isn't tuned every so often bad things can happen. Here's what I suggested in October 2000:

I passed yet another broken-down bus on the streets of Jakarta the other day – driver, conductor and mechanic staring bemusedly inside the blackened engine of what should really be in a museum. It reminded me of computer users.

Most users are happy enough with their computers until they break. Then they get upset. My advice to them – and to the drivers where I live – is to service your machinery and you won't get upset so often.

And these days it's not hard, or expensive. Once purely the domain of geeks, system software now is readily accessible to the average user. The drawback: With weird, unappealing names like "Win Reg Scan," "JetDefrag" and "SmartDefender" such programs don't exactly leap off the shelf into your arms. But when you get beyond the titles, this comes down to something quite simple: Your computer is begging for a regular checkup, just like your car.

There are several options, but most involve the same elements. First off, your hard disk needs checking to ensure that none of the data on it is out of order, what's ominously called "corrupted." (If you turn your computer off without closing down Windows first, chances are your computer will perform this check automatically next time you turn it on.) If you have corrupted files, nothing alarming will happen at first, but if not corrected, over time your hard disk is asking for trouble.

To make the hard disk run more smoothly, there's another step that most system-check software adds to the process: defragmentation, or defragging. This process scans your hard drive and tries to compress data so the free space is consolidated. Then programs and data can run more smoothly and any new additions have the elbow room to take root. Run this once a week and you should notice a difference, especially if your hard disk is quite full.

System suites such as Ontrack Data International's Fix-It Utilities also will back up vital files so if you do run into trouble after, say, installing new software, chances are you can return to previous settings and forget the whole nightmare ever happened. (Fix-It, now owned by VCom, is up to version 6.)

This software also removes hard-disk clutter – files that you probably didn't know were there and almost certainly don't need. Coupled with this is usually a feature that lets you recover stuff you deleted but now need again. It's been a lifesaver for me on several occasions. (In Fix-It, this is usually an add-on to the existing Windows Recycle Bin, which also acts as a half-way house between deleting files and oblivion.)

Probing more deeply into this world, you'll no doubt encounter The Registry, which is the central file where details of all of your programs are stored. Unless you really know what you're doing, you don't want to go there; it's for techies only. Instead, let your system software automatically fix errors, clean it up, or even defrag it. Once again, you'll notice small improvements in performance every time you do. It's surprising what a mess other programs leave behind. (Ontrack's Fix-It claims to have an "enhanced Registry editor that simplifies direct modification of the

☞ **gussage** (*n, Dorset*) A balloon message appearing in the system tray that tells you, completely unnecessarily, that something has happened. *I got some more gussage when I tried to install the printer.*

Windows registry" but it still looked mighty tricky to me.)

Then there's the scary business of protecting your computer from serious attack from within or without. System suite software nowadays usually includes a virus-protection component that tries to guard against viruses, worms and trojans carried on incoming files and emails. It's well worth keeping this program on the go all the time, and don't forget to update regularly. This month saw the arrival of a variation of the so-called Love Letter virus that caused havoc a few months back.

More controversially, there's a feature claiming to protect your computer from crashes – moments when one or more active programs seize up, freezing your computer. It's controversial because some users complain that such utilities cause more problems than they solve. Indeed, Symantec's new version of Norton SystemWorks ($60 for the basic version) has dropped CrashGuard. I, for one, don't bother with these antifreeze features anymore, but I always mourn their absence when there's a crash.

Indeed, that's the bottom line with all of these programs: They're not much fun to use but you sure miss them when they're not around.

Here's another piece from December 2002 on ways to get your computer moving faster without splashing out:

Intel has just unveiled a new version of its Pentium 4 processor, the first to operate at 3 gigahertz, or 3 billion ticks a second. To put this into English, the processor is the brain of the computer, and the faster its clock ticks, the faster it processes data: For comparison's sake, the 80486 chip, the first that was fast enough to support your familiar Windows environment, worked at no more than 133 million ticks a second when it was introduced in 1989. But what does this mean for ordinary Joes like you and me?

Well, a lot of it is hoopla. Intel and its main competitor, Advanced Micro Devices, are locked in a sometimes comical battle to be the first to get there fastest. There are enough enthusiasts (and suckers) who will pay a premium for the newest thing: The 3.06-gigahertz Pentium 4 costs about $650 wholesale. You could buy a brand-new computer for that. There are advantages: With this latest chip Intel has introduced a feature it calls Hyper Threading. No, it's not Ethel Girdle sewing very fast; it's a technique which should help folk who run more than one heavy-duty program – a big spreadsheet, a graphics package, a CD burner – at a time. Intel reckons 75% of users do this kind of thing – it's called multitasking – quite a lot, and while I think that figure's a tad high, I'll admit I'm one of them.

That said, unless your computer dates back to before the Web, or still has one of those large floppy drives that went out with the Cold War, you should resist the urge to splash out, until you've completed the Loose Wire checklist, culled from an unscientific poll of independent computer experts:

- Computers slow down for many reasons. The most basic one is because of the hard drive. However fast your processor is, if it can't read the data off the hard disk quickly, it can't do the tasks you're asking it to do. So make sure you keep your hard drive in good condition. This means not overstuffing it with data and programs: If you're no longer using programs you installed (or came pre-installed when you bought the PC), think about removing them. You can always reinstall them later.

- Second, clean the hard disk of temporary or unwanted files. (In Windows XP you'll find the program Disk Cleanup in the System Tools subfolder of the Accessories menu.) Both of these tasks will free up a surprising amount of space on your hard disk, leaving more room for programs to run smoothly. The next step is to run Disk Defragmenter (it's next to the Disk Cleanup icon), which will shuffle what's left on your hard drive so that the computer can find programs and data faster and write new data more easily. Performing these three tasks every week or so will go a long way to speeding up your computer.

- If you still feel things are a bit too slow, you should consider adding more memory. Memory, usually called RAM (or random-access memory) is where data and programs are placed when you open a new program or document, so that the processor can access it quickly without having to search through the hard drive. It makes sense that the more RAM you have, the less hunting around the processor has to do, making your programs run faster. Windows XP recommends you have at least 128 megabytes of RAM, but since it's so cheap (about $30 for 128 megabytes), I'd suggest at least doubling that. In many cases this is as easy as opening up the computer and slotting the RAM in, but you may want to get help.

- It also follows that you don't want too many programs running at the same time since they all sit around in RAM, not doing very much. Many programs will load automatically when you start your computer and you should be ruthless in hunting them down and stopping them. A good program to keep an eye on how much RAM you've got spare is RAM Idle Professional, $20 from TweakNow (www.tweaknow.com).

As Joshua Feinberg, author of *What Your Computer Consultant Doesn't Want You to Know*, says: "Most consumers don't need the Pentium 4" or even its predecessor, the Pentium III.

One final word of warning: Replacing your computer may solve some of the problems you're having with your present one, but there are downsides. For one thing, you have to migrate all your programs and stuff. And while a spanking new computer may work like a dream, when it's full of your old stuff it may start to move and feel like your old PC once the hard disk and RAM start to bulk up.

What's more, new computers bring new problems: On balance I'm happy with my Acer laptop running Windows XP, but God (or Bill Gates) only knows why it spontaneously reboots from time to time, taking all my hard work with it, not to mention the weird memory freeze-ups when programs start blinking at me for no good reason. And while I'm at it, my old IBM ThinkPad with Windows 98 was never quite so mercurial as to hide

☞ **chew stoke** (*n, Somerset*) Software supposedly designed to solve computer problems but which actually makes things worse (*see also* **chew magna**).

whole folders of files from me without asking first. Until computers start working with the reliability of auto-flush toilets, I'd recommend the devil you know over the devil you don't. Hyper threads or no hyper threads.

Not bad advice, even if I say so myself. I hear a lot of people saying "my computer's going slowly, I'm going to buy a new one", and each time I wonder whether they apply the same approach to other parts of their life: their car? Their lawnmower? Their Friday nights? Instead, look under the hood. And, as this column from March 2003, explains, start with the hard disk:

As a technology columnist, I'm often approached by beautiful women at parties who plant lipstick on my cheeks before murmuring conspiratorially: "Darrrrling, I need your advice." Every time it happens to me my heart sinks. I know I'm about to be asked the same question again: 'Why is my computer running slowly?" Each time I look deep into their eyes and say one word: "Defragment."

It's the most important thing you should do to your computer's hard drive, and also, statistically speaking, the thing you're least likely to do, short of eating it. Unlike most people, Peter Kastner, chief research officer at Boston-based technology consultancy Aberdeen Group, takes his defragmentation pretty seriously. "Picture a child's box of alphabet blocks, all lined up A-Z," he says. That's what the files on a new, or well-maintained, hard drive should look like. "Now, take out blocks to spell a word. The box has holes in it, just as a disk drive does as files are deleted or moved. Now, put the blocks used to create the word back in the box – the first letter of the word going into the first slot, the second letter into the second slot, etc. When completed, the alphabet box is no longer in alphabetical sequence. This mixed-up condition is a fragmented hard drive."

Of course, the longer it takes your computer to find all the bits that make up a file – a Microsoft Word document, for example – the longer it will take to load. "If you notice your computer takes longer than normal to load a file, this is probably why," says Harry Husted, a computer consultant and author who runs his own PC help site (www.thecomputersociety.com).

The solution is defragmentation. “When the disk is arranged neatly, like the initial alphabet box,” Kastner explains, things can move at least a third faster. That’s why it’s good to get “data files, especially programs, grouped in the order they will be called on.” The sad thing is that the latest version of Windows, XP, is not so good when it comes to looking after your hard drive.

As hard drives get bigger and operating systems like Windows get more complicated, there are more programs running in the background, meaning more data is being moved around, stored and accessed. Don’t believe me? Hit the Control, Alt and Delete keys together once if you’re running XP and click on the Processes tab. You’ll see a long list of weird file names, all of them programs running in the background. All are storing hundreds of little alphabet bricks around the place, messing up your lovely pristine hard drive – however much empty space you have to play with.

Sadly, the defragmenter program that comes with Windows XP isn’t effective at cleaning this up. It won’t make sure that all the free space on your computer is in one place – which would make it easier to keep your hard drive fresh. What’s more, it won’t even touch some files, and may require several goes before it can defragment the whole drive.

In brief, you’d be well advised to do a bit of defragmenting. If you’re a light user, the defragmenter that comes with Windows is probably all you’ll need. Just make sure you run it regularly – once a week, if you can. If you use your PC a lot, buy an extra program. Here are some options:

Raxco Software’s PerfectDisk 2000 (www.perfectdisk.com) claims to address a lot of the problems with the Windows XP defragmenter, and I’d second that.

Its main competitor is the better known Executive Software’s Diskeeper (www.diskeeper.com) which works harder at defragmenting existing files, rather than freeing up space to make life easier for programs to run. That said, it has a great set-and-forget option, which means that once you’ve

☞ **great missenden** (*n, Buckinghamshire*) Expression uttered when Microsoft (again) changes your home page, default browser, email program etc. without asking you. *Great Missenden! What Redmond-based mega multinational software corporation changed my homepage again?*

set it, you need never think about defragmenting since Diskeeper does everything in the background. I didn't even notice it was running, though I did notice my computer behaved better.

As Kastner says: "Any PC user who does not regularly defragment their hard drive must enjoy looking at the screen waiting for something to happen. Many think they need a new PC when all they need is to undo a year or two worth of fragmentation." If that doesn't impress folk at parties, I don't know what will.

Nowadays the best defragmenter for Windows is Diskeeper (www.diskeeper.com) although for many users the inbuilt defragmenter works fine. But if you're still not sure what the problem is, here's a checklist I put together in April 2003:

I was halfway out of the door, and very pleased to have fixed a computer, when the owner called me back. "Hang on," she said. "These squarey bits are much too small. They weren't like that before." I sighed, put down my backpack and reached for the mouse. This must be what it's like fixing a broken-down car on a windswept highway, rescuing the family inside from frostbite and certain death, only to be told by the occupants that while the engine now worked, the radio didn't.

Welcome to the thankless world of Helping Friends With Their Computer Problems. It's a fool's errand, take it from me. In the past few weeks I've attempted to fix four computers, with a success rate of 25%. Of course none of this is the user's fault. No one really prepares us for when things go wrong, and while on that one occasion I was able to fix the main problem and those squarey bits, my friend is none the wiser about what to do if it goes wrong again. So here, for one time only, is my Idiot's Checklist Of Things To Do When Something Goes Wrong With Your Computer. Of course I claim no responsibility for any advice you may follow, and do not lure me over to your place to fix it (unless it's with an offer of some Battenburg Window Cake, to which I'm rather partial).

☞ **full sutton** (*n, the East Riding of Yorkshire*) The complete process of turning off a computer, removing all peripherals, waiting a minute and then rebooting.

1. Try turning the computer off and turning it on again. I know it sounds obvious, but six times out of 10 this fixes it. (If necessary, unplug the power cable, remove the battery if it's a laptop, and then leave the computer for five minutes first. This drains the memory, as well as allowing you to get yourself a cup of tea.)

2. Assuming your computer now does load as normal, you have either fixed the problem, or you're having a problem with a specific program or a specific device you've plugged into your computer. The trick now is to isolate the problem. In most cases, you'll get an error message alerting you to the problem – usually a separate window ("this program has performed an illegal operation and will now go to jail" or somesuch). Take note of which program is causing the problem. It's not always obvious.

3. In my friend's case, it was Eudora, an email program. Every time she tried to check her mail, it crashed with a message, that while cryptic ("an unhandled error has occurred") at least informed me who the culprit was. The next trick, then, is to see whether someone else has had the same problem. Assuming you have an Internet connection (if you don't, call up a friend who does), check the manufacturer's website and go to their Support page. Search for something relevant like "crash" and "check mail." No point in reinventing the wheel: If someone else has had the same problem as you, chances are it's recorded somewhere on the Net.

4. In Eudora's case, they do a great job of listing possible options for fixing your problem, and after trying about eight of them, everything worked. But if this doesn't happen, you can still try stuff out yourself. For example, try closing all other programs you don't need, including, if you're in Windows, all the ones in the system tray (usually by right-clicking the icon and selecting Exit).

5. Still no joy? Run an updated virus check on your whole computer, and sit tight until it's done. Don't have a virus checker installed? Shame on you,

but try this free online one: www.trendmicro.com/en/products/desktop/housecall/. If you have a virus aboard, that may be your problem.

6. No virus? Try reinstalling the program or device in question (make sure you have the original program file or CD-ROM first). To do this, open the Control Panel in the Settings menu, and Add/Remove Programs. Once the program's uninstalled, reboot your computer and reinstall the program. If it's a piece of hardware, open the System icon instead of Add/Remove Programs, find the Device Manager tab and right-click on the device that doesn't work. Select uninstall. Once you're done, reboot. You may have to now reinstall the drivers that make the device work.

7. Still not working? Try cleaning up the Registry – the place where Windows stores all the settings that make your programs run (or crash, depending on your point of view). Here's a free program, EasyCleaner, that does a good job of it: www.toniarts.com/ecleane.htm. Once the program has run its course, reboot and try the program again.

8. If it's still not working, try checking the hard disk for errors (Accessories/System Tools/Scan in Windows; Windows XP won't have this option). If that's still not helping, try removing some of the components of the program in question. Eudora, for example, has extras called plug-ins that may be causing the problem. Microsoft Outlook and Word have similar add-ons that are often the culprit. Remove those and you may be okay.

9. Still no luck? I hate to say it, but you may have bigger problems. You could try reinstalling Windows, but before you take that kind of step you may want to try consulting a professional, since you're entering Scary Territory.

More on reinstalling operating systems in a future column. In the meantime, print this checklist out, stick it above your computer and stock up on Battenburg Cake, in case I'm dumb enough to come round.

Another likely explanation if your computer is running slowly, and there's lots of hard disk activity, is a shortage of memory, as I talk about in this March 2006 piece, called, predictably enough, "Thanks for the Memory":

The shop was hidden in the back of the mall, away from all the flashy outlets selling spanking new laptops, projectors and handheld gizmos. And the most glamorous thing going on inside was a woman from a phone-cleaning service adding perfumed pads to the shop's solitary handset. But for me, it was a glimpse of heaven (the shop, not the Perfumed Pad Lady). Somewhere amid the glass cabinets stocked to the gills with identical looking blister packs were two slices of silicon that would, I hoped, solve all my computer problems – for less than $100.

My laptop had been playing up for months. It wouldn't exactly stop midflight, but it would go so slowly sometimes that I would either sink two cups of coffee waiting for it to catch up with me, or else restart it and sink four cups of coffee waiting for it to reload. And we aren't talking rubbish here: A classy laptop with a fancy chip, a decent-size hard drive and what I always thought was more than enough memory for my needs – 512 megabytes. But this last bit was where I was wrong. That is why I was lucky I met The RAM Dude.

Now first off, just in case you don't know, memory – Random Access Memory, or RAM – isn't the same as your hard drive. Your hard drive, measured these days in 10s of gigabytes, sometimes 100s if you're a serious hoarder, is where you store your data. It's like a big cupboard. RAM, on the other hand, is where your computer puts stuff you're actually working with. It's like a sideboard in the kitchen, where you chop, pound and season. The heart of the computer, the Central Processing Unit, or CPU, is where the processing gets done. That, as you might have guessed, is the stove. No cooks worth their salt would start cooking without getting everything they are likely to need out of the cupboard and onto the sideboard. Your computer is the same. It will load programs and documents into memory

☞ **abson male** (*n, South Gloucestershire*) Offspring who's never around when you need him to fix your computer.

when you open them, so that when you ask it to crunch some numbers, play a music file, or edit a picture, it can do it without having to run back to the cupboard all the time.

So memory is important. If you don't have enough, your computer has to make it up, creating what's called virtual memory by swapping bits of data between your memory and your hard drive. As you can imagine, delays start to occur. So it's a simple equation: The more memory you have, the smoother your computer will run.

Of course there are other factors, too. If your computer chip – the wafer that includes the CPU – is slow, your computer will be, too. How much space you have on your hard drive is also important. If it's crammed full of data, the computer has a hard time finding what it needs, further slowing things down. But while everyone tends to focus on the speed of your chip and the size of your hard drive, not many people focus on adding RAM.

That is why I found myself in an unglamorous shop at the unglamorous end of a mall, talking RAM with the shop's owner, the self-styled RAM Dude. Well, actually, I didn't, because he wasn't there. But we talked over the phone and by instant messaging, and The RAM Dude, actually a very businesslike local agent for U.S.-based Corsair Memory Inc. named Winston Setiawan, explained to me some of the ups and downs of owning RAM.

The bottom line is that computing ain't what it used to be. A few years ago, Mr. Setiawan says, the average user would have a word processor running, and perhaps Microsoft Outlook. Now, he points out, that user would also keep three or four browser windows open and play MP3 music files. "That," Mr. Setiawan says, "is going to need a lot of RAM – if he wants things to run smoothly." If you also throw in, as in my case, Google Desktop Search and free Internet telephony software like Skype, it's no wonder my 512-megabyte memory was creaking.

So what is enough? I polled a few experts on the matter, and, like experts everywhere, they didn't agree. But there seems to be consensus that

☞ **bootle** (*n, Sefton*) Time waiting for a reboot.

if your computer comes with only 256 megabytes of RAM, it isn't enough. It's a bit like buying a nice new car and then putting old, bald tires on the wheels instead of new ones. Melissa J. Perenson, senior associate editor at PC World magazine in the U.S., sums it up when she says that 512 megabytes is the bare minimum. Her magazine recommends one gigabyte for starters. So that's what I've got.

And this is hardly going to break the bank. True, if you buy your memory from the manufacturer of your computer, you may balk at the price tag. But don't be put off by that. Lenovo (the owner of what used to be IBM's Personal Computing Division), for example, tried to charge me $133 for 512 megabytes of RAM, whereas I got the same thing – minus the IBM/Lenovo sticker – for $49 from The RAM Dude. Just make sure you buy the right RAM for your machine – check www.crucial.com, the website of Crucial Technology, the consumer division of U.S. RAM manufacturer Micron Technology Inc., for details of what your computer needs.

One final word. Mr. Setiawan reckons you'll get a 10% to 20% increase in speed, as the computer doesn't need to keep juggling data between disk and memory (cupboard and sideboard in our analogy). That's quite a significant improvement, but don't expect miracles. As Scott Testa, co-founder of software and Web-based consulting company Mindbridge Inc., puts it: "It simply enhances performance and saves time."

Me? I'm now off coffee altogether and my computer responds with alacrity to more or less whatever I throw at it. Now, all I worry about is placing the perfumed pads on my telephone.

backup

Backing up data is not an exciting topic, which I've left it to the end of this section. This chapter is based on a series of pieces I did for The Wall Street Journal Asia *in 2006 in response to readers' laments. I had hoped to cover the whole thing in one column but it ended up being many more, since as I polled my council of Wise People – a motley collection of sources, readers and friends – I realized that there were as many different ways to back up as there are people. I started out by looking at the overall problem, and trying to convince readers that it was a subject which is relevant to everyone:*

I can usually tell when someone hasn't backed up their data. It's their expression – a combination of Hangdog, Abused Party and, when certain questions are asked, Hard Of Hearing. Conversations usually go like this:
"I think some of my data may be missing."
"When did you last back up?"
(Silence) "Sorry? Are you talking to me?"
"Yes."
"Er...recently, I think. Last week. Last month, maybe. Six months ago?" (Awkward silence as we stare at dead computer.) "Was I supposed to back up? Doesn't that happen automatically? Do I have to click something? Nobody told me. Can you fix it?" (Accompanied by Pitiful Stare.)

Backup, or lack thereof, is the biggest single source of computer-related distress. A recent survey commissioned by software vendor Symantec Corp. showed that more than 90% of users store personal data on their computers, and nearly a quarter of them have lost some of that data in the past six months.

The Art of the Backup has several components. One is The Fear. Fear of losing stuff. This is the kind of fear that only people who have experienced serious data loss can have. Up until then, most people whistle their way through the day thinking that everything is dandy. Then WHAM, they come home to find their computer missing/refusing to start/burned beyond recognition along with their home. Before that, those people generally assume that data loss happens to others. But trust me: It will happen to you.

What could go wrong? Well, everything dies, including hard drives. It could be age, it could have been part of a bad batch of drives, it could be a virus. It could be a power surge. A lightning strike. Flood. Fire. Your 18-month-old kid trying to hammer a nail into your laptop while you're taking a nap. You may accidentally destroy the data yourself in a fit of housecleaning. Or theft: My laptop was stolen – when I was at lunch – by a guy who walked into my office, unplugged all the peripherals and wandered out, waving cheerily to my colleagues. Really.

So get The Fear.

Another component of the backup is Organization. If you don't know
where your files are, y
what files are importa
your MP3 music files
books, your browser bc
messaging chats.

Another componen
you're going to back up
are you going to use?); v
drive? CD or DVD? On
going to back it up; and
drives, if you choose not

What is the best backup option? I'll explore each of them in coming months, but the short answer is: Do what works for you. If you fear Acts of God demolishing your home, it might not make sense to back up to gadgets that sit in the same room or building as the original data. If you have a slow Internet connection, you might want to avoid online backups – where you upload your data to a service that will store it, usually for a fee. If you've only got a few files you want to back up, then a little USB key drive might be the way to go. If you need backups not only of the data you have, but of older versions of the data – for legal reasons, say – you may want to consider backing up to DVDs or CD-ROMs, dating your backups so you can easily find the stuff you need. My advice: Build in a bit of redundancy. Don't rely on just one kind of backup: Everything fails, eventually. CDs decay, USB key drives break, hard drives stop turning, online backup services go down, go bad or go bust. Use two different approaches and, if you can, back everything up twice.

Where should you keep your backups? Not next to your computer if you can help it. If the device – USB key chain or hard drive – is plugged into your laptop, there's a danger it will be felled by whatever takes the original. Whatever the media, the devices should be labeled and stored in a dark cupboard and, preferably, in a fireproof box. CD-ROMs and DVDs should be labeled using a special CD-labeling pen – with an ordinary, solvent-based pen, the ink will leak and ruin the data – and kept in proper CD boxes.

The last component is The Habit. If you don't get into the habit of backing up, you'll face the problem of Big Data Holes. This is when you still have a backup in the event of catastrophic data loss, but the backup you have is more than six months old, meaning you have all the data you need except the vital bits. I'd recommend backing up once a week.

So: Put all these elements together, and you too can become a Backer Upper, without the need to cultivate any pathetic expressions. Good luck.

☞ **wimbish** (*adj, Essex*) The expression you adopt when you try to get a friend to help you with your computer.

That laid the groundwork:

A few weeks back, I wrote about the principles of backing up your data and promised I would then tell you in more detail how to do so. But first, let's address the worst-case scenario: You lose everything when your laptop catches fire. (It happens – trust me.) Then your concern isn't just losing the photos of Timmy's first steps; it's getting your whole life back. If your hard drive dies – and it will, one day – you will be looking for a way to restore things to as recent a state as possible. Backing up individual files is important, and something we'll go into later, but the cornerstone of your strategy should be having a backup of your whole computer.

This is why the first step I want to tackle is the disk image: taking a snapshot of all the data on your hard drive and recording that snapshot on a separate device, whether it's another hard drive, or disks such as CD-Rs or DVDs. This isn't about copying files from one place to another, but using software that creates a kind of replica of what's on your hard drive, but compressed into a single file, which can then be restored should something go wrong.

It's not particularly popular among nongeeks, because it can be rather challenging to do, but it makes a lot of sense. For one thing, the prices of hard drives have fallen precipitously. For another, the process has gotten easier and isn't as time-consuming as you might think: When I took a snapshot of my 40-gigabyte hard drive, it took about half an hour. The payoff is obvious: Even if your hard drive crashes, or weird stuff starts happening because of a virus, you can restore the backup image and you'll be back in action in a few hours.

So how does one do this? Well, first you need the hardware. You need your computer, with either a CD burner or DVD burner attached to it. Or, even better in my view, a hard drive connected directly to your computer. (If it's a desktop computer or one of those laptops that have space for two hard drives, it can be inside. If not, the hard drive can be an external one.) Then you need the software. For Mac users, Carbon Copy Cloner (www.bombich.com/software/ccc.html; free, but donations welcome) has a good reputation. The most popular Windows program is Norton Ghost (www.symantec.com), but I had problems launching it, so much so that I ditched it. Another promising-looking program, FarStone Technology Inc.'s RestoreIT, also failed at the first hurdle – installation problems this time. One that did work for me was Acronis Inc.'s True Image Home, which has an acceptable interface and one of those wizard things that take you by the hand and lead you through the process. This makes it all quite simple: Select "backup" and then just answer the questions.

These programs will then create what is called a disk image on your other hard drive or the CD/DVD. The image is one file, large because it's a snapshot of all your data, but quite a bit smaller than the data it is capturing because it's compressed. It will probably still be too big for any one CD to hold, and it may be too big for a DVD – in which case the software slices the image file into smaller bites that can fit on each disk.

Now you have a backup of your entire hard drive. Should something go wrong with the original, you can restore it to the state it was in when you made the image. But you need to take one more step first, so you can restore the backed-up version even if your main hard drive is no longer functioning: Create what is called a boot-up disk. This is (usually) a CD-ROM that, if it's inside your CD-ROM drive when you turn your computer on, will bypass your computer's hard drive and load the basic operating system files that make it run. This backup CD is your spare key to the computer. Keep both the disk image and the boot-up disk in a safe place.

Now, it's important to note what these disk images are and what they aren't. A disk image will save all your files – including your all-important program files – from any disaster that may befall your hard drive. In more recent versions of the software you can look inside the image file to retrieve individual files, should that be all you're looking for. But of course they're also only as good as the time you made them: If you made a disk image six months ago, it isn't going to know what's been going on in your computer since then. Finally, a disk image isn't infallible. David Weinberger, a fellow

☞ **lychpit** (*n, Hampshire*) CD-ROMs that aren't properly labelled and so sit in a pile until you get the time to see what's on them, if ever. *I did a fylingdale (p.200) but it's in the lychpit.*

at Harvard Berkman Center, a Harvard Law School project that researches the relationship between the Internet and society, uses them, but says they have sometimes failed on him. The reason can be anything from a faulty image file to flaky storage media. "Sometimes you can get the data back and sometimes you can't," he says.

That's why you need to follow the ABCs of disk imaging: A) Do it as often as you can and, if you have the space and time, make two copies each time. B) If you're backing up to a hard drive and you can afford the space, don't overwrite previous images; if one of them fails, you'll still have another. If you're backing up to a CD or DVD this shouldn't be an issue; just make sure you include dates on the label. And, most importantly: C) Don't rely on any one system. A disk image is just your first line of defense.

That's why I need to write some more columns about this. Which I did, a couple of weeks later in a column called "Time to Play Librarian":

Two weeks ago, I wrote about the first line of defense when backing up your files: the disk image. I'd recommend you start with that if you're looking for a thorough regimen to protect yourself against data loss; it's the quickest way to recover from something bad happening to your computer, whether it disappears, combusts or just dies of old age. But making a disk image has its limitations: It's not really practical if you're on the road, and more importantly, in this multimedia age, it may not capture all the files you have spread across lots of different hard drives, disks and computers. That's why you need to think about what kind of files you have, and how much you need them.

After polling a range of people in and outside the technology business, I reckon the best way of tackling this comes from Sydney Low, who runs a spam-and virus-free email service out of Australia called AlienCamel.com. "There are essentially three types of files on your computer," says Mr. Low. The first are Files That Make Your Computer What It Is – operating system files such as those that make your printer work, and programs like Microsoft Word or Adobe Acrobat. Without the operating system, your computer won't run. Secondly, there are the Bread and Butter Files: working documents that you interact with on a daily basis, alter, edit and add to. These are vital, living organisms, and need special attention because you might not just need one version, but several (if you ruin one revision and need to rewind to an earlier one, for example). Finally, you have Heirlooms: music files, photos, videos and so on that are captured once and then never changed. (Of course, you may want to edit them, but you never want to lose the original.)

Let's take the first type. In most cases, you're not going to be too bothered by these files. The most likely cause for ruining your operating system and program files is a virus or an act of God. In which case, if you're creating a disk image every few days (or even weeks) then the easiest route back to sanity is to restore your whole hard drive. Or, if the worst comes to the worst, you can reinstall the applications using the original disks. The only potential hiccups here are that if you do need to reinstall, you've got to make sure you have the program disks or, if you downloaded the software from the Internet, access to those programs, as well as the serial numbers and any preferred settings and passwords you need to make them run the way you want to. There's no easy way to avoid this hassle, but it pays to keep A) a copy of all downloaded software on a disk separate from the place where these programs are installed, B) the original CDs of any software you bought that way, and C) a list of all the programs you commonly use and their serial numbers – in a place that isn't your main hard drive. Backing up, you see, isn't just about backing up the files you have, but also the files and information you may need.

That brings us onto the second category: the Bread and Butter. If you've seen anyone trying to calculate in their head all the vital documents they've just lost to a crash, you'll know how painful it is to lose your Bread and Butter Files. The easiest way to define a Bread and Butter File is: Do I use the file regularly, or am I likely to need to use it again? Here, again, a list is a good place to start. First, there are the types of files you use a lot

☞ **fylingdales** (*n, North Yorkshire*) Backup sessions. *How many months of fylingdales do you have?*

– Word files, spreadsheets, presentations. Then there are the programs you use where the data is lumped together in one big file: Microsoft Outlook, and its PST files – the ones that contain all your Outlook data – spring to mind. Those files usually contain contacts, calendar items and emails all in one place, so losing one could be catastrophic. This could be a long, long list, but the most important thing is that it's exhaustive. You don't want to find you've backed everything up except the presentation that your boss needs you to revise for the annual general meeting.

The revision bit is important, too. Often it isn't just about retrieving a file, but retrieving a version of a file. Things happen, from deleting a vital paragraph to your boss suddenly preferring an older version of a document that you thought she'd long lost enthusiasm for. Backing up your Bread and Butter Files has to anticipate this by saving multiple versions of files, so that you can, if necessary, retrieve a long-forgotten and now-priceless version of a file.

Having made the list of documents that fall into this category, you then need to figure out where they are. This isn't as easy as it sounds. Keeping your files in some sort of order is never easy, and has gotten less so with the advent of desktop search, which effectively allows you to be lazy because you can find stuff just by tapping a few keywords into something like Google Desktop Search. I'm a strict disciplinarian when it comes to keeping files in orderly folders, and I spend a few hours a month keeping those folders in order. Beyond my clear lack of a social life, there's a good reason for this: Backing up. If you keep your files in a limited and logical set of folders, it makes backing them up much easier. For one thing, you're more likely to follow a system of naming that makes sense and avoids duplication and confusion; for another, copying one folder with lots of subfolders is a lot easier than moving lots of individual folders.

Selecting Mr. Low's third category of files – Heirlooms – follows similar rules, although it's somewhat easier. Whether it's MP3 files, videos or photos, it pays to keep them in some sort of folder hierarchy. Pictures, in particular, can quickly get out of hand and there's a danger, if you don't keep them in well-labeled folders, that you overwrite older pictures because your digital camera has assigned the same file name to different sets of snaps. Music files can quickly get messy for different reasons: Different software programs and music websites may assign different systems of naming song files, so that you end up with lots of copies of the same song, often for no apparent reason.

But, as with Bread and Butter Files, there's no point in starting a backup regimen until you've checked that you know where all these files are. They could be hidden in subfolders in weird places; they could even be burned to a CD or stored on an external drive. The easiest way to reduce this chaos? Launch a search of different file types on your computer via the Search function: Microsoft Windows XP, for example, lets you search for all pictures and photos in one go, and will capture not only the obvious JPG format but photos in lesser-known formats that you might also want to save. Once you've tracked down all the photo files, start putting them in some order.

Then you're ready for the Big Backup – which you'll have to wait a couple more weeks for.

I imagine readers were really, really holding their breath.

Two weeks ago, I wrote about backing up files on your computer ("Time to play librarian"). Specifically, I talked about how to choose what files to back up by dividing them into work files and "heirloom" files (ones you capture once and don't change, such as music and photo files), and how to manage those files so they're easier to back up. The reason for making this distinction between workaday files and heirlooms is that when it comes to backing up, you need to adopt two different approaches.

Let's take the second one first. Photographs and videos are really important. Music files less so – losing a copy of David Gray's latest album is less catastrophic than losing the only photo of your son's first birthday. But the three types have one thing in common: They are "one shot" files that you're unlikely to change or tamper with.

☞ **boulge** (*n, Suffolk*) A surfeit of data on your hard drive that, however much you try to delete, doesn't go away. *I cleaned it out last week but I've got another boulge.*

Backing them up, therefore, is fairly easy. You need the original file (photo, music or whatever), the place where you want to back it up to, and the software to do the backup. I've discussed before the importance of ensuring that you include in the process all of the files you want to back up, because Murphy's Law dictates that the file you don't back up is the file you'll lose and the file you'll most need. It's important to think about where you're going to back up these heirlooms. The options: an external hard drive, a CD-ROM or DVD-ROM, or online. USB key drives are still too small to handle the quantity of stuff you're likely to be dealing with, but there's no reason that your iPod couldn't become a backup drive for photos, for example.

Software? There's lots of stuff out there, both for Windows and Macs. What the software you use needs to have, though, is an interface you can understand. Then it should give you two other important options: The first is to compress the backups using standards like Zip (this squashes the file down so it takes up less space without losing anything; when you unzip the file, it's restored to its original size). The second is to schedule future backups. Windows programs I've used that include these features: SecondCopy (www.secondcopy.com), which I found the simplest to use; WinBackup (www.liutilities.com); Argentum Backup (www.argentuma.com); and Handy Backup (www.handybackup.com).

If you're simply making a straight copy of all the photos, music files and videos on your hard drive, then it's a simple enough procedure. Select the folder or folders you want to back up and the place you want to back them up to. Depending on how many files there are, the backup could take anything between five minutes and five hours. Once that is done, you need to plan the next one. Once you have two copies – the original and the backup – of each file in place, you'll be moving into something called synchronization, which simply means making sure that what you've got on one drive or disk is the same as the other. That way you are sure you've got two copies of your files – which is what backup is all about.

Of course, it's not that simple. You may well hit the point where your photos, music files and videos are taking up too much space on your hard drive and you decide to move some or all of them onto another drive. This is where things can get confusing. Having a diagram – of where you're backing up stuff from and to – makes things a lot easier, and ensures you don't miss anything out. (The worst thing that can happen, of course, is when you're trying to back something up from one place to another and manage to delete both copies. It happens more often than you think.)

While you can never do too many backups, you can have too many backups. What I mean is that it's good to have lots of backups, because the media they're on often fail. But if you're not organised about how you keep these backups, then you'll quickly drown under a pile of DVDs, or bloated external hard drives with lots of copies of files on them, and find that amid such chaos you are never quite sure what still needs to be backed up, and what can be deleted to make space. So, frantic and chaotic backing up is less helpful than frequent and orderly backing up. Hundreds of copies of the same picture of Junior on the swing may sound harmless enough, until you have to thumb through them to find the picture of Junior's sister on the swing.

These rules all apply to your working data, too – files such as word-processing documents and spreadsheets that you use all the time. But there are some differences. Firstly, you'll only need to back up photos and so on once a week at the most. Working data could be backed up once a day. (You can set your backup software to do this overnight.) Secondly, the synchronization will be slightly different; in many cases, you may want to create unique backups of your data so they don't overwrite earlier versions. Thirdly, you may want to create an extra backup of a select few files onto a portable key drive, allowing you access to your most important working documents even if you're away from your computer and your backups. This last tweak should be in addition to your ordinary backups, since the flash drives in USB key drives, which can lose data through wear and tear, aren't as reliable as a fixed hard disk.

That gives you the basics of backup. Where you back them up to – drives, disks, online – is an important decision, but the simple rule of thumb is: don't trust any one medium.

☞ **fryerning** (*n, Essex*) The noise a hard drive makes as it's about to die.

PART THREE

getting what you need

browsers

Browsers are what we use to look at Web pages – most of the time. They started out as static beasts – we couldn't do much with them apart from, well, browse – but they have evolved, albeit slowly, as the World Wide Web has grown from a static, text and link-based medium into an all-singing, all-dancing rival to the television in visual appeal. So why bother wasting a chapter on the browser? Well, given how much time we spend with them, it's worth getting to know them better, and to find one you're happy with. Moreover, its history is an interesting one, telling us a lot about how the Web has evolved since I started writing about it. You might be inspired by some of these stories to test alternatives, or at least to think in terms of tweaking and adding to yours to have a better browsing time. First off, here's how browsers looked to me in April 2000, when Microsoft was busy destroying Netscape, the browser that had dominated the Internet for several years:

Brace yourselves for another round of the browser war. The only hitch: No one can quite agree on what we're fighting over anymore.

For those of you who missed the last round, this is basically a slugfest between Netscape, which is now a division of America Online, and Microsoft's Internet Explorer. For years, Netscape pretty much ruled the roost – until 1996, that is, when Bill Gates finally overhauled Internet Explorer and, more importantly, began offering it free of charge.

But last week Microsoft was found guilty of unfairly using its monopoly power in the way it markets its browser, the software tool used to locate and display Web pages. Court appeals are likely to drag the case out, but already the battleground has shifted. It just isn't clear where it's going.

Previously, browser manufacturers fought over the ability to direct you, the user, where they wanted you to go, usually to their home page. Things have grown a bit more sophisticated since then. Now, as more and more devices have Internet access, savvy software companies are cutting deals directly with the makers of palm devices, mobile phones and anything that may end up accessing the Web like your television and car.

This will be a harder game to dominate. Most of those devices don't use Windows, or any stripped-down version of it, so there's no pressing reason to use Internet Explorer. And even with Windows, Microsoft is facing fresh challenges.

An Oslo-based company has for the past five years been producing a browser called Opera (www.opera.com), which is small and fast (half the download time of its rivals, according to my own tests). They have just launched a beta release of version 4 of their product. Even Netscape (www.netscape.com) is doing battle again. Last week it released Netscape 6 – it skipped version 5 altogether. Is it that it can't count or that it's throwing the gauntlet down at Microsoft, whose Internet Explorer remains at version 5?

Having these new browsers around should make things interesting. But I don't see either of them succeeding in a face-to-face challenge with Internet Explorer. Opera may be fast but it isn't free – it's the only browser that isn't. Netscape's version 6 sports a whole new look that may take some getting used to. To me it looks strangely old-fashioned. But all this may be irrelevant because of changing perceptions of what a browser actually is.

Some software makers already piggyback Internet Explorer. NeoPlanet (www.neoplanet.com), for example, is a free, small browser that actually uses most of the Internet Explorer functionality under its hood. All you'll see, however, is a snazzy program that can change its look with your mood, courtesy of downloadable "skins." Clever stuff. Not only does NeoPlanet steal users' attention from under Mr. Gates's nose, but it anticipates a growing feature of the Internet: customization.

This is one reason why the browser wars are getting more complex. It's no longer a head-to-head battle to the death. As users see the Internet as a source of information that comes in different shapes and sizes, so will programs come in different shapes and sizes. Tickers and minibrowsers already format information in discreet corners of computer screens. Other new browsers, such as Porthole (www.webcharms.com), will allow users to view a slice of a Web page.

Moreover, the browser itself is moving toward being more than simply an interface for viewing a Web page. It's likely to become the main program for you to view all kinds of information in different ways. Enfish Technologies is taking the first step in this direction with Onespace (www.enfishonespace.com), which it soon will release. Onespace will keep tabs on existing data, but also will collate information from the Web and serve it up in configurable layouts, all on one screen. It's a logical progression for the browser: a single window displaying all the data you need. And you can tell it's a browser because it will be free.

OK, I was wrong about Onespace but the general idea has held true. The browser has become a lot more dynamic as web pages, and even applications that use the web, have become more interactive. And what has proven to be most interesting is Microsoft's failure to stamp out all rivals in the browser war. This is because of some intriguing innovations that have made the browser the vanguard in broader interface design. First to really challenge the status quo, in my view, was Opera, which I wrote about in more detail in early 2003:

Just when I thought software had become as innovative as a bacon sandwich, something came along to prove me wrong. There is software out there that is innovative and that actually makes things easier. It's a Web browser made by a Norwegian company called Opera Software ASA and its latest incarnation, released last month, is a real gem.

Why is it so good? For starters, it's small. The installation program takes up less than 3.5 megabytes of memory. This not only means it won't take up much space on your computer; it's also a good yardstick to measure how well the program has been written. This doesn't, however, mean the program is just a no-frills way of surfing the Internet. It's got more, and better, features than its heavyweight competitor, Microsoft's Internet Explorer.

For example, take the "forward" button on your usual browser. In other browsers it will only take you back to a page you've already visited, and then left. Right? Opera, however, instead tries to figure out from the page you're visiting where you'll go next, so that by clicking on the forward button you'll go there automatically. It works like this: Say you're looking for Britney Spears websites on Google. The first page of matches appears, but to reach the following pages of the other 2,010,000 matches you'd have to scroll to the bottom of the Google page to find the "Next" link. Not with Opera: Its "forward" button has transformed to a "fast forward" button which will take you to the next page of matches, and then to the next, and so on. Simple, elegant, and useful.

If you find moving the mouse to the "forward" button is a hassle, try this: Hold down the mouse button, and move the mouse slightly to the right. In Opera, that gesture means "page forward" and you'll automatically go to the next page of Google's Britney Spears matches. Indeed, there are other mouse gestures that make navigating a lot easier. Prefer using the keyboard? Opera lets you move around the screen and access links using the Shift and arrow keys. Smart stuff.

Opera has, like Internet Explorer, an optional panel on the left side of the screen, but unlike Microsoft's this is seriously useful. It contains all the usual information – what sites you've visited recently and your bookmarked sites – but it can also list all the files you've downloaded, as well as all the links in the page you're currently viewing. So, say you're viewing your home page at Yahoo!, replete with links to news from your home town, current valuation of your portfolio, your favorite cartoons, etc. All those links are now listed separately in the left-hand panel, meaning you don't have to wander around the page to get what you're looking for.

The main appeal of Opera, however, is its speed. Because it's small it loads fast, and because it's written to keep things simple, most Web pages load very quickly. An information-packed newspaper website take minutes to load in Internet Explorer; Opera zaps it onto your screen in a second.

So what's Opera's plan? Surely it doesn't think it can take on Microsoft? "We can never beat a company with the distribution and marketing resources of Microsoft," says Pal Hvistendahl, Opera marketing director. "However, we can fill the void that users who want something different than Internet Explorer are looking for. Just as not everybody should have to drive the same brand of car with the same features, we give an alternative."

Opera is playing smart. Aware that the mobile phone is encroaching on the space currently occupied by PDAs and laptops, Opera is hoping its browser is a tempting choice to an industry wary of giving too much elbowroom to Microsoft. Nokia's Communicator has Opera as its browser, for example, while a Korean version of Opera comes preloaded on the Sharp Zaurus PDA. Indeed, a feature of Opera is the way Web page developers can, at the press of a button, see what their full-screen Web page would look like on the small screen of a PDA – a touch that speaks volumes about the way browsing is heading.

In fact, all of these innovations should find their way into other programs, like word processors and spreadsheets. Each is a significant improvement to the way we work. I'm assuming Microsoft will adopt them, but if not, I'd buy Opera's version of Word, if they made one.

Downsides? Some websites won't allow you in unless you're using Internet Explorer. Another: the browser costs $40, against Microsoft's Internet Explorer, which is free. The good news: A free version is available, fully functional, so long as you're willing to put up with an unobtrusive window spouting ads at you. My advice? Try it out for a month and, once you're hooked, shell out the $40 for the unsponsored version. Innovation like this deserves all the support it can get.

Opera wasn't the only challenger, although at the time it was the only one that seemed to threaten Microsoft in the mainstream market. I wasn't to know this, but it wasn't Opera that would end up scaring the pants off Microsoft, but one of the open source programs mentioned above. But it wasn't to hit the scene for another year. It was called Firefox, and I sang its praises shortly after its official launch in early 2005:

No question about it, the word "browser" is a really bad name for something that's your entree to the Internet, that is, the way you get around the World Wide Web. It makes it sound like you're window-shopping, with no idea what you're looking for. But the Web is nothing like that anymore: It's a mall, a library, your bank, your office, your local polling booth, a museum, a travel agent, not to mention a place to rub shoulders with the criminal underworld.

Of course, I can't think of a better name for this program apart from Web Access Hub (WAH), or Generic Realtime Universe Facilitator (GRUF). This leads me to make a serious point: The term "browser" has made the browser itself boring. And in turn, it's made actually using the Internet boring. But it needn't be.

Not much has changed with the browser since Microsoft's Internet Explorer took over the show years back. Now it's on nearly every Windows computer, and it hasn't changed much since. That's left an opening for a series of rivals, the latest of which is Mozilla Firefox. Firefox was officially launched by the Mozilla Foundation on Dec. 7; within 10 days it had been downloaded one million times. At the time of writing that figure has risen to 21 million. It's available in 27 languages.

This is a feat, though not exactly an overnight sensation. Ben Goodger, the 24-year old lead engineer behind the project, credits the dedication of thousands of volunteers. "It's been an enormous challenge for a huge number of people," he wrote in a recent email interview.

These people are all devotees of the Open Source movement, contributing everything from designing desktop icons to downloading nightly builds (the latest, albeit intermediary version of the software) and testing – "a great way to find and report bugs as they occur," says Mr. Goodger. This means that Firefox might be a homemade product, but it works better than most Version 1.0 programs. There are some beautiful bits and pieces in there, such as tabbed browsing, a built-in search box, and a small button to advise you of updates. And, it's all free.

But while Firefox is a shining example of a smooth, sleek, stable interface, it's the bits you can add on that, to me, make the difference. These are called extensions and they are put together by ordinary users to add extra functions to the browser. For example, a currency converter, appearing as a toolbar in your browser, lets you convert one currency to another without having to visit a website; the tool goes to the website for you, and shows you the result in the toolbar.

This might not sound all that revolutionary, but the beauty is that with so many extensions available, you're bound to find one that suits you. For example, if you want to keep little chunks of text you find on the Net, try the QuickNote extension. If you need to count the words in a chunk you've selected from a Web page, or the whole page itself, check out Word Count. Obsessed by the weather? Try ForecastFox, which gives you quick access to detailed local weather information.

Another extension will automatically copy any text you select in a Firefox window so you don't need to, saving you a mouse-click or two. Another one will automatically look up whatever word you've selected in an online dictionary. My favorite? A widget that will display headlines from news feeds at the bottom of your Firefox browser.

All of these extensions are tiny in size, can be downloaded in seconds, even on a slow connection, and installed – and tweaked – seamlessly.

This is great, but is the all-volunteer, feel-good movement that got Firefox under way likely to last? Yes, says Mr. Goodger, who points to financial support for the Mozilla Foundation from companies like Sun, IBM and Novell, as well as growing industry usage. Increasing concerns about the security of Internet Explorer in the face of determined and inventive scammers also help make Firefox attractive. "Firefox is more than a flash in the pan…We're just getting started," says Mr. Goodger.

☞ **skipsea** (*v, the East Riding of Yorkshire*) The very quick movement a colleague will make if you approach his desk too quickly as he tries to close the browser page for the gossip/sports/porn site before you see it. *I think Bob's not working hard enough. I walked pasted his cubicle so fast he skipseaed his coffee on the floor.*

Microsoft spokespeople have said they aren't worried about Firefox, but the company has already started trying to look less like a Goliath and more like a friendly neighbor. Microsoft's website showcases browser plug-ins, produced by other people, that work with Internet Explorer.

The problem is that it's a pretty pathetic offering: 41 so far, and a third of them you have to pay for. The priciest, at $50, is a tool that lets you collect and sift through your browsing history. Compare this with the extensions developed for Firefox: between 185 and 261, depending on who you listen to. All are free.

What does this mean? Browsers are starting to look innovative and special again. They aren't perfect, but there's some interesting stuff going on – and not just Firefox. Opera (www.opera.com) is a fine option, as is K-Meleon (kmeleon.sourceforge.net), another Mozilla offshoot that has just had an official, though more muted, launch.

My advice? Don't be afraid to try out other offerings. Moreover, there's no rule that you have to stick with one browser. I have four installed on my computer and I use all of them, depending on what I'm doing and my mood. I suggest you do, too. I also suggest you give them their proper name: WAHs or GRUFs.

Since then Opera and Microsoft have offered new versions of their browser. But as the Web evolved, so have the ways we use it. These have in turn influenced the shape of the browser. The first contender has taken Firefox and welded onto it some of the vision I had for the browser back in the early days: not just a passive browser but a place where you can actually work and interact. It's called Flock, and it got a column all of its own in November 2005:

One of the fun things about the Internet is that just when you think the game is over, somebody moves the goal posts, shoots the ref and says the rules have changed. At least that's the way I see it with a new browser called Flock.

You're no doubt familiar with the Web browser wars of the mid-1990s. Microsoft's Bill Gates came to realize the importance of the Internet late, but quickly got up to speed and crushed the poor old Netscape browser by offering Internet Explorer for free. The epilogue is that despite some upstart threats from a Scandinavian company called Opera and an open source free-for-all called Firefox, Internet Explorer still dominates the Web. In sporting parlance, it's a bit like Microsoft has parked a big bus in front of the goal, so no one else can score.

But I don't think that's the whole story. For the browser, you see, is emerging from a passive click-and-read experience to a place where you can get your work done and even share it with others.

From online collaboration to well-tooled word processing programs, there's a growing array of applications you can access over the Web that involve no expensive or time-consuming software installation. And all of these run inside a browser program.

This means the browser wars are far from over. They've just shifted from being big heavy guns and massed pitch battles, to a subtle game of technology and vision – one that could turn an otherwise solitary experience, browsing, into a powerfully sociable activity. And a likely victor is a small California outfit called Flock and its browser of the same name.

Flock (www.flock.com) is the brainchild of Belgian programmer Bart Decrem. Armed with some seed money, he and his team have released an early version of a browser that's impressive. It's perhaps not as remarkable as some of the hype it has received on some tech websites, but it illustrates a new front in this drawn-out campaign: The browser is a place where you do stuff, too.

Flock, for example, includes built-in tools that let you post entries to your Web log, or blog, directly from whatever page you're viewing. (Usually you would either have to buy third-party software to do this, or else visit your blog and create an entry on the Web page itself.) It also lets you add photographs to your online Flickr account (www.flickr.com), a popular website that collects photographs and, via a clever tagging or labeling system, lets other people see thousands of photographs by category.

☞ **netherthong** (*n, West Yorkshire*) Images on a website that aren't pornographic, but might be construed so by co-workers glancing into your cubicle.

I've gone on about tagging before (see Organizing on page 120), whereby users label their favorite Web pages, music or photos, which makes it easier to search and sort through. There are still some people who don't get it, but I have no doubt it's a big thundering train of innovation that will help carry the Internet to a place where information is much easier to share. Tools like Flock understand this.

Take your Internet bookmarks, for example. These are stored in your browser and save you time when you're surfing the Web. But when sites like del.icio.us (del.icio.us) came along, bookmarks became something you could share. Flock has taken this to the next stage by saving you a step: Save a bookmark in Flock and it automatically adds it to your del.icio.us account. Now you, and anyone else if you choose, can see what you're interested in. You can make use of what others are bookmarking too, making it a kind of social bookmarking.

I can see this isn't going to be for everyone. Flock isn't quite ready for public release. I wouldn't recommend you try it until it's publicly available later this month. And even when it is, not everyone will be persuaded it's the Holy Grail. Despite there being some other nice touches, such as being able to search pages you've recently visited, some critics have said these features could easily have been added into the free browser Firefox (www.getfirefox.com), rather than become the springboard for a new browser.

True, also, that tags, blogging, Flickr and social bookmarking are still in their infancy, and perhaps too geeky for many. But throw them together and I think we are beginning to see a new set of rules for how the Internet works – making it easier to access stuff and easier to create Web pages, to share what you know, what you've seen and what you've heard. In short, by leveraging the "social" side of the World Wide Web and the tireless efforts of some of its more creative denizens, the browser is fast becoming the place where we'll get some of our best work done.

Flock is now officially out and definitely worth trying out if you are blogging or uploading pictures regularly. I'm sure in the months and years to come there will be more browsers, and I'm sure Microsoft will continue to dominate, if only because it's the default browser when you load Windows. But Mac lovers will testify that Internet Explorer is not the be-all and end-all, and even if you're not a software fanatic you will be surprised by how much easier and more fun browsing can be if you try one of these alternatives. My favorite? Firefox, by a long chalk.

surfing

Surfing. It's another way of saying "browsing". You'd think we would have better words to describe this but they're pretty much the same thing. Neither really captures the different elements involved of looking for and at web pages. But while you can't really browse (or surf) without a browser (see previous chapter) there has always been a movement towards improving on that by adding widgets, gizmos and other bits and pieces of computer code. Not all of them have been successful. Take my first column on the subject, for example, written in March 2000 when the dot com bubble was at its bubbliest:

Stripped of hype, the Internet is about two things: information and communication. It's about finding things you need and it's about communicating with others. But perhaps the most rewarding part of it is the serendipity of it all: the chance hook-up with people you weren't looking for, the chance discovery of things you didn't know existed. And the Web, being the Web, is fostering plenty of tools to help you do just that.

Take information gathering, for example. Unless you're a brave explorer with time on your hands, chances are you'll be visiting websites where you know your way around already. Indeed, without an address to tap into the browser, you're stuck. That's why Yahoo!, for example, which earned a name for itself early, has remained one of the most popular websites since its launch in 1995. The result: There's a kind of highway of big sites – Yahoo!, CNN, Altavista – that everyone visits, while many of the byways get ignored. So how can you find the byways without getting lost and wasting time?

There's a number of small, mostly free, programs you can try. These piggyback on your existing Explorer or Netscape browser to act as independent agents gathering data relevant to what you're looking at in your browser. One is Alexa (www.alexa.com), a browser plug-in that provides on-the-spot information about sites and products as you browse. Alexa has been around for at least two years, but it's only since its acquisition by online bookseller Amazon.com that it's started to prove its worth. Load the free software and you'll see a bar that appears either to the left of your browser or below it. As you browse, information will appear in the bar about a given site, including the address and telephone number of the company that owns it. (Not always the kind of information you find on a company homepage.) Also listed are several sites with related themes: Alexa even allows users to add their own. Visit the Alexa homepage, for instance, and the Alexa bar, bafflingly enough, offers you a link to Privacy International, a London-based watchdog on surveillance by governments and corporations. Follow that link and you're already off the beaten track.

Another tool is Flyswat (www.flyswat.com), a program with similar pretensions and a rather different approach. Once the software is loaded you won't be aware of its presence save for a small toolbar at the top of your browser – a fly in the system tray, so to speak. When you load a Web page with any text in it, chances are you'll see some of the words underlined in yellow (not to be confused with the blue, underlined text that usually indicates a hyperlink). Click once on this text and a small window will appear with a range of links to pertinent information: if the word is a place, Chicago, say, it will have links to travel guides; if it's a major company, it'll have a checklist of useful links, such as one to the company's Securities and Exchange Commission filings. The downside of Flyswat: not much so far on Asian companies or issues, but that's something Flyswat officials say they are working on.

Both these programs are fairly useful. And there are others: neoButler (www.neobutler.com), for example, tracks your browsing habits, sends you emails suggesting similar websites and stores pages you visit for quick recall. But none of these search tools offers the opportunity for that chance meeting with another wandering Internet soul, who may provide valuable information you may have wasted hours trying to find yourself. This is where so-called browser companions such as uTok and ThirdVoice come in. Both are widgets that turn a website into a cross between a church bulletin board and a blank wall in a public restroom.

ThirdVoice (www.thirdvoice.com), which has its origins in Singapore, has already made waves with a program that allows users to post invisible notes to any website they visit. Anyone else with the same software can read those notes. (The notes appear as little arrows wedged into the site's existing text and have raised concerns about issues ranging from free speech to who really owns a website.) uTok (short for Users' Tree of Knowledge) does much the same thing, but the notes will appear as an adjunct to the program's own window, not on the Web page itself. (uTok can be downloaded from www.utok.com). ThirdVoice's website announced plans to release a complete overhaul of the software next month that will, apparently, combine its existing functions with those of companions like Flyswat and Alexa.

None of these programs involve direct "chat" (software that allows users to type messages to each other and react instantaneously). For that you need to download programs like Gooey (www.gooey.com) or Instant Rendezvous from Mulitmate.net (www.getir.com). But what they do offer is a sometimes banal, sometimes uplifting forum for the exchange of ideas, tips, and views. Scour Microsoft's homepage, for example, with ThirdVoice running and you can read an energetic debate about the merits of Microsoft Windows vs. Apple software. (Yes, it still seems to be an issue.) Where uTok goes one better though is in its ability to do keyword searches through all posted messages. Type in Indonesia, for example, and you get an impressive list of quite interesting comments about the country and its recent withdrawal from East Timor. Post your own comment to a site, and if you chose not to do it anonymously, any subsequent comments will be forwarded to you.

These programs are neat, and highly distracting, but they only hint at the possibilities of the Web for bringing people closer to information and to each other. They remain somewhat fiddly and unstable. For now, this prevents them from reaching their goals of uniting people with similar interests, claims to the contrary notwithstanding.

At some point these toys will become serious tools that will make it easy for users to hook up with others to pool knowledge and experience. That will take time, and probably in the end it will cost you, the user, money. For now, with all these freebies on offer, you could do worse than try one, and see where it takes you. Get serendipitous.

Perhaps unsurprisingly, given the time, none of these tools survived. I was wrong about that, but not about the idea, which has reemerged in the past year or so with products that allow you to post comments to websites, much in the same way their extinct ancestors did. For more, check out a list of social annotation tools on my blog at www.loosewireblog.com/2006/03/a_directory_of_.html.

But the most basic part of browsing – finding a place you like, and remembering where it was so you can go back – has always been a candidate for innovation. In the early days we would store such places as bookmarks (Microsoft preferred to call them "favorites") which would appear as a drop-down list in a browser menu. This was fine if you didn't have many sites to go back to, or you didn't want to share them with other people online, but as the Web grew, and our desire to access and share such lists grew, this was not such a useful method. Thus in 2004 was born the idea of "social tagging", a mini-revolution that, more than anything else in my view, ushered in a new kind of browsing and a new kind of saving information. Here's how I saw it in January 2005:

Wouldn't it be great if you could actually find stuff on the Internet? Sure, Google is a wonderful tool for searching for some things – say the home page of a company, or how to make Battenberg cake. But more often than not, you'll get way too many hits for what you're looking for, and end up frustrated.

☞ **burton coggles** (*n, Lincolnshire*) Special eye equipment for wearing during Internet surfing.

It isn't surprising, really: Google is now indexing more than 8 billion Web pages, against 2 billion three years ago and 3 billion two years ago. That's a lot of pages. As David Weinberger of Harvard University's Berkman Center puts it: "We've been struggling for several years with the Internet's size and complexity." So is there a better way of finding stuff?

Well, not exactly. I think that Google is still the best search engine. But some believe that might be looking at the problem the wrong way. What if there was a better way of organizing, and not just indexing, the Web? Google, after all, merely indexes the words it finds on a Web page, and those on pages linked to it. So if you're looking for recipes for Battenberg cake, that's easy enough. But Google doesn't try to figure out what the words actually mean, or what the pages are about.

In short, using Google is like going into a library and hiring a very fast runner, who isn't smart but happens to a be a very fast reader, to sprint around finding all the books that have the word "Battenberg" in them. Wouldn't it be better to just wander over to the catalog and look up the subject of cooking marzipan-wrapped yellow-and-pink-square sponge cakes?

It would, but so far there's no catalog like this. But there's an idea of one. It's called the "semantic Web," and it's simple enough: To categorize information on the Web by adding tags – cake, marzipan, recipes, whatever – to Web pages. But with billions of pages out there, and thousands more added every day, this is not a task that anyone is volunteering to do. Until recently.

Last year a couple of free Internet services started doing something interesting, entirely independently of each other. Flickr (www.flickr.com) is a website for storing your photographs; del.icio.us (simply http://del.icio.us) lets you store bookmarks to your favorite Web pages. They share two features: Both let users add tags to what they are storing, and by default share that data with any other user.

So, say you upload a photo to Flickr, you might add a word or two to categorize it – say, scuba, or marzipan. The same applies if you add a Web page to your del.icio.us bookmarks. But because both of these tools are public, it also means that you can see what other pictures, in the case of Flickr, or Web page links in the case of del.icio.us, have the same tags.

This wasn't intentional: Joshua Schachter, a 30-year old New Yorker who set up del.icio.us, did it primarily because he wanted to keep track of his bookmarks. But suddenly you could see not only what you are gathering, but also what other people are gathering. "The motivation was mostly because I was solving a problem I had, and then I solved it for everyone," Mr. Schachter says. Social tagging was born.

Others realized that this was a grass-roots kind of classification that could be extended. Instead of someone hiring dozens of drones to sit at a computer and surf the Internet categorizing Web pages and photos so that people could find them more easily, people were doing it on their own, voluntarily, just by adding whatever key words came to mind when they added a Web page or photo.

Instead of a committee sitting down and deciding on some hierarchical system of categorizing stuff, it was ordinary people adding whatever tags sprang to mind, on the fly. A sort of egalitarian taxonomy – which is why some people are calling it "folksonomy", which may or may not catch on. It's not perfect but it works: As Gen Kanai, a Japanese-American based in Tokyo who has been working on tagging, puts it: "The user does a bit more work tagging, but it results in a wealth of information once the tagged information is cataloged and associated with other data that has the same tag."

So what does all this mean for you and me? Well, imagine that you're interested in scuba diving. You add a few relevant websites to del.icio.us and tag them "scuba". Suddenly, on your del.icio.us bookmark page, you can see not only all your tags, but how many others have tagged the same pages. And you can see what other pages have also been tagged "scuba".

You've not only stored your bookmark somewhere you can find later, but you've helped point others to the same page. And, most important, you can then see a whole library of pages others have considered worth bookmarking. Suddenly tagging becomes something simple, social – and useful. Says San Francisco programmer Bowen Dwelle: "It gives people a comprehensible way to link things together. And, most important, it gives people a way to link to other people, and – potentially – to be grouped together."

Now, all this remains small-scale, and fragile. First off, how can we be sure everyone is adding the same tags to things – marzipan, and not almond paste, say? Second: This is just two websites, a tiny fraction of the whole Web. True, but this is just the beginning. This month, a search engine called Technorati started using tags from Flickr and del.icio.us to categorize the millions of blogs, or online journals, that it indexes. That turns Technorati into a kind of homepage of every conceivable topic you can imagine people writing about:.

Most important, this social tagging thing, if it takes off, could make finding information much easier. Instead of relying on search engines, we can rely on other surfers submitting interesting sites as they find them. A bit like having some seriously fast, smart speed-readers running around the Internet on our behalf armed with piles of index cards.

I was still cautious about social tagging back then because I wasn't convinced it would take off, but it has. And it doesn't have to be about tagging for others; as I wrote in an accompanying box at the time:

You don't have to be overly excited about tags to use del.icio.us: Just think of it as a good way to keep your bookmarks in a place you can find them. And there are alternative sites that offer this service. Check out Simpy (www.simpy.com), Powermarks (www.kaylon.com/power.html), and Spurl (www.spurl.com). For a more complete list, and some more thoughts on tags, visit my blog at loosewireblog.com. All of these solve two basic problems: how to keep tabs on your bookmarks if you use more than one browser, or more than one computer, and, second, how to find them again easily.

Still, tagging is the future and once you see it in one place you see it, and its potential, everywhere. If you have a Gmail account you'll notice how

☞ **heworth without** (*n, North Yorkshire*) The big empty sound when you open a box of software and realize there's no such thing as a manual anymore.

you can add what Google calls "labels" to emails to find them later. So, if you wanted to keep all your family emails in one place, you could add the label "family" to those emails. If you were an organized sort of person, you would put these emails in a separate folder called "family" anyway, but the beauty of labels, or tags, is that you can assign more than one. So if Auntie Joan happened to be your boss, an email from her could get a "family" tag as well as a "work" tag. Beginning to see the benefits yet?

Tagging is now de rigeur *in every online application or service, and I think it's had a huge impact on the way the web is searched. Oftentimes now it's easier to find, or monitor, a topic by looking for tags than by doing keyword searches of Google. But it only solves part of the problems with browsing, How about if you want to save stuff you find while you're browsing? Here's how I saw the problem in 2006:*

One of my gripes about the Web is that it's not easy to save and retrieve small items of information – clippings, sentences, pictures, whatever – when you're surfing. You probably know the feeling: You find something on a Web page that interests you – a photo, a news item, a recipe for gob-stoppers – and you think to yourself: "Well, that's interesting. I want to keep that bit of information. Now how do I do that?"

If you're savvy you highlight the text with your mouse and try to copy and paste it somewhere you won't forget it, or if you're in a hurry you just save or print out the whole darned page, further littering your desk and denuding the planet. The only thing you can be sure of is that you'll never, ever find that bit of information again until years down the track when you're clearing out your desk and you can't remember why you wanted it in the first place. So near and yet so far: The Internet offers us a glimpse of the wisdom accessible at our fingertips and then snatches it away from us.

So what can we do about it? Actually, we have several options. The idea behind all of them is to build software into your browser so you can save stuff you come across, slot it away somewhere you can find it again, and then be able to view it when you need it. Given that most of us use a browser – Internet Explorer, say, or Opera or Firefox – to traverse the Internet, this makes a lot of sense.

But within this narrow field, there's a lot of different approaches. There are the big guns, for example, like Onfolio (www.onfolio.com) or EverNote (www.evernote.com). These, in a nutshell, let you save and organize lots of stuff.

Onfolio is nicely designed but pricey unless you're a professional – clearly its intended market. I have a soft spot for EverNote, not least because its interface is quite a departure from the usual approach: First off, your clips are saved not in a tree hierarchy, with branches and sub-branches, but in one long stream. Secondly, you can access your clips via a timeline on the right-hand side of the screen, where little markers indicate when you saved something. This gives you extra ways of navigating your saved stuff.

But there are other ways of doing this. Most of us just want to grab stuff quickly and drop it somewhere with a name or label that makes finding it again easy. If you're a Firefox user, I'd suggest something called ScrapBook (free from amb.vis.ne.jp/mozilla/scrapbook), a plug-in (a small splodge of computer code that adds to the browser's features, but less than a full-blown program) that's simple enough for most users but packed with lots of cool extras to satisfy geeky types.

Put together by Taiga Gomibuchi for his master's thesis at the Tokyo Institute of Technology, ScrapBook appears as a column in the left hand side of your Firefox browser and lets you save anything, from whole pages to selections of text or graphics, in folders that you create on the fly. You can then come back to what you have saved and prune it – cutting away, say, ads or other bits and pieces you don't want, so just the information you want to keep remains. This is all done easily via a sort of square-outlining lasso that magically corrals the separate elements that make up a Web page. Click on a selected element and it disappears, leaving just the stuff you're interested in. Sounds complicated? It's not at all. In fact, the biggest problem I found was the addictiveness of pruning unwanted foliage from Web pages I'd saved.

This pruning approach is also part of another great tool called Clipmarks (free from www.clipmarks.com). Clipmarks also works via a plug-in (which also works in browsers other than Firefox), but instead of setting up shop in the left-hand side of your window, it will lodge itself as a set of three buttons at the top of your browser. Click on the left button and you'll see something like the ScrapBook pruning tool appear next to your cursor, only this time you're using it to save the bits you're interested in, rather than to delete the bits you don't want. Click on the section you want to clip and it will change to green, with a "Clipped" sign superimposed over it. Once you've finished clipping the bits you like on the Web page – or any number of Web pages – you click on the middle button at the top of the browser to save what you've collected. Another window appears, letting you add a title and some labels to what you've saved, as well as any remarks you want to make. You can also save the material into a specific folder; unlike ScrapBook, Clipmarks stores this on the Web rather than on your computer.

There's another element to all this. By saving it online, via a free account you set up before you start, you can access what you've saved from anywhere with an Internet connection. But you can also share what you've saved with others by making your Clipmarks public. Others can then comment on what you've saved, turning Clipmarks into as much a social Weblog as a repository of bits and pieces.

Clipmarks is very well thought-out, and its co-creator Eric Goldstein promises more tweaks. A new version of Clipmarks, which was launched this week, allows users to search either in folders or by the labels attached to clippings, making it remarkably easy and quick to find and view what you or other people have saved. As Mr. Goldstein puts it: "Google lets you find information; we let you manage it." Looks like I might be a step closer to having one less gripe about the Web.

encyclopedias

Encyclopedias, you'd think, would naturally lend themselves to the Internet. They're about finding information – I only have a couple of friends who read encyclopedias end to end, and they're not the kind of people who go out much. Not just that encyclopedias are reference tools; they're also information that needs to be updated, so the Internet connectivity thing, you'd think would mean they would be even more popular as CD-ROMs or online than in the hardbound, foots-squashing book kind. But, at least initially, that didn't seem to be the case, as I found when I found myself spending a long, cold winter at my parents' house in England in early 2001:

Not everything at my parents' home is stuck in the 1950s; the Concise Oxford dictionary, for example, dates back to 1949; the family drawing pin tin has been identified as pre-Boer War and the hairdryer, a model which ceased production in 1964, has only recently been replaced after the dog caught fire during a particularly awkward bathing exercise.

Such possessions (except the dog) are timeless, but there are limits to the usefulness of the family encyclopedia, which is a 1952 vintage. Don't, for example, bother looking up computers: There isn't an entry. Or, for that matter, Alan Turing, father of all things computed, who had just won the recently concluded World War II pretty much single-handed. By way of consolation, the authors give typewriters and typography a generous seven pages, and, after noting excitedly the recent arrival of "the all-electric typewriter" conclude "the general design of the typewriter seems to be fairly settled." Well, sort of.

Fascinating fireside reading, but not all that practical if you want an update on, say, the population of major cities, how many people have access to paved runways or whether the Soviet Union still exists. This is where CD-ROM encyclopedias come in handy – at least in theory.

Buy a CD-ROM or DVD version of, say, Microsoft's Encarta Encyclopedia Deluxe, and you not only get an up-to-date encyclopedia the size of a sandwich, but you can download updates on a daily basis.

This is on first sight a great solution to the dust-gathering tomes of yesteryear, and has made many a student burrowing for material happy. Indeed, Encarta and its main rivals are aiming squarely at the school research project market: most encyclopedia CD-ROMs come with built-in research software that allows the user to compile (read crib) data from the encyclopedia directly into the student's homework report.

But there are problems, and not just with little Timmy stealing all his homework from Bill Gates. With all that free information on the Internet, who wants to shell out $50 for a CD-ROM? It's been a particular teaser for Britannica, who have been forced to provide much of their product on their website for free. Indeed, a lot of what you'd find in Encarta is also on the Microsoft website (www.encarta.msn.com), just as searchable and downloadable as if it were on your CD-ROM. In fact, if you've got a fast Internet connection you might get that information quicker than if it were sitting on your CD-ROM drive, especially if you use a new crop of free miniprograms such as Atomica (www.atomica.com) or uDefine (www.udefine.com) which do the searching for you.

Still, there is a market there. Not all the cool stuff you'll find on a CD-ROM encyclopedia is on the Internet. Encarta's Deluxe 2001 version comes with an excellent dictionary that's a mini encyclopedia in itself. Microsoft's atlas is also bundled together: a quality, multimedia product that drills effortlessly down from the global view to your village. There's comparative data you can mix and match to measure the differences between countries and peoples, or you could take to the skies on virtual tours over continents and oceans.

This package pretty much knocks any competitors out of the ring. Britannica Deluxe 2001 comes in a distant second, offering charts and comparative data but little of the pizzazz. The spruced-up interface isn't intuitive and breaks basic rules: in several layouts it wasn't possible to copy text easily, undermining the package's claim to help students looking for research material. The other package I tried, the very British Hutchinson's Encyclopedia, was even more disappointing and buggy, telling me at regular intervals I'd committed a "stream read error," whatever that is.

My major gripe with all these CD-ROMs however, is more fundamental: For all their claims to be the latest version, there's a lot of information that's old hat. Hunting down a recent figure for the population of Jakarta, for example, wasn't easy. Britannica's British version gave me a 1981 figure that's roughly half what it is now. Hutchinson was slightly better, offering a census 1990 figure. Only Encarta seemed to think it was worth giving me a recent estimate, and even then that was three years old.

If such programs are so cavalier about this kind of information, how can we trust on them on less checkable stuff? Most of the Britannica data for constructing charts and graphs I looked at was at least five years old; some of its currency valuations at least two years old. Software glitches don't seem to be tackled from version to version, either: An Encarta Atlas tool for measuring distances throws up messy-looking marks as it moves over the map, a bug I recall from the 1999 edition.

What's the point of us updating if data and glitches aren't? These are great products, and worth buying as easy-to-reach reference tools, but if encyclopedia manufacturers want us to buy updates they must put more into ensuring each new edition is up-to-the-minute and working properly. Otherwise, I'm going back to reading about typewriters in my Dad's Everyman's.

This was already beginning to change. Not at my parents' house, which was stuck with their old Everyman's. But on the Internet people started breaking down the fences around information. The first effort was not hugely successful, but it was a start. I wrote about the copyright issue, and the knowledge it was creating online in this February 2002 column called "Copylefties Are In the Right":

Today I unearthed the secret recipe for cola, just as Microsoft was being asked to give up its secret recipe for Windows. Now it may be my caffeine-sozzled brain, but I think this proves an important point: We should redraw the rules of software copyright.

It's like this. Copyright, some folk believe, is stifling innovation and concentrating power in the hands of big corporations. The task of taking on these guys fell, naturally enough, to people known for their lack of respect for authority, questionable sartorial taste and unusual personal habits: programmers. In particular, someone called Richard Stallman who objected to software companies keeping the code behind their computer programs a closely guarded secret. How, he reasoned, are these programs going to get better if we don't know what's going on under the hood? So he invented something called open-source software which was free for anyone to copy and alter.

The trick in this concept is that whatever changes you make to the software must also be copyright-free, or copyleft in the argot, or else you might find your efforts co-opted further down the line by someone who does impose a copyright. See www.gnu.org/gnu/thegnuproject.

This works well for software. The Linux operating system is a good example. Programmers get together and tweak, gaining kudos for their sweat and tears – and not much else, since there's not much money in this – as the software gets perfected. But does it work for other things?

Graham Lawton, in a *New Scientist* article, which itself is copylefted (www.newscientist.com/hottopics/copyleft/copyleftart.jsp), reports mixed success: So-called open music has not got much further than the short-lived file-sharing Napster phenomenon, in which Internet users could download songs converted to small files called MP3. An effort to build an online encyclopedia put together by volunteer experts (www.nupedia.com) has flopped, as experts show little inclination to give away their expertise for free.

But that might say more about experts than about whether open-

☞ **iffley** (*adj, Oxfordshire*) Questionable reliability of some Wikipedia entries. *The site is good on science and pop culture but some of their entries on public figures are somewhat iffley to say the least.*

sourcing works. The frustrated editor of Nupedia has taken a different tack, launching an online encyclopedia that can be added to, and edited, by anyone – expert or not. In less than a year there are some 23,000 entries (www.wikipedia.com).

And it's not just wacky stuff: The entry on Enron is informative, balanced and up to date. On the day of writing, there have been more than 20 entries made or altered, from Alphonso I of Aragon to Zhuyin (a type of Chinese phonetics). Nupedia thrives on peer review. If someone spots an error, they can fix it straight away. It's not as fancy as a CD-ROM encyclopedia, but it's probably more current – and free.

So, back to Microsoft's woes. In brief, attorney-generals in some American states pursuing an antitrust case against Microsoft are demanding access to the secret source code behind Windows in order to verify claims it's not technically feasible to offer a stripped-down version. This, in the words of one law professor, "is the equivalent of demanding of Coke that they turn over the formula."

Which, I suspect, proves the point of the open-source crowd. Microsoft has been claiming that its Internet browser is so integral to Windows that it can't be unhooked; its opponents say it's just a device to dominate the browser market. But as long as the code remains secret, no one is really going to know whether a) Microsoft is telling the truth and b) open-source programmers could fix all the problems us normal folk have with Windows if only they could get their hands on it.

Microsoft has every right to protect its property but perhaps there could be a statute of limitations on older versions of its software, allowing enthusiasts to develop the underlying code in a way that doesn't challenge existing markets.

Oh, and the secret recipe for cola? A company called Open Cola posted it on their website (www.opencola.com/products/3_softdrink/formula.shtml) as a gimmick to promote software, but now finds itself selling truckloads of the fizzy drink. And that just goes to show that revealing your secret recipe doesn't necessarily hurt your bottom line. Microsoft, take note.

From 23,000 articles in 2002 Wikipedia grew exponentially. When I next looked, exactly two years later, it had reached 200,000:

Wouldn't it be great if there was a place on the Internet where educated folk pooled their knowledge for nothing, conscientiously building up a huge, orderly and free database on subjects as varied as wind gradients and the yellow-wattled lapwing?

Actually, it's already happened. It's an online encyclopedia called Wikipedia (www.wikipedia.org), and it probably qualifies as the largest ever collaborative effort on the Internet. Late last month it reached a milestone: 200,000 entries (compare that with 60,000 at MSN Encarta Premium, Columbia's 51,000 entries, and Encyclopedia.com's 57,000 articles). By the end of this year, Wikipedia is expected to have about 330,000 articles.

But of course, quantity doesn't necessarily equal quality. So I ran a few checks on some recent topics. What about bird flu? Britannica's online (www.britannica.com) service found 75 responses to "avian influenza", none of which seemed to have anything specific. Encyclopedia.com had nothing. I couldn't log onto the MSN Encarta website at www.encarta.com because, I was told: "Your market is not currently supported." The three-CD deluxe version of Encarta had nothing on bird flu, even after I updated it online. And Wikipedia? Entering "bird flu" or "avian influenza" in the search box took me straight to the right page, with information about infection, bird flu in humans, prevention and treatment, and a link to the World Health Organization's avian-influenza fact sheet. The page had been modified the previous day to update statistics on fatalities to add the suspected case of human-to-human transmission in Vietnam.

This, I have to say, is impressive knowledge management. And it wasn't a fluke: I tried "ricin", the toxin that was recently found in the United States' Senate mail room. On Britannica it took me a couple of jumps before I found out that ricin is a poison derived from the castor-oil plant; Columbia Encyclopedia only mentioned this in passing, as did Encyclopedia.com. Encarta Deluxe did a much better job, with an article that had been updated two weeks before. (However, if I hadn't updated the contents, and had used only the CD's data, I wouldn't have found anything.) Wikipedia still won, though, with a page dedicated to the subject, and updated to include the discovery of ricin traces in the homes of a suspected terrorist ring in London last year.

So how does all this happen? How can such a huge database be maintained, and stay free? Wikipedia was set up three years ago by Jimmy Wales, a 37-year-old Internet entrepreneur who lives in Florida with his three-year-old daughter, a Hyundai and a mortgage. He wanted, he says, "to distribute, for free, a complete and comprehensive encyclopedia in every language of the world, easily and affordably accessible to even the poorest and most oppressed people." (He admits it sounds corny and made up, but all good things do…)

Anybody visiting the site can update, add or edit any entry as they see fit, via an online form. They don't even have to register first. The reason it works is, in part, because the software is really easy to use, and saves all copies of whatever has been changed or deleted. (This is where the 'wiki' bit comes in: It's Hawaiian for "quick," and Wikiwiki is the open-source collaborative software that Wikipedia is run on, but that's another story.)

The most obvious concern, with all this freedom, is abuse. What is there to stop people with bad intentions, or just bias, altering, defacing or deleting content? How can we be sure that what we're reading is accurate, if anyone can contribute? The answer: peer pressure. It's not that this kind of thing doesn't happen; it's just that it's fixed so quickly most people won't notice. That's because the software is set up so that, while anybody can change anything they want, other folk can see what has been changed and, if necessary, alter it or change it back. With about 200 regulars watching the site, and another 1,000 or so frequently monitoring, there are a lot of folk watching out for wreckers, zealots and the misinformed.

Recent research by a team from IBM found that most vandalism suffered by Wikipedia had been repaired within five minutes. That's fast: "We were surprised at how often we found vandalism, and then surprised again at how fast it was fixed," says Martin Wattenberg, a researcher in the IBM TJ Watson Research Center, in Cambridge, Massachusetts.

Of course, this doesn't mean everything is going to be accurate. Or unbiased. But once again, the sheer volume of people actively involved tends to lead towards some sort of consensus based on facts. And the rules, such as they are, tend to help rather than hinder. The goal, for example, of all posts is NPOV, which stands for Neutral Point Of View. There is no hierarchy, beyond Wales as a kind of benevolent dictator. But even he doesn't interfere much. Instead, users talk out controversies online, and only rarely pull the plug on someone. As Wales himself puts it: "There's an institutional danger if we start kicking people out that ideological considerations might play a role that we don't want them to play. An encyclopedia is a neutral reference standard."

While such discussions can be heated, they reveal the high calibre of contributors: I trawled around and found some recent spats about Belorussian President Alexander Lukashenko, the Arab-Israeli conflict and atheism. If that's the level of debate, the material can't be bad.

So where is all this going? Wales has just raised $50,000 in donations from users and fans to upgrade computers (he asked for $20,000) and hopes to raise some more by selling a version of the database to Yahoo! In the long run, however, he wants to find a way to get a hard copy of the encyclopedia to folk who don't have easy access to information. He's kind of hoping someone like talk-show host Oprah Winfrey might be interested in helping out. Over to you, Oprah. And if you know something about something, do your bit by adding, editing or correcting entries. I tried it, and the warm fuzzy feeling you get is great.

Of course with success brought criticism. How reliable could something that was put together by any old person? So, in June 2005, I polled some people who might know what they were talking about:

Can we trust Wikipedia, the free online encyclopedia that is now one of the most popular sites on the Internet?

Wikipedia, in case you haven't heard of it, is built and maintained by anyone who wants to contribute, on the fly. Literally, anyone: Go to www.wikipedia.org, view an entry, click the "edit this page" tab, change it. Literally, on the fly. In the time it's taken me to write these three sentences (four minutes, say) entries have been updated or altered more than 150 times, including the addition of three games to the entry on Tiling Puzzles and a tweak to an entry on the Foustanella, a Greek kilt.

Wikipedia, as you might have judged from the subjects above, is a massive body of work, in 200 languages. The English version is fast approaching 600,000 articles – double the number two years ago. And it's no longer fringe: Hitwise, an Internet monitoring company, has seen Wikipedia rise from 13th most visited reference website in 2004 to second, behind only Dictionary.com.

So, is it reliable? Well, first off, we shouldn't get too defensive about the infallibility of more traditional encyclopedias. British newspapers had a field day a few months back with the Oxford University Press' massive new edition of the Dictionary of National Biography, quoting experts on Jane Austen, Florence Nightingale, George V, Edward III and Patrick O'Brien as saying entries contained factual errors, were "written by the constitutionally illiterate" or, in one case, "was entirely fictitious." Earlier this year the BBC reported that a 12-year-old boy in London had spotted five errors on two of his favorite subjects – central Europe and wildlife – in the print edition of the Encyclopedia Britannica, and wrote to complain.

I've found Wikipedia to be pretty good on the few subjects I know a little about. But you aren't interested in what I think. So I polled some people who might have something to say: random academics from diverse disciplines in North America, Australia and the United Kingdom. I asked them to look up five to 10 subjects in their field and offer their impressions. Here's what they said:

☞ **chaldon herring** (*n, Dorset*) A Wikipedia entry on meaningless ephemera that you end up reading anyway. *What did I do in the office today? Devouring dozens of chaldon herrings, most of them about Star Trek characters who have one line to say and then never reappear. Fascinating.*

- Claudia Eberlein, a theoretical physicist at the U.K.'s University of Sussex, checked entries relating to quantum and laser science: "I must say I am impressed! Not everything was 100% accurate, but it was close enough for a general knowledge encyclopedia, and in places it was much more detailed than I would possibly have expected."

- William J. Jackson, an expert in Hinduism at Indiana University-Purdue University at Indianapolis, says he was "pleasantly surprised at how accurate the information is – not because I assumed Wikipedia would get things wrong, but because often sources from the West often seem put together by people who haven't studied the other culture in depth."

- Ray Trygstad, Director of Information Technology at the Illinois Institute of Technology, focused on several areas of interest: Internet & Web, Information Security and Navy/Naval Aviation. He was impressed with accuracy and balance, but felt that some entries were thin or nonexistent: "The information security article was an outstanding introduction to the field and very well balanced...The helicopter article was very complete and very accurate although there were some additional areas that could be discussed."

- Komninos Zervos, a lecturer in CyberStudies at Australia's Griffith University, looked up digital poetry (poetry that in some way uses the computer) and found it "a good starting point to a new and developing field of new media/cyber/digital/web poetry" although he found it "still very patchy mentioning types of digital poetry."

- Charles Chapman, manager of digital marketing at Massachusetts' Babson College and an occasional tweaker of entries covering emerging technologies found entries on his subject matter 95% accurate. "I can't say 100% because there was missing information, rather than incorrect information, on some of the topics I researched. I was happy to find most everything correct."

- Chris Ewels, a nanotechnology expert at the University of Paris, was lukewarm on entries on nanotechnology ("started well, then lumpy") and transmission electron microscopy ("it's a good, very introductory description, but is missing many important features of this type of microscopy"), but was impressed by density functional theory ("would give this 100% on all fronts – very accurate, detailed, well written"). Overall, he was impressed by how far Wikipedia has come since he last checked: "I must admit I didn't realize to what depth information was available."

I would take those responses as a general thumbs up. If the experts can't pick big holes in Wikipedia, I'd say the rest of us can use it. This doesn't mean, of course, that we should use the information in it without confirming it elsewhere. As Andrew Lih, director of technology at Hong Kong University's Journalism and Media Studies Centre and a long-time contributor to Wikipedia, puts it: "It's a good starting point for things; it isn't a good authority."

Why is something so easy to tamper with so good? This is easily answered: Guardians of the site constantly monitor the updated information by viewing a real-time feed of changes and can quickly spot a vandal or heavily biased contributor and undo the damage, or refer the case to others. Vandalism usually stays there for only a few minutes, or even less.

Indeed, comparing it with an existing encyclopedia may be missing the point of Wikipedia. It isn't written by individual contributors – who, like everyone else, may be fallible – but by a vast network of people of varying expertise whose contributions are open to challenge and review by anyone else. In other words, it isn't about what qualifications you have. It's about what you contribute. If your contribution is good enough, well-sourced enough and balanced enough to survive the challenges of others, then it's probably pretty good stuff. There's always room for improvement, but then any print editor who has had to issue a correction would acknowledge that.

Wikipedia, for what it is, is an impressive monument to collective scholarship and curiosity.

blogs

Blogs. I hate the word now as much as I ever did, and they have turned out to be bigger than I could ever have imagined, but reading back through my columns on the subject, I feel I earned at least some of my wages with my predictions. Here's what I wrote in February 2002, when blogging was such an obscure sport saying the word in polite company was likely to get you a slap with a handbag:

The Internet is like a teenage party: lots of groping around in the dark hoping to bump into something worth telling your friends about later. And like a teenage party, chances are you'll be hanging around sipping warm Coke with the complexion-challenged in the kitchen, unaware that all the action is taking place in the basement.

Weblogs may be the answer to this finding-the-action problem. Weblogs are Web pages built by real people, blessedly free of corporate-speak and ubiquitous images of tall, shiny skyscrapers, smiley people gazing intelligently into laptops, or besuited business types shaking hands.

Weblogs are where the real action is. They are the creation of individuals, usually musings on national, local or personal events, links to interesting articles, a few lines of comment or discussion collected and presented by one person. Weblogs are a milestone in the short history of the Internet.

☞ **adswood** (*n, Greater Manchester*) A blog that has so many advertisements you can't actually find any content. *His blog is pure adswood.*

They first appeared in 1997, according to Rebecca Blood in her excellent history of the Weblog form's development (www.rebeccablood.net/essays/weblog_history.html). By early 1999 it was shortened to "blog." Blogs took off with the advent of Web-based programs to set up and maintain sites without fiddling around with lots of formatting.

Although the media hype has faded, blogs show no sign of going away. Of those 350,000 blogs, 20% were published in the last month. Williams says new users are signing up at an average of 1,300 a day.

It's not hard to see why. Blogs are probably unique in that they allow ordinary people to put things on the Net easily, and yet to feel that the space in some way reflects and belongs to them. "There are other things that can work on the Web – it's a highly flexible medium, obviously – but the blog format is one of the 'natural' formats for Web publishing, and this is a big reason it's taking off," says Williams. Given that the original promise of the Web as a leveling medium – as open to ordinary folk as to big press barons – has faded in recent years, this is good news.

Part of a blog's charm is simplicity. In most cases it's just text, simply but elegantly laid out. Pages are quick to load. The content is concise and measured. The more you read a blog you like, the more inclined you are to trust the author's choice and follow the links offered. And, of course, it's free.

There are, of course, downsides. The sheer plethora of blogs makes finding one you like difficult. Indexes of blogs are few and far between and most don't give much idea of what lies therein, beyond a usually short and obscure title. And there's a lot of rubbish out there – overly introspective bleatings of the terminally unhappy, irrational whingings – as well as blogs that don't get updated and just take up Web space.

So where is it going? I'd like to think that blogs do what the much-vaunted portal of the dotcom boom failed to do: collate, filter and present information from other sources, alongside comment. Bloggers – those that

☞ **pickering nook** (*n, County Durham*) Blogs of complete strangers you stumble upon and read with awed fascination when you should be giving birth or mowing the garden. *Sorry I haven't finished the project...I got stuck in a pickering nook. You should check it out.*

blog – will be respected as folk who aren't journalists, or experts in their field, but have sufficient knowledge and experience to serve as informal guides to the rest of us hunting for stuff on the World Wide Web.

There's not much money in this, though doubtless they're likely to upset the media barons who realize that their carefully presented, graphics-strewn home pages are being bypassed by blog-surfers stopping by only long enough to grab one article. But that may be the future: The editor that determines the content of our daily read may not be a salaried Webmaster or a war-weathered newspaper editor, but a bleary-eyed blogger in his undershirt willing to put in the surfing time on our behalf.

Who knows? We may even be willing to pay to read their blogs. As long as there are no grinning, laptop-carrying hand-shakers in sight.

I'm a little surprised how accurate this turned out to be. I must have been on something at the time. A few months later, prodded by readers, I offered a primer in how to blog – most of which is still relevant, although so far my grandchildren haven't shown quite as much interest in my early blogging years as I predicted:

One day your grandchildren are going to sit on your lap and ask you, "Grandpa/Grandma/Generic Grandparental Figure, what did you do during the Great Blogging Revolution?"

OK, so they might not, but there's no harm in being ready. Blogging is here to stay and, like it or not, we're in the middle of new means of gathering and disseminating information. And it's about time we got up to speed and started a bit of blogging ourselves.

For those of you not yet up to speed on the phenomenon, Weblogs – Web logs – are usually basic websites maintained by individuals who chronicle anything, from their own dating disasters to the world of wireless communication. They pepper their text with links to other websites, include

☞ **blindbothel** (*n, Cumbria*) Comments left on blogs that don't make any sense. *Most of the comments were interesting but there was a lot of blindbothel as well.*

their own comments, and those of readers. Blogs reflect the Internet at its best: an informal medium for informed ideas, anarchic, commercially nave and compelling. They're also quite polite, a bit like the Internet of old. Perhaps because each blog is individually owned and managed, the interactions that take place seem to be less churlish and aggressive than some of the material you'll find on news groups and other public forums. Hooray to that. So what do you need to get started?

First, you need to find someone to host your blog. This is not difficult. And not expensive; indeed, several sites dedicated to blogging offer a basic package free. If you sign up, in most cases you'll end up with a site mixing the name of your blog with the host's name, followed by a .com (for example, loosewire.typepad.com).

Once you've signed up, you'll be asked to select a template – sometimes called a skin or a theme – that determines the basic layout of the page, including colors, columns, and text size. These can be fine-tuned later, depending on how fiddly you want to get. Once that's done, you'll be asked to fill out basic fields, such as the name of your blog, a brief description of the site and a few details. You'll also be asked how public you want the site to be – ranging from allowing any Tom, Dick or Harry to add their comments directly onto the site, to only you who can add material. When this is all done, your site is basically ready.

Adding content can be done the same way, by logging into your site and making a new posting. You don't need to know any HTML – the basic programming code that goes into preparing Web pages – as in most cases you can add links to other sites that you mention in the text, just by selecting the text in question, clicking on a button and typing in the website's address. This linking to other sites is a core part of many blogs, which themselves consist of little more than a list of links to other sites. That's not to say this is not important or useful stuff. On the contrary, such sites are lovingly prepared by aficionados who generously pepper their links

☞ **blindcrake** (*n, Cumbria*) Comments on blogs that aren't grammatical, but sound like they may have been written by people in possibly life-threatening situations. *What do you do when someone leaves some blindcrake? Call the police?*

with informed comments. This, in my view, is blogging at its best, since it provides a degree of objective expertise you're unlikely to find elsewhere. Indeed, providing links to other sites has become so central to many blogs that services have sprung up to make it easier – check out BlogRolling (www.blogrolling.com), for example.

It's not all sunshine and haymaking. Teething troubles are unavoidable. I've tried a host of hosts, finding some wouldn't let me set up archives of old postings on anything but one of its own hosted sites, for example. That said, most hosters are intuitive and user-friendly without being twee.

I'm now a convert. Once you're over the psychological hump of actually putting your own content onto the Internet, you may find yourself hooked – and prepared to look your grandchildren in the eye and say with steely certainty: "I was blogging."

Indeed. Of course, our grandchildren are probably already blogging by now, even if they're still in the womb. Everyone seems to be doing it. But what started to make it really interesting was when companies allowed employees to blog, or else failed to stop them from blogging. One such success story was Robert Scoble, who did more for Microsoft than probably any PR firm. Here's a piece I wrote after chatting with him in July 2004:

Once upon a time there was an evil bespectacled king called Bill who ran nearly 98% of the world, imposing on it bloated software solutions and enslaving it in usurious licensing agreements. Resentment of Bill was so widespread that all the king's public relations and philanthropic works couldn't put his image back together again. Then, one day, along came a rather chubby computer marketer called Robert Scoble who, via his blog, turned it all around. Suddenly everybody liked the king again and bought all his products. (Well, at least, they didn't resent him quite so much, and even spoke to him at parties.)

☞ **praze-an-beeble** (*n, Cornwall*) Comments posted to a blog where the posters seem more interested in currying favor with the poster than making a serious contribution. *His blog's not worth reading; the comments are just one praze-an-beeble after another.*

OK, it didn't happen quite like this. But the arrival of Scoble at Microsoft a year ago has certainly made a difference. Scoble, you see, writes a blog (scoble.weblogs.com, later moved to scobleizer.wordpress.com) which is about him, Microsoft, technology, cars, more or less anything. He gets three to four thousand readers a day, which in the blogging world (we bloggers call it the blogosphere) is no mean feat. When Scoble helped launch an internal Microsoft news channel in April called Channel 9 (channel9.msdn.com), it got tens of thousands of visitors on its first day. The reason for his success? Credibility.

"If there's a reason that Microsoft hired me, that's it," says Scoble. "They knew they couldn't just come in and pay some guy to write a blog. It had to be an authentic blog by someone who had some street cred." This credibility comes from Scoble not being afraid to be rude about Microsoft-he's written about how it should be broken up into separate companies, something that is definitely NOT the party line. He's been rude about the marketing efforts of some of his colleagues (he called the Microsoft Media Center one of the most underpromoted products he'd come across) and, shortly before leaving for holiday, gave a personal take on the company's recent cost-cutting measures. To Scoble, it's all about being authentic: "If I tried to spin, my readers would call me uncle. They would unsubscribe or call me a corporate shill."

Of course, Scoble's not the first to do this, even within Microsoft. Corporate blogging has been around a few years, and there were already two dozen or so blogs at Microsoft. But after his arrival, "things really took off," he says. He doesn't claim credit for this: Microsoft, he says, hired him after one of their executives saw the success of his guerrilla marketing efforts on behalf of computer manufacturer NEC. The executive, he said, "told me later he was seeing that I was changing customer opinions about NEC and he wanted me to do the same at Microsoft." The weapon? His blog. Last week, Microsoft launched its own directory of Microsoft employee blogs, the Microsoft Community Blogs Portal. It currently lists 366.

☞ **scruton** (*n, North Yorkshire*) Someone who leaves pedantic comments on your blog. *Who was that scruton who said you were using conphlagmatized in the wrong context?*

It's hard to quantify, but Scoble's presence on the Web is gradually changing perceptions about Microsoft. It puts a face on the corporate behemoth and blurs the lines between what is the corporate message and what is the private view of someone who happens to be an employee. So does Scoble consider himself a Microsoft spokesman? "I think it's pretty clear that I am a spokesperson for the company…I'm not talking on behalf of Microsoft but I can affect things on behalf of Microsoft," he says.

Scoble's experience is now being replicated elsewhere. Slowly, companies are waking up to the benefits of allowing-even encouraging-their employees to blog. Sun Microsystems, for example, has dozens of employees blogging: So many, in fact, that one employee has fashioned a blog of all the Sun blogs, so that if you really, really care about what's going on in Sun, you can read it all in one big lump. Soon companies won't be able to afford NOT to have some sort of blogging presence.

And it doesn't stop there. Corporate blogging is not just about getting the message out. It's about the dialogue within an organization. Whether the blog is a personal one, written anonymously out of office hours, or an officially sanctioned journal stored on the company's servers, it will evolve as the writer and readers interact, heading off onto alleyways and side roads as discussions gather pace. Those discussions can only help the organization, however casual they appear to be.

Blogs are the word-of-mouth, water-cooler discussions of old. And, like water-cooler discussions, they can be about anything, from company gossip to what cars to buy, what movies to see. Only they're on computers, which means they reach a much larger group of people, and unless they're secure inside a corporate network, they can't help but leak to the outside world. In short, blogs start a conversation both inside the company and through the walls into the outside world. And, because it's a conversation, it flows back in as well. The result: "They realized that if they could bring in a human connection they could change perceptions of Microsoft," says

☞ **angmering** (*v, West Sussex*) The posting of comments on a popular blog hoping to attract traffic back to one's own, less popular, blog. *He's just angmering for traffic back to his blog, whatever it is.*

Scoble. But they were smart enough to realize it worked both ways. "And they could build a better product because they're getting better feedback."

Not everyone likes this new world. I've spoken to three people who were fired for keeping blogs. While all the cases are different – and their blogging activities may have been the excuse and not the reason for their dismissal – it highlights the nervousness some employers have about their staff keeping an online journal that, however tangentially, discusses company business. But this only illustrates the power of blogs, and how they'll change the way we do things, whether we like it or not.

Amen to that. Scoble became such a success he reinvented the idea of fame, at least on the Internet. So I took another look at the phenomenon of bloggers a year or so later, in May 2005 piece entitled Secrets of Internet Fame:

Is being famous on the Internet the same as being famous in the offline world?

I was given to thinking about this when I checked out a new website called Preople.com. (No, that's not a spelling error.) It was set up by a Dutch entrepreneur called Boris Veldhuijzen van Zanten, who would get into regular arguments with a friend over who was more famous. "He was on the radio, I was on TV. He was in a magazine, I was on a panel," Mr. Veldhuijzen van Zanten explains.

So the pair typed their names into Google, as does everyone these days, to see who had the higher number of search results. "My name gives you about 1,500 hits. His 1,200. So I was more famous," Mr. Veldhuijzen van Zanten recalls. This gave him an idea for a website where people could measure their online fame: Preople.com was born, using Google and a "secret recipe" of other variables. (I'll now pause while you run a search on your own name. Don't be ashamed: Everybody does it.)

☞ **buttercrambe** with **bossall** (*n, North Yorkshire*) Twin techniques used by PR firms to try to persuade bloggers and others to write nice things/stop writing nasty things about their clients. *The PR guy was buttercrambing but when I told him I wasn't going to change my mind he started to bossall.*

All very cute, but does it mean anything? Just because a lot of websites mention your name, does that make you famous? Not really. But it does highlight an interesting phenomenon: Being well-known online isn't exactly the same thing as being well-known offline. The best test is this: Spears, Houston, Depp, Beckham, Blair. It's likely you've heard of most of these people, and could give them their right first names. But how about Ito, Scoble, Doctorow, Kottke, Rubel? Heard of any of them?

This is the thing. Those second five are members of the "technorati", the blogging A-list of people who are famous online. Not as famous as Britney, Whitney, Johnny, David and Tony, but famous. Joi Ito, for example, is a Japanese entrepreneur who gets as many hits on Google as his prime minister, Junichiro Koizumi. Compare the two names in Factiva, a database of mostly offline media co-owned by Dow Jones & Co. and there's no contest. Doing a search across all dates, the Japanese prime minister gets more than 750 times as many mentions as Mr. Ito. Another example: Robert Scoble is a American marketing executive from Microsoft who writes an online journal, or blog. Who's more popular? He, or his boss, Microsoft CEO Steve Ballmer? Offline, Mr. Scoble gets mentioned about 150 times less than Mr. Ballmer on Factiva. Online, it's a different story: Mr. Scoble is ahead, scoring 651,000 against Mr. Ballmer's 599,000.

Clearly there's a disconnect between the big names online and those offline. But what does this tell us? First off, we probably shouldn't get too worked up about online fame. Britney Spears is still the most famous person online as she is, probably, offline. But something is changing.

The Internet, it seems, is much more effective than the offline world at propelling people to limited fame; to being famous in certain circles. As Alex Halavais, a blogger and assistant professor of informatics at the University of Buffalo, puts it: "The Internet makes those circles much easier to draw." The explosion of blogs – online journals, short for web logs – has speeded up this process. Now anyone with expertise in a subject,

☞ **blagdon** (*n, Somerset*) A blogger who is always sending you links to their blog in a blatant act of self-promotion. *I stopped reading him. He's just a blagdon.*

from knitting to online gaming, can gain respect and influence by writing about it online. This is different from how one might gain influence or fame offline.

As Mr. Ito the Japanese entrepreneur puts it: "The ability to cause people to get attention online is probably the main definition of fame. In the real world, it probably means more about the ability to influence the flow of money." Offline, in other words, fame and money usually go hand in hand (when was the last time you met a famous poor person?). Online, it's more about what you say: "The way you become famous on the Internet," Mr. Ito reckons, "is probably mostly done by being interesting."

I polled a few other technorati and there seems to be general agreement. David Weinberger, a writer, blogger and consultant, talks about how "Internet fame is about the appeal of someone's 'voice'." Mr. Scoble – the Microsoft blogger – says "I don't look at it as a numbers thing but a chance to talk to the people you want to." Steve Rubel, a PR consultant in the U.S. who has gained prominence by writing a blog that straddles PR, technology and journalism, says it's not about preaching but "about the conversation" with readers. In other words, developing a following online is nothing like developing a following offline, where your remoteness, mystique and inaccessibility are likely to be part of your appeal.

Online, it's the opposite: It's all about holding a discussion, allowing people to add comments to your blog entries, writing knowing that however big a name you are there will be people who disagree with you – and giving them the space and respect to do so. Fame online, in some ways, is nothing like offline fame. (This may explain why the other thing I noticed about these guys is they don't like being thought of as famous. All were keen I emphasize they hadn't sought this high a profile, and thought fame was the wrong word. We just couldn't agree on an alternative.)

So where does this take us? Mr. Ito says that as the Internet becomes more ubiquitous – via wireless connections and mobile phones – "cyberspace" as an idea will start to die. Then the gap between prominence online and

☞ **blore** (*n, Staffordshire*) A blogger who is less than entertaining. *She used to be quite a lark, but now she's just a blore.*

offline will start to die. Indeed, for Mr. Ito that's already the case: In his work on government committees in Japan he has already found his online "fame" smoothing the way with bureaucrats and old-world moguls.

Meanwhile, in his social life Mr. Ito can't remember visiting a city anywhere on his travels where bloggers and other followers of his online writings hadn't already set up a dinner or other gathering for him, using his appearance as a chance to meet and chat. All this is arranged ahead of time via readers on his website; he just turns up. It sounds a bit like a world tour without the groupies or heavy sound equipment, I suggested. Yes, said Mr. Ito. But it's not just about him. "It's not about worship, but about the likelihood that something interesting will happen."

Now, that sounds like a new kind of fame.

Since then Scoble has quit Microsoft for a small podcasting (see p. 262) startup, so it'll be interesting to see whether he was famous for being the Microsoft blogger or whether he had a strong following for his writing. And, as I pointed out at the time, fame isn't always desirable: Some of the sleaziness of offline fame does creep in, with Internet adding the ingredients of scale and speed. Take the fate of a Canadian teenager Ghyslain Raza, whose private 2002 recording of him wielding a golf-ball retriever as if it were a Star Wars light saber found its way onto the Internet, and from there to millions upon millions of home computers. Then there's American Gary Brolsma, whose bedroom lip-syncing to a Romanian pop song last December catapulted him into similar levels of reluctant fame. These were relatively spontaneous bursts of fame, although they were aided in part by websites such as Waxy.org, whose Andy Baio makes a point of trying to trace the individuals in such video clips.

But blogging has created its own stars, many of whom have found modest fortune in the "real" world. For me it's been a somewhat weird journey. My employers allowed me to blog back in 2002 mainly because they didn't know what it was, I suspect. But I've been careful not to write anything that would embarrass them too much or get anyone into legal trouble. And it's not as if

☞ **petsoe end** (*n, Buckinghamshire*) Blogs that haven't been updated in more than a year. *The guy doesn't seem too committed. His blog is a petsoe end.*

my blog has made me famous; indeed, given I try to write for a non-geeky audience, it's surprising that it gets read at all. And I have reservations about it. It does take up time. And does working on a blog detract or add to what you write elsewhere? And popularity is elusive; some can become very popular quickly, while others languish for years. That said, it's been an interesting journey, and a great discipline to get into. The best rule of thumb: Write for yourself primarily, but try to make it interesting for others. A good blog will always find an audience.

rss

First there was push. Then there was shove. Then there was pull. And again there was push. If that doesn't make any sense, perhaps these columns might. It's the history of getting information to you. Sometimes known, simply, as RSS. First off, a piece called "When Push Comes to Shove" from April 2002:

I think I can safely say it, though others have been saying it for years: Push is dead. In which case I'd like to be the first to say: Long live push.

For those of you who weren't following closely, push was much hyped in the mid-1990s when computers were first being hooked up to the Internet in a big way. The idea was simple enough: instead of users going to websites to get information – pull – the information could be sent – pushed – to the user. You could then sit back and watch it all – cricket scores, share prices, headlines – scroll across your screen. For the corporate world it was an opportunity to also push ads, special offers and branding.

So what went wrong? First out of the starting gate, PointCast earned lasting opprobrium because its software hogged computer and Internet resources. PointCast retired hurt, and was eventually bought by EntryPoint in 1999, which a year later merged with Internet Financial Network Inc. to form InfoGate. This stopped offering its free ticker in mid-April, and now can only be found in the technology behind the subscription-based USA Today NewsTracker ($40 a year from newstracker.usatoday.com), which somewhat fittingly looks like the PointCast of old.

Actually, it's not push that is dead. It's the gravity-defying business models and catch-all products that don't offer anything other people can't offer for free. InfoGate fell by the wayside because it didn't make any money. USA Today's NewsTracker won't, in my view, attract users because you can get the same thing free elsewhere – try the BBC's excellent Newsline ticker (www.bbc.co.uk/newsline – *currently unavailable as it going through a major upgrade at time of press*).

Why then has yet another scrolling-ticker business thrown open its doors to the public in the same week as InfoGate closed them? Enter KlipFolio from Serence, a small Windows program that at first blush is not much different. The scrolling is familiar; the clicking on a headline to see the full story is the same. The only visible change is that each Klip contains information from one source only, so instead of one big scrolling ticker with everything in it, from CNN to your local rag, Klips are small and independent.

Below stairs, it's very different: a content-service provider (what you and I would call a website, whether it's a magazine, news service, an auction site or whatever) adds some lines of Klip computer code so that every time they add some data to their website (a news story, an updated stock price, a new item for sale) that data is added to the Klip's scrolling headlines.

Users, meanwhile, select which Klips they want to view on their screen, which will then update in real time with the new story, price or item for sale. Simple. Serence operates merely as the provider of technology to the content-service providers. For the user, the Klip software is free (www.Klipfolio.com), though Serence says some providers may charge for content in the future.

So what's so different about this? Well, first off the software looks and works beautifully. Secondly, the back end is simple enough for content-service providers to be able to incorporate it without any extra computers, technicians or PhDs. This means that Serence is just an intermediary; it just provides a site where users can find what sources are available, and it licenses the software to the providers.

Where I believe Klips might really take off, however, is in delivering more specialized content. Sure, we can monitor websites, get stuff by email, even have stock prices sent to our mobile phone, but imagine having a Klip that monitors, say, the prices of fast-moving items on an online auction site, or jobs in a particular industry.

What's more, Serence has priced the product so that even individuals who produce specialist newsletters can jump aboard for about $100 a month. Indeed, as blogs become more organized, Klips may emerge as a great way for individuals to provide a valuable real-time service which grateful users may pay for.

If that happens, it may well mark the coming of age of push: an information-delivery service that gives me stuff I need, doesn't take up space and doesn't go out of business.

Actually, I was wrong about this. Around the time I was writing this, something called RSS was taking root. Me being a bit slow, it took me a year to get it into print. Here's my first crack at explaining it, from July 2003:

This is not another column about spam, but that's where I have to start. Spam, or junk email is, we're all agreed, the bane of our lives. But what if the problem is not so much spam, as email itself?

Look at it like this: Email is our default window on the Internet. It's where pretty much everything ends up. I have received more than 1,000 emails in the past week. The vast bulk of that is automated – newsletters, newsgroup messages, despatches from databases, press releases and whatnot. The rest is personal email (a pathetically small amount, I admit), readers' mail (which I love, keep sending it) and junk. While it makes some sense to have all this stuff in one place, it's hard to find what I need, and it makes my inbox a honey pot for spammers. And when I go on holiday, it all piles up. Now, what if all that automated stuff was somewhere else, delivered through a different mechanism you could tweak, search through easily, and which wasn't laced with spam? Your inbox would just be what is email, from your boss or Auntie Lola.

Enter the RSS feed. RSS stands for Really Simple Syndication, Rich Site Summary or variations of the two, depending on who you talk to. It's a format that allows folk to feed globs of information – updates to a website, a blog, news – to others. These feeds appear in programs called news readers, which look a bit like email programs.

This also makes sense for those folk who may not subscribe to email alerts, but who regularly visit any number of websites for news, weather, movies, village jamborees, books, garden furniture, or whatever. Instead of having to trawl through those websites each morning, or each week, or whenever you remember, you can add their RSS feeds to your list and monitor them all from one place.

RSS feeds aren't just another way to deliver traditional information and have become popular in part because of blogs. While many blogs are more like personal diaries, others are written by people who know what they're talking about, and have become a credible source of information and opinion for industry insiders. Many of these bloggers now offer updates of their websites via RSS feed. "There's an awful lot being created by individuals who are key figures in their markets," says Bill Kearney, who runs a website, www.syndic8.com, that lists more than 20,000 such newsfeeds.

Blogs and RSS have, despite their unwieldy names, helped to level a playing field between traditional news suppliers – news agencies, newspapers, news websites like CNN – and those in or monitoring a particular industry. Some call it "nanomedia": An often-cited example is New York's Gawker (www.gawker.com) which collects gossip and news from the Big Apple, many times scooping the local dailies. Indeed, blogs themselves came of age this year, first during the Iraq War when a young Iraqi translator calling himself Salam Pax ran a massively popular blog (dearraed.blogspot.com) from Baghdad, offering a compelling perspective on the conflict. Later *The New York Times* felt the growing power of blogs when the plagiarism crisis prompted by reporter Jayson Blair was fuelled by blogs and other Internet sites, all in real time.

We don't want to go too far. There's a lot of dross in blogs, and therefore a lot of dross in RSS feeds. And while the software has improved in recent months – check out news readers such as Newzcrawler (www.newzcrawler.com) or Feedreader (www.feedreader.com) – it still feels slightly experimental. But as the format matures, I think our once-bright hopes for the Internet as a democratic, intelligent medium might be realized.

Part of it means throwing away what we traditionally think of as "news". Corporations are beginning to sense that blogs make an excellent in-house forum for employees. Small companies have found that running a blog for their customers – say a real-estate agent sharing news and opinions about the neighborhood property market – pays better than any newspaper ad. Individuals – consultants, columnists, one-man bands – have, through well-designed, well-maintained blogs, built a critical mass of readers, some of whom become paying customers or subscribers. Teachers are finding RSS feeds useful for channeling subject matter to classrooms and sharing material with other teachers.

Is there money in it? One Canadian company, Serence (www.serence.com), targets its form of RSS feed, called Klips, to companies automating specific tasks – monitoring competitors, prospects or industry news, accessing critical internal data. There is, of course, a danger that what ailed earlier formats ends up ailing RSS feeds: This month, one company started carrying ads in an RSS feed, with mixed results. In the end, I think, some of this data will be good enough to pay for, some will be supported by ads, and some will continue to be done out of love.

RSS's strengths are simplicity and versatility: It can be added on to other programs – the browser, Outlook, or be delivered to your handphone, hand-held device, or even as audio on your MP3 player. It's a lot more powerful than email, and – we hope – will be guaranteed spam-free. Hurrah.

Some advice I offered at the time for those of you wanting to get into the RSS world still holds true:

Newzcrawler and Feedreader, both mentioned in the main article, are the best programs to start with. Feedreader is still in development, but felt pretty stable to me. To add a RSS feed, just paste in the link (more on this in a bit) and it should start showing up immediately. Newzcrawler even lets you send stuff from other people's feeds to your own blog or RSS feed. Each program adds the feeds in a slightly different way, but in most cases you'll be asked to copy a link (the website address that appears at the top of your browser) into the newsreader. These links usually end in a full stop, then three letters: RSS, RDF or XML (don't worry which; they all do the same thing).

This sounds scary. If all this is a bit daunting, try Serence's KlipFolio (www.serence.com), which is a bit more polished – though still free to the end-user. Now into its second version, it supports Korean and Chinese language Klips. Download the software and then browse the various Klips on offer. An Outlook user? Try NewsGator (www.newsgator.com) which folds all your RSS feeds into an Outlook folder. Or if you're brave, check out clevercactus (www.clevercactus.com), which is an Outlook-style personal organizer with RSS built in. Here's a provisional list of newsreaders: www.hebig.org/blogs/archives/main/000877.php.

How do I find interesting feeds? A couple of places to start: Feedster (www.feedster.com) is the Google of the RSS/blog world. Another option is Syndic8 (www.syndic8.com), a more select, and searchable, list of feeds. You'll notice a lot of sites offer their own feeds so you don't have to go hunting for them. Can't find a feed for a site you're interested in? Check out MyRSS (www.myrss.com) which allows you to build a custom feed for any site, even if it doesn't have a feed. It's pretty straightforward, too.

How do I set up my own newsfeed? First you need material, which means setting up a blog. That's easy enough: my favorites are Weblogger (www.weblogger.com) or Blogger (www.blogger.com). Once you've set up a blog, both sites offer simple options to add an RSS feed automatically. That's it. If you're a company thinking of setting up a feed, you may want to talk to the pros. The coding is quite simple, but there are ways to add your logo, and other corporate stuff, to ensure some quality control.

Not that RSS caught on, or has caught on, to the mainstream. It does remain somewhat nerdy. Here's an update I wrote on it all a year later:

It's been more than a year since I wrote about RSS, but if my immediate entourage is anything to go by, the wonders of Really Simple Syndication (or sometimes Rich Site Summary) have yet to hit the mainstream Loose Wire readership.

Every time I mention RSS to Colin, for example, he says something like, "Can you tell me what it is again? And can you speak slowly this time?" Of course, this could just be Colin, but this week I thought I'd show you some short cuts to the future of how we get our information.

Basic stuff first: RSS is just another way to get data from one place to another, whether it's from my blog, the BBC's news headlines or Amazon's top best-sellers. What's so good about it? Well, because everyone has (more or less) agreed on the standard, you can find RSS feeds all over the Internet now, which you can then pull together in one program called a newsreader. Look for the little orange button: [XML] And while RSS started out as a way to subscribe to blogs, now it carries a much larger range of information, not all of it nerdy. Some examples of RSS feeds launched recently: news sources from ESPN to *The Wall Street Journal* and *The Washington Post*, a British employment-agency roster of new technology jobs and even the United States National Hurricane Center's tracking of Hurricane Ivan.

This all sounds great, being able to grab the information you're interested in and have it all updated for you, in one place where you can read it. But there are a couple of obstacles that make it less easy than it ought to be. The first is that to read all these feeds you need to install a special program, called a newsreader.

Actually, that isn't true any more. There are several products that let you pull RSS feeds into your existing set-up, whether it's your browser or your email program. Bloglines (www.bloglines.com), for example, collects all your RSS feeds and lets you view them, put them into nice tidy folders and even keep the articles you want to hang on to, all within your browser. Indeed, some browsers now include RSS as standard: Firefox (the open-source browser), Opera (the tenacious Scandinavian David to Microsoft's Goliath) and even Apple's Safari all now offer a way to read RSS feeds without any extra software.

The other obstacle is how to find the RSS feed you want and then put it somewhere you could use it. Some newsreaders and even online services still make this a bit tricky, requiring you to locate the feed, copy the address (all RSS feed sources are in the form of a Web address) and then paste it into the reader. But this too, has changed. Bloglines, for example, includes a directory of feeds, and, even better, includes a little tool called a Bookmarklet (I'm not crazy about the name) that lets you add a feed to your collection easily. (A tip: Adding a feed is called "subscribing," but one of the beauties of RSS is that you don't actually have to give out any personal information – even an email address – to subscribe to a feed. Even better, ending your "subscription" involves nothing more tricky than just deleting it from your RSS list.)

So, just to walk you through the Bloglines Bookmarklet thing, because this is the way a lot of these services let you add RSS feeds. In all browsers nowadays there's a bit of space, usually between the viewing part of the browser (the main window where you see your Web pages) and the menu bar and the bar with the Back, Forward and Home buttons above it. This space usually lists a handful of different websites you might access frequently, and is usually preloaded with some sites – usually ones touting the business of the browser manufacturer.

But it's also a good place to store more complicated bits of code that act as short cuts: in this case, adding an RSS feed. So, drag the Bookmarklet link to the top of your browser with the mouse. This will add an extra button called "Bloglines" or something like it. Now, if you're reading a Web page and you see a feed you like the look of just click on the [XML] next to the feed name or description, click on your new Bloglines button and you'll be able to add that feed to your list without further ado.

I'm not going to pretend RSS is perfect but it's definitely on the way to the big time. Expect to see a lot more than just items of news delivered in the future, and expect it to be delivered to places other than your browser.

RSS will power delivery of business information within companies, as well as video and audio, and it will be delivered to your mobile phone, your car, the fridge and a panel in the bath, just behind the taps, where you can view updates from the BBC while you soak. OK, I made that last bit up, but it could happen. RSS is here to stay, and it's well worth getting out of the bath for.

It is here to stay, and in some ways it has become a victim of its own success. It makes it easier to deliver information, and that makes it easier to put out information, which increases the amount of information, which in turn shifts the problem to the end user who feels he or she should be reading all that information. Here's a suggestion from May 2006 about how to cope, titled, suitably enough, "How to Read 35 Million Blogs":

The blogging revolution is about five years old now, and already it's out of control.

Blogs have proved wildly popular; the total number out there is doubling every six months, according to Technorati Inc., a company that tracks more than 35 million of them. And this creates a problem: How can anyone find what they want among all that information?

Of course, it isn't as if we don't have tools to help: Most blogs nowadays – and a lot of mainstream websites, including parts of the site of this newspaper – are available as RSS feeds. These allow you to subscribe to those blogs you like and receive updates from them without having to repeatedly revisit them, via a browser or a separate program called a news reader, which collects the feeds together rather like an email program collects your emails. But all this has done is make it easier to add more stuff to our growing list of what we feel we need to read.

A recent case in point: Monday morning, I again tackled my blog surplus. As I started looking through the blogs I track to decide which ones to weed out, I got reading. And following links. Within half an hour, I had removed three blogs but added nine new ones. By lunchtime I had committed myself to 274 feeds – 17 more than I had started the day with

– containing 3,624 items. But hey, it isn't hopeless. I only have 3,582 more blog posts to read. At present reading speeds, and assuming nothing happens between now and then, I should be up to speed by November 2033.

This is the problem with blogs. They're too good. Sure, among those 35 million-plus there are probably some real turkeys. But find one good one, and you'll quickly find dozens more. By definition, each blog isn't hermetically sealed, since it contains links to other blogs. Like me, you'll get sucked in very quickly, following links like paper trails until the early hours.

The challenge, then, is to turn the blogging world into a place where you're only able to read what you can manage, and to ensure that what you're reading is the best there is on the subject.

One solution: BlogBridge. On one level it's just another (free) news reader. It lets you collect and organize RSS feeds into folders according to theme (Technology, Sport, Squirrel Waterskiing, etc.). But BlogBridge goes further.

First off, BlogBridge calls its folders "Guides" or "Reading Lists". These aren't just static collections of feeds, but are lists carefully collated by experts in the relevant fields, whose credentials you can read on the site. Instead of subscribing to a single feed, you subscribe to an expert's Guide or Reading List. Conversely, if you felt you were an expert on Squirrel Waterskiing, you could share your list of exciting blogs and other feeds on the subject as a Reading List, allowing other Squirrel Waterskiing enthusiasts to download it into their BlogBridge program.

Nothing too revolutionary here, since it is already possible to share groups of feeds, although only really for the seriously nerdy fringe. But one of the neat tricks with BlogBridge is that any Reading List you subscribe to can be dynamically updated. If the expert in any particular field decides to replace one feed with another, or add a feed, those changes will automatically be reflected in your Guide. The responsibility for monitoring those 35 million-plus blogs (and the millions of other RSS feeds out there) has shifted from the reader to a sort of uber-reader, the informal expert who has put the Guide together. As the guy behind BlogBridge, Pito Salas, puts it: "This is a bit like being a publisher, but in the blog mentality of being decentralized."

It isn't perfect. BlogBridge is Java-based, meaning that it will work on all platforms, but also that it isn't overly pretty to look at. Subscribing to a list could be easier. And right now there aren't that many lists to choose from. There's a danger that BlogBridge ends up getting swamped with bad lists, or too many lists, or lists that aren't what people are looking for. And, of course, there's still the danger you'll get swamped with more than you can ever read.

Still, I suggest you check it out, whether you're new to RSS or not. Don't get too excited about the Squirrel Waterskiing list though; I'm still working on it.

podcasting, etc.

Beyond all these different ways of presenting and delivering information, there are one or two other terms that are proving, or may prove, as revolutionary. One is called podcasting, which I wrote about in June 2005, having been somewhat skeptical for about a year about how popular it was going to be. How wrong I was:

Podcasting is one of those ideas that didn't exist a few months ago but is now so commonplace that you wonder why we didn't think of it earlier. For those of you still in the dark, Podcasting is basically a way to syndicate audio files – recordings, to you and me – on the Internet in a way that makes it easy for listeners to find and get what they want, when they want. The recordings themselves are in the popular MP3 format, meaning you can transfer them to your MP3 player or iPod. Hence the term podcasting. The new bit isn't the file format, but the way you can subscribe to a particular podcasting service, in exactly the same way you can subscribe to an RSS feed, as I explained earlier. Think of it as radio on demand: being able to listen to more or less anything you like wherever you like, whenever you like.

Podcasting has taken off in a big way. Now everyone seems to be doing it, from one-man operations to the BBC. Texas-based consumer researcher the Diffusion Group last week predicted the number of people listening to podcasts would rise to 57 million by the end of the decade from 4.5 million this year. While it is probably a good idea to take such figures with a grain of salt, there is no question that podcasting has caught the imagination of a large and varied group of people. One online directory, Podcast.net, lists more than 1,400 podcasts in the entertainment category alone, ranging from a show entirely dedicated to "the screen's greatest team, Spencer Tracy and Katharine Hepburn" to a live music jam.

Why so popular? Well a lot of people have MP3 digital music players already, and most of them know how to get music onto it from their computer, either by grabbing it from a CD or by downloading it. Getting a podcast from your computer to your MP3 player or iPod is no different. Finding the podcast material online is a little different, but it still involves a technique that a growing number of people are familiar with: RSS is the tool for subscribing to blogs and stories from newspapers and other websites. Recording podcasts and turning them into RSS feeds is also easy, although it could be simpler.

I suspect there's another factor at play in podcasting's popularity. Users are beginning to look at the Internet and technology a little differently. Blogs have made it really, really easy to build impressive looking websites with little or no knowledge of HTML, the fiddly code behind a Web page. Digital photography and video cameras have gotten cheaper, easier to use, and, perhaps most importantly, more closely tied to the Internet, so posting a photograph from, say, your mobile phone to a Web page doesn't involve cables, complicated formatting or a degree in computer science. All this multimedia dexterity has helped blur the distinction between consumer and producer: Now anybody who wants to can be a publisher.

This is having another important effect. Before, during the dot.com boom, everyone was looking for the money. Everyone was thinking big scale. Nowadays, not everyone thinks like that. The buzzword du jour is "the long tail," shorthand for the idea that not every business needs to worry about finding a huge audience for its product, (the fat end of the long tail) but instead could find success in catering to smaller, more specialized or localized chunks of the audience (the thin end of the long tail).

And while many people are still looking to monetize this long but thin tail, those actually in the long tail seem to be more interested in just doing stuff for other people interested in their slice of the long tail. Like blogging. Like posting pictures to a site such as Flickr.com. Like podcasting. Why should I care if the podcast I produce on my obsession with the lesser spotted woodpecker (Dendrocopos minor to its fans) is listened to by only 10 people if they are all fellow enthusiasts?

In any case, podcasting isn't just radio broadcasting about woodland-based birds. Podcasting offers a way to deliver all sorts of interesting audio content, from commentaries of tours, museums, movies, books and airline flights to lectures and schoolwork.

Take the kids of Musselburgh Grammar School, just east of Edinburgh, who use podcasting to make an entertainment show for parents and the local community or create audio guides to the town in French and German for tourists, while the teachers use the medium to create language-listening exercises. That's just the start, says Ewan McIntosh, a language teacher at the school. "The kids keep having other ideas on how it could be used."

Or consider Frank De Graeve, a 26-year-old Belgian whose website (www.podguides.net) is dedicated to creating and collecting audio-walking guides. Using MP3 players that also display pictures, such as Apple's iPod Photo, users can see a map of where they are, and quickly jump to podcasts that match numbered locations.

This is all just a beginning. Audio guides (what are sometimes called sound seeing tours) could offer extra information or instruction about more or less anything you are doing, from exercising to cooking to watching a movie. The television series "Battlestar Galactica" even offers podcast commentaries by its producer of each episode, to be listened to while watching the show. I can see a lot of other people offering similar commentaries – from erudite observations to trivia – to other TV shows, movies, sports events and concerts, indeed anything that can be synchronized (railway trips? airline flights?).

☞ **brightling** (*n, East Sussex*) A podcaster who is endlessly energetic and enthusiastic about all things geeky. *He's young, he's a brightling. He'll get over Web 2.0.*

I'm sure a lot of current podcasters will lose interest in the medium. But as it matures and users stop thinking about just recreating a radio station in their bedroom and explore the outer limits of what can be done, I reckon podcasting will become as exciting and fulfilling a way to get information as blogs are now. Like blogs, people will agonize about how to make money from it while others go ahead and do interesting things with it.

In order to subscribe to these podcasts, you will need a piece of software called a podcatcher which enables you to search, subscribe and organize podcasts. One of the more popular podcatching programs is actually Apple's MP3-playing iTunes. A recent update to embrace and integrate podcasts into its online Music Store has really helped push them into the popular consciousness, whatever that is. At the time of writing there are over 50,000 different podcasts with topics ranging from News & Politics to Comedy to Music. Subscribing couldn't be easier: just find the podcast you want and then click the "subscribe" button. Once the episodes download to your computer, you can easily synchronize them with your iPod and listen on the go. Like the podcasts, iTunes is free (www.apple.com/itunes) and since it works on both Mac and Windows platforms it's worth checking out, even if you don't have an iPod. For a list and discussion of podcast directories, check out http://tinyurl.com/hutl6; if you want to use Windows software other than iTunes to sort and download podcasts, check out this list here: http://tinyurl.com/93fux.

Talking of iTunes and iPods, the two devices have helped prod along another revolution: videocasting. Here's how I saw it in a February 2006 column called "Surrender to the Madness":

The other day I succumbed to iPod madness. It's just easier, I decided, to buy one of the latest models than to have all my friends yak on about theirs and for me to, somewhat lamely, grunt about the fact that I had one of the very first ones, back when my friends still thought an iPod was a fancy contact lens case.

And besides, I was sucked in by the idea that I could not only store and listen to all my music on it but now also watch videos. My wife, quite reasonably, asked what exactly I would watch on it, and when. But she didn't understand. She wasn't there when my friend Mark showed me his iPod, replete with an episode of "The Office" (not the original U.K. version but a U.S. episode: boring) and a video of his wedding (not boring). I want one of those, I thought to myself (the iPod, not the wedding). So I got one: a gorgeous black 60-gigabyte number with color display. Now I can be as smug as all my friends.

But that's not the only reason the iPod, and Apple boss Steve Jobs, are so successful. After all, there have been lots of MP3 music players around which store just as much as an iPod can; some can even play video. Apple wins folk over because it makes things simple. Take podcasting, for example. Until Apple cottoned on, broadcasting via downloadable MP3 files was a niche activity. Although the "pod" bit came from iPod, the idea didn't come from Apple, but it really took off when Apple made it very, very easy to find and download podcasts via its iTunes software. Now there are thousands of podcasts available, some of them quite good.

Apple made MP3 players sexy. It made podcasts easy. And it has now made watching video on a color screen the size of a matchbox at least plausible. And I've joined the legions of people who are watching re-runs of "The West Wing" on a display that's smaller than my phone's. I never used to watch anything on my PDA, phone or watch, so why do I now think this is the best thing that ever happened to me?

Partly it's because Apple makes it easy to buy reruns of "The West Wing" and "The Office". So long as you have Apple's iTunes software, Apple's iPod and an account with Apple's online store, it's all quite simple to pay for and download these files to watch on an iPod. Apple has taught us again that ease of use counts for a lot more than cost or user ingenuity.

I must confess I've really gotten into the whole Watching-Something-on-the-Bus-Just-Because-I-Can thing that video iPods have created. I've watched several episodes of a wonderful BBC TV series on the British countryside and art; I've watched old soccer matches I recorded off the TV and downloaded to my iPod (possible if you have a DVD recorder or something like the $130 Neuros MPEG-4 Recorder 2 device, which plugs into the TV and records shows digitally – it's available from www.neurosaudio.com); I've also watched a guy in Hong Kong called Simon Chan play the popular German drinking song "In München Steht ein Hofbräuhaus" on the accordion.

Having said that, the process of getting a piece of video onto your iPod that hasn't already been shrink-wrapped into the right format by Apple isn't quite as easy as it could be. I used a Windows program called ImTOO DVD to iPod Suite (www.imtoo.com) to convert DVDs so I could watch them on my iPod. It was straightforward, but you would be well advised to let it run overnight since it ain't fast. Indeed, it's worth pointing out that Apple only makes easy those things it wants you to do: If you don't like being locked into file formats and other restrictions, you may want to check out the less beautiful but more versatile Archos range of video players and recorders (www.archos.com), which do most of the things an iPod can, and more.

But there's no question this is the start of something big. Just as podcasts are probably going to change the way we listen to audio, video iPods will change the video business. Expect to see people devising different kinds of content for watching in small matchbox-sized rectangles on public transport – and I'm not just talking Hong Kong people with accordions. *Eastern Daily Press*, a newspaper in Norfolk, England, for example, now offers daily video bulletins of the local news, turning it into a quasi-TV station (www.edp24.co.uk). I found more than 250 websites registered containing the word "vodcast." And you've got until Feb. 20 to get your entry in for what is billed as the world's first film festival specifically for iPod content (www.theflux.tv/ipodfest).

Expect to see the way we behave on public transport changing, too, as people don an array of two- or one-eyed visors for viewing on the move. Check out eMagin's Eyebud 800, to be launched later this year for about $600 (www.emagin.com). And a $15 adapter, available in most Apple accessory stores, will plug your iPod into any TV for use as a portable video storage unit. Or there's the iSee 360i device, due out later this quarter for about $250 (w3.isee-ato.com): Slide your iPod into it, flip it over and you have a larger screen – 9.1 centimeters rather than the iPod's 6.3-centimeter one.

I'm off to see what the accordion-playing Mr. Chan looks like on that. Let the madness continue.

Videocasting, or whatever it's called, has not perhaps been quite as popular as podcasting, mainly because watching something on a small screen doesn't appeal to everyone. But loosely connected to it is another kind of casting that I have high hopes for: screencasting. Here's a column I wrote about it in June 2006:

I'd quite understand if you feel you've heard enough about new gizmos, programs and paradigm-shifting delivery mechanisms. A lot of it may sound great to geeks, but to ordinary Joes who just want to get through their business day without their computer crashing, a lot of it may seem a little, well, hyped. This week's offering may sound like another one of those, but I'm pretty sure it isn't – although the name might give you a shudder. It's called screencasting.

Screencasts are really simple to grasp. And in some ways they aren't new. But I think they represent a great way to use computers to train, educate, entertain, preach and otherwise engage other people in a simple way. Something the Internet, and computers in general, have so far largely failed to do.

Screencasts are little movies you create on your computer. In most cases, they are movies of your computer. You use special software to capture the keystrokes and mouse clicks you make on your screen, demonstrating, say, how to use Google (the screen bit of screencasting). Then, once you've edited and added a voiceover, you upload it to your website and let everyone else watch it (the casting bit).

Why might someone want to do this? Well, if you've ever tried to explain to someone over the phone how to fix some problem on their computer, you'll appreciate the benefits of a little movie that they can watch themselves and follow. Instead of frustrating directions – "OK, move the mouse to the bottom right-hand corner of your screen where you can see some little icons, right? Click on the yellow one that looks like a pregnant ant." "Hang on a minute. What's an icon?" – you can just make a quick screencast, email it to them and let them watch on their computer what they should be doing. (Of course, this doesn't help if their problem is that their computer doesn't work.)

It needn't just be helping Mom open her email. Software manuals could be replaced by libraries of screencasts, from "Overview of why this product rocks" to "How to change the font size of the fourth tab from the left without messing everything else up." Websites or online services could quickly introduce new users with screencasts that run through their main features.

Actually, this kind of thing is already happening. Dreamed up by programmer and technology writer Jon Udell in 2004, screencasts have quietly taken off. Now a search of Google Video throws up more than 200, while online video repository YouTube has nearly 70. For an example, check out one from Mr. Udell, of how a single Wikipedia page changes over time (weblog.infoworld.com/udell/gems/umlaut.html).

Big companies such as Microsoft Corp. are waking up to the idea, using screencasts to demonstrate new products to early adopters. One online poker website runs screencasts of notable games (www.pokerscreencasts.com).

Mr. Udell himself acknowledges that the idea of making such miniscreen movies isn't that new: He has just helped define and develop the genre, by experimenting and showing how it can be used, to a point where people are waking up to what screencasts can do.

There are several screencasting programs of varying capabilities available, some free (Wink, from www.debugmode.com/wink) and some not (Camtasia Studio, www.camtasia.com); for a fuller list, check out loosewireblog.com. They let you define what part of your computer screen you're going to record, record it, and then add extra features to the recording, including a voiceover, a video of you using your Web cam, or little text boxes and arrows to help users see what you're doing.

Mr. Udell is exploring the idea of screencasts beyond the computer screen, making what he calls "mini-documentaries" of everyday experiences. Indeed, as screencasts move away from being just movies of your computer and toward capturing the real world, they find themselves overlapping with the abundance of homespun video offerings that can be found on websites such as YouTube. Screencasts, however, tend to focus more on demonstrating than entertaining; for example, they could cover sports events by weaving drawings of moves on a whiteboard into what is happening on the pitch. Screencasts would also be great for anyone trying to teach remotely, whether it's e-learning or training election monitors in Africa.

As Mr. Udell, the father of screencasting, put it in a recent article: Blogging has shown us new ways to communicate via text and photos. Podcasting – recording audio and sharing it as you would share your blog – and its video equivalent, videoblogging, have shown us new ways to communicate by sound and video. Screencasts give us an opportunity to share what we know, and what we do with computers and the Internet. Or as he wrote on O'Reilly Digital Media, an online magazine: "When the subjects of our videos are experiences that intersect with cyberspace, or occur primarily within it, we'll use screencasts to describe and explain them."

Lastly, another term you might hear more of: BitTorrent. As we start moving more and more files around the Internet, and as those files grow from small text and picture files to big music and video files, we need a way to do it that isn't too slow or expensive. This is where BitTorrent comes in, as I try to explain in this October 2005 piece:

One of the biggest revolutions taking place on the Internet has, strangely, caused barely a ripple. It's called BitTorrent.

If you've ever heard of BitTorrent it's probably alongside a word like "evil". After all, isn't BitTorrent the Internet protocol of choice for online video, music and software pirates swapping their illegal wares? Well, yes. That's true. But it's only part of the story.

BitTorrent, in fact, is the thin end of a big wedge that will pry open the way television, movies and lesser things such as software find their way into your home. This makes trying to close down BitTorrent a little like banning photocopiers because people can copy books on them. Getting upset about BitTorrent ignores the No. 1 rule about new technologies: Don't shoot the medium.

So what is this thing called BitTorrent? BitTorrent is a standard devised by a young American named Bram Cohen as a way to move large files around the Internet efficiently – for free. Your average Web page or email is only a few kilobytes. Even an MP3 file is about three megabytes, which takes only a minute or two to download, even on a crummy connection.

But what about bigger files? Imagine you have a 100-megabyte file – a short home movie, say – you want to make available to 100 of your acquaintances. You could email it to them, clogging up their inboxes and losing their friendship forever. You could post it to a website, and then send them a link so they can each download it, one by one. This is obviously better than email, but it still means that 100 people have to download the file from your website. It may not crash the computer hosting your website, but it'll slow it down, especially if all those 100 people want to try to download it at the same time. It's a bit like inviting them all to come around and simultaneously use your ice machine. They may get their ice, but they aren't going to be happy to have to wait.

Now imagine you break up that 100-megabyte file and let people download different bits of it to their computer, then share bits with each other until everyone has the whole file. Dude A, say, downloads the first bit, Dude B the second, Dude C the third, and so forth, and then Dude B can grab the first bit off Dude A and the third bit off Dude C, etc., until everyone is sharing what they have with anyone who hasn't. It's a bit like in the ice machine analogy, the ice is split up and dumped off at different houses, so anyone can pick up what is needed and share it with others until everyone gets ice. In short, everyone becomes both a customer and a distributor. This is what is called a peer-to-peer (or P2P) approach – the peers are sharing the files with other people, as well as the workload of moving them around the Internet.

This is what BitTorrent does – amazingly efficiently. It divides up the task of moving files around. This means not everyone needs to download the file from one place in one go, taking the pressure and expense off the guy trying to distribute the file. And it means everyone gets the file much faster, because they are spreading the job over dozens of computers. This is the BitTorrent protocol – a standard that makes this kind of transfer possible. And this isn't a pipe dream. Since Mr. Cohen wrote a piece of software (also called BitTorrent and also free) to use this standard in 2002, it has been hugely popular. Depending on who you talk to, it accounts for around half of Internet traffic at any one time.

Of course, not everyone likes this. This is a big load for the Internet to bear. And most of the traffic isn't exactly legitimate. Big files are usually video files, which take up a lot of space. And many of them are TV programs or pirated movies. BitTorrent is good at moving these files around, which is why movie moguls don't like it. But this doesn't stop it being a powerful medium, which is why BitTorrent is also now a company and seeking to be a legitimate concern. "The challenge for them is how to shrug off the perception that it's a tool for piracy and instead be regarded as a legitimate and acceptable distribution technique," says Andrew Parker, founder and chief technology officer of United Kingdom-based CacheLogic Ltd., which provides tools to ease the load on Internet service providers coping with all the extra traffic BitTorrent creates. The company seems to be convincing the industry of its viability: Last week BitTorrent Inc. landed $8.75 million in venture capital financing.

So why might this all change our world? Simply put, suddenly anyone can be a broadcaster. No longer do you need a network to get your product out. Just compress your show into a computer file, add the BitTorrent protocol, and put it on the Net. Users just click on a link and download it to watch when they want. Ashwin Navin, chief operating officer of BitTorrent Inc., says he's already persuaded media companies to sign up. He sees BitTorrent spawning lots of new TV programs as small and big producers alike make use of its low-cost distribution channel. "This tool empowers the creative folks, especially those that don't want to pitch their idea for years before they get their big break."

Indeed, things already are moving in this direction. The British Broadcasting Corp. in August announced plans for MyBBCPlayer, a system that uses a similar P2P protocol and that would let viewers legally download some BBC TV programs. Mark Pesce, a lecturer in interactive media at the Australian Film, Television and Radio School, has no doubt it's going to change not just the way TV is distributed, but how TV programming is made. "BitTorrent is here to stay," he told a conference of filmmakers in Montreal last month, "and what it does changes everything about everything in the creative industries."

Sounds like a revolution to me.

PART FOUR

getting out of trouble

nigerian scams

Scams and trickery predate the Internet, as does our gullibility. It's not a very exciting or fun subject to deal with. My problem as a columnist is to try to make it interesting, and where possible, funny, even if the only thing we're laughing at is ourselves. A perfect example of how scams evolve is the Nigerian 419 scam, which has been around longer than the World Wide Web, and I'm sure will still be around long after it. Here's how I had a crack at the subject in 2002, including the full email exchange in the text. All are real emails.

I wish people would stop being so cynical. Why do they assume that every spam email they receive is a scam? Just because the pitch "Hi, friend! You've already won a trip to the moon!/Need toner? We've got toner coming out of our ears!/Find the dirt on anyone, including your mother!" isn't reassuring, it doesn't mean these people aren't just trying to make an honest living.

At least, that was what was going through my mind when I decided to respond to one of a new wave of so-called 419ers. These missives, named after a clause in Nigeria's penal code, used to arrive as mail. In the old days postal companies would intercept them – easy to spot with their fake stamps – and use them, literally, as landfill.

These days free email accounts allow any aspiring fraudster with access to an Internet café to try their hand. Where they used to be from purported Nigerian officials with access to siphoned or missing funds, now you're just as likely to get emails about unclaimed millions found by special forces in Afghan caves. All you, dear reader, have to do is give a bank account number and, er, the money is yours.

But, I reasoned, such emails couldn't all be scams, surely? Okay, I've read of people being fleeced for thousands of dollars. Sure, the United States Secret Service receives 100 phone calls a day from potential victims, and estimates some $750 million is lost globally each year. Sure, Nigerian money-related fraud is the fastest growing online scam, according to the National Consumers League.

But, what the hell, I reasoned, I'll give this one a shot. Besides, the addressee was none other than Dr. Maryam Abacha, the widow of Gen. Sani Abacha, Nigeria's ruler from 1993-98. "Dr. Abacha," I learned from the Internet, is a light-complexioned beauty of Shuwa Arab stock. She also popularized the Aso-Oke by wearing it to official functions, but I'm not quite sure what an Aso-Oke is. More relevantly, the Nigerian government in April said it had reached a deal where the Abacha family would hand over $1 billion, and keep $100 million, in return for an end to criminal proceedings into the embezzlement of government funds.

Given this, I was delighted to be approached by such a fine person, and was only slightly intimidated by Mrs. Abacha's insistence on WRITING HER E-MAILS IN CAPITALS:

ATTN:WAGSTAFF,

I AM DR. (MRS.) MARYAM P. ABACHA, THE WIFE OF THE LATE NIGERIAN HEAD OF STATES, GENERAL SANI ABACHA WHO DIED ON THE 8TH JUNE 1998 OF HEART PROBLEMS WHILE ON ACTIVE DUTY. I AM CONTACTING YOU BECAUSE OF MY PRESENT NEED TO ENGAGE IN A MUTUALLY BENEFICIAL BUSINESS RELATIONSHIP WITH PERSON WHOM I HAVE NOT HAD DEALINGS BEFORE AND WHO DO NOT HAVE ANY POLITICAL INDIGNATION IN MY COUNTRY, NIGERIA.

SINCE THE DEATH OF MY HUSBAND MY FAMILY HAS BEEN

SUBJECTED TO ALL SORTS OF HARASSMENT, INTIMIDATION AND PERSECUTION BY THE NIGERIAN GOVERNMENT. THIS IS BECAUSE THE PEOPLE IN THE GOVERNMENT NOW ARE PEOPLE WHO BELIEVE THAT MY HUSBAND VICTIMIZED THEM WHILE HE WAS IN POWER. THEY HAVE FROZEN NUMEROUS BANK ACCOUNTS AND SEIZED MONIES AND ASSETS RUNNING INTO HUNDREDS OF MILLIONS OF DOLLARS BELONGING TO MY FAMILY UNDER THE EXCUSE THAT MY LATE HUSBAND STOLE THE MONEY. IT IS IN VIEW OF THIS THAT I SEEK THE ASSISTANCE OF HONEST, GOD FEARING PEOPLE LIKE YOU TO HELPMESECURE MY FAMILY'S ESTATE.

PRESENTLY I HAVE WITH ME THE SUM OF US$85 MILLION, WHICH I WISH TO TRANSFER ABROAD AS DISCREETLY AND AS EXPEDITIOUSLY AS POSSIBLE AND I WISH WITH YOUR HELP TO APPLY THIS FUND TOWARDS INVESTMENT PURPOSES IN YOUR COUNTRY. THIS MONEY WAS MY HUSBAND'S SHARE IN A DEBT BUY BACK CONTRACT DEAL BETWEEN MY HUSBAND AND A RUSSIAN COMPANY IN OUR COUNTRY'S MULTI-BILLION DOLLAR AJAOKUTA STEEL PROJECT. THE RUSSIAN COMPANY RETURNED MY HUSBAND'S SHARE OF US$85 MILLION AFTER HIS DEATH AND LODGED IT IN MY LATE HUSBAND'S SECURITY COMPANY OF WHICH I AM A DIRECTORANDHIS NEXT OF KIN.

WITH THE INTENSIFICATION OF THE NIGERIA GOVERNMENT PROBE INTO MY FAMILY'S FINANCES AND THE CONSEQUENT DETENTION OF MY SON MOHEMMED ON TRUMPED UP CHARGES, I ACTED FAST TO WITHDRAW THIS MONEY FROM THE SECURITY COMPANY'S VAULT AND I HAVE DECLARED THE SECURITY COMPANY BANKRUPT. NO RECORDS WHATSOEVER EXIST CONCERNING THIS MONEY BECAUSE I HAVE PERSONALLY DESTROYED ALL DOCUMENTATION CONCERN.

NOW I WISH TO SOLICIT FOR YOUR ASSISTANCE TO TRANSFER THIS MONEY OUT OF NIGERIA AND INTO YOUR ACCOUNT TO BE APPLIED TOWARDS INVESTMENT IN YOUR COUNTRY. FOR YOUR ASSISTANCE I PURPOSE TO GIVE YOU A COMMISSION OF 15% OF THE TOTAL SUM INVOLVED, WHICH YOU SHALL DEDUCT IMMEDIATELY THE MONEY IS PAID INTO YOUR ACCOUNT.

PLEASE, I IMPLORE YOU TO EXERCISE THE UTMOST DISCRETION IN KEEPING THIS MATTER VERY CONFIDENTIAL, WHATEVER YOUR DECISION WILL BE. CONTACT ME IMMEDIATELY THROUGH EMAIL:MARYAM_ABA2002@EUDORAMAIL.COM

YOURS FAITHFULLY, DR. (MRS.) MARYAM ABACHA MNI,CON.

All I had to do, it seemed, was help her smuggle $85 million into my bank account, and I would get 15% of the proceeds. That should make my bank manager happy, I thought. I immediately dashed off an offer of help, but to be on the safe side, used a pseudonym:

Maryam

Thanks for your email and I'm very excited to be able to help you and get absurdly rich as well. I'm very sorry to hear about your husband. Did you get along OK? It was nice of the Russians to give you back all that money. I find it very hard to get them to give anything back. Especially nuclear Chechnya! (That was a joke!)

Could you send a picture too, so I know what you're like? I'm single too, so maybe we could hang out.

Yours, Egbert Dimple

PS. And how do I know this is not one of those scam things I hear about?

☞ **scammonden** (*n, West Yorkshire*) Email that could be scams but might not be.

My new penmate wasted no time in replying, sending me a picture of Abacha in swaying gowns – it might have been the Aso-Oke – answering the phone (*see overleaf*).

DEAR EGBERT,
THANK YOU FOR YOUR REPLY MAIL, WHICH IS YOUR RESPONSE TO MY LETTER OF INTRODUCTION AND PROPOSAL. I SHALL BE SENDING MY PICTURE TO YOU AS REQUESTED LATER TODAY,IT'S GETTING A BIT DIFFICULT TO SCAN AND ATTACH INTO THE SYSTEM.

WELL DUE TO TIME SENSITIVENESS OF THIS PROJECT, I WILL GO AHEAD TO EVEN DIVULGE SOME CONFIDENTIAL INFORMATION TO YOU THAT WILL BE BENEFICIAL FOR THE QUICK REALISATION OF THIS PROJECT AND TRUSTING THAT AM IN GOOD HANDS.I WANT TO TRUST MY INSTINCT IN BELIEVING THATYOU ARE THE RIGHT PERSON TO HELP ME IN REALIZING THIS PROJECT.

I WOULD LIKE YOU TO KNOW THAT THE WHOLE FUND HAS BEEN MOVED TO SWITZERLAND INTO THE SECURED VAULT OF A FINANCIAL SECURITY COMPANY IN ZURICH. MY STORY AND THE STORY OF MY HUSBAND SHOULD NOT BE NEWS TO YOU ANYMORE.ALSO THE HARD TIMES AM FACING IN THE HANDS OF THE PRESENT GOVERNMENT IN MY COUNTRY SINCE MY HUSBAND'S DEATH FOUR YEARS AGO. AS IT IS NOW,WHAT IS LEFT FOR ME, MY CHILDREN AND MY IMMEDIATE DEPENDANTS IS THIS SECURED FUNDS IN SWISS. THIS EXPLAINS WHY I WANT TO BE EXTRA CAREFULLY IN MY DEALING WITH ANYONE. WHEN ALL ARRANGEMENTS HAVE BEEN CONCLUDED. WE WILL HAVE TO MEET TOGETHER IN SWITZERLAND AND GO TO THE COMPANY

☞ **fazakerley** (*adj, Liverpool*) The peculiar literary style adopted by most Nigerian scammers that manages to mix a grasp of current events with an exaggerated faith in the reader's gullibility. *The email was very fazakerly, right down to the references to the Lebanese crisis.*

FOR WITHDRAWAL OF FUNDS AND SUBSEQUENTLY SET UP AN ACCOUNT / PREFERABLY A PROTECTED ACCOUNT THAT WILL ACCOMMODATE ALL THE FUNDS IN SWITZERLAND AND GIVE US ALL THE NEEDED SECURITY THAT WE WILL NEED. YOU HAVE TO PREPARE AND BE SURE YOU SINCERELY WANT TO HELP ME, KNOWING THAT YOU WILL ALSO BENEFIT FROM IT AT THE END.

THE SWISS COMPANY IS GLOBAL FINANCIAL SECURITY COMPANY ZURICH, AND THE PERSONS TO CONTACT ARE MRS. ANGELA STEPHAN OR MR. MARTIN WILLIAMS.THE TELEPHONE NUMBERS ARE 0041-797-602814. REQUEST TO FIND THE CONDITION OF DEPOSIT, WITH DEPOSIT ALPHA CODE GVJGTES, IN ADDITION YOU SHOULD INFORM THEM OF YOUR READINESS TO COME DOWN TO SWISS FOR WITHDRAWAL OF THE DEPOSIT AND ASK THEM OF ALL THE NECESSARY REQUIREMENT TO COME WITH. IF YOU CAN DO THIS, THEN WE ARE VERY CLOSE TO REALIZING THIS PROJECT. AND YOU SHOULD ENSURE THAT YOU LIMIT YOUR DISCUSSIONS ONLY ON ISSUE OF THIS PROJECT PLEASE.

I WILL AWAIT YOUR RESPONSE.

BEST REGARDS,

MRS. MARYAM ABACHA.

I was hooked.

Maryam

Thanks for the picture, and I must say I think you're beautiful. I like the outfit too. It must be hard to stay looking nice with all this trouble going on.

I know this may sound odd, but do you think it would be possible for us to start dating at some point, what with your husband no longer on this Earth. Please excuse me if that's a bit forward of me.

Best

Egbert

This seemed to cause some surprise.

DEAR EGBERT, THANKS FOR YOUR MAIL AND THE NICE COMPLIMENT.REALLY I CAN NOT SAY EXACTELY WHAT YOU WANT AT THIS TIME.YOU HAVE COMPLETELY KEPT ASIDE THE MEAN REASON WHY I CONTACTED YOU IN THE FIRST PLACE.

I REALLY DON'T KNOW YOU SO MUCH TO START TALKING ABOUT DATING.AND I CAN'T SAY FOR NOW IF THAT COULD WORK OR NOT.BUT I BELEIVE THAT WE SHOULD NOT FORGET FIRST WHAT GOT US TOGETHER.NOW YOU CAN TELL ME A LITTLE ABOUT YOURSELF.HOW OLD YOU ARE AND SO ON AND POSSIBLY SEND ME ALSO YOUR OWN PICTURE JUST LIKE I DID.THIS IS IMPORTANT PLEASE.

FINALLY I WOULD LIKE TO KNOW EGBERT IF YOU HAVE CONTACTED THE SWISS COMPANY AS I INSTRUCTED.

YOUR QUICK RESPONSE WILL BE APPRECIATED.

WARM REGARDS. MARYAM.

Sensing an opening, I sent back a picture – not of myself, for modesty's sake, but a random photo culled from a Google search of the keyword "hunk."

I also called up her friends in Zurich, who weren't quite so friendly. It might have had something to do with the time difference.

My dearest Maryam

Your message brought me joy that there might be a future for us, after all this messy financial business is done. I want you to know now that I'm not just after your money. I just want us to have a future together. You deserve to be happy again.

I attach a photo of myself as requested. It's not a good one, I'm afraid, but I hope you can tell I've been working out! It's not easy having a surname like mine in these parts!

Lastly, I have contacted the people in Switzerland as you requested. But he seemed a bit sleepy, and told me to call back. Perhaps he has been too busy – you should give him a holiday! He also wasn't very helpful when I asked him whether this was one of those money fraud scams that I read about somewhere. Please, my dear Maryam, tell me you haven't got caught up in one of those awful rackets?

I can't wait to hear from you again. Somehow the sun shines brighter now, knowing you will reply to my emails.

Eggy (as my friends call me!)

Mrs. Abacha, if it was she, was keen to impress upon me the legality of our arrangement. Somewhat less keen on our budding romance:

DEAR EGGY, THANKS ONCE MORE FOR YOUR PROMPT REPLY.AM REALLY HAPPY TO KNOW HOW INTERESTED YOU ARE WITH MY AFFAIR.UNFORTUNATELY AM UNABLE TO

☞ **bittesby** (*adj, Leicestershire*) The process of momentarily considering replying to a scam email, even as you know it's probably a scam. *For a moment there I was bittesby, the offer sounded so good.*

OPEN THE PICTURE YOU SENT,MAYBE TOMORROW I WILL GET THE COMPUTER BOY TO ASSIST ME WITH THE ATTACHED PICTURE SO THAT I CAN SEE YOUR PICTURE AND WHAT YOU LOOK LIKE.

YOU DID NOT TELL ME HOW OLD YOU ARE IN THAT MAIL. HOWEVER I WANT YOU TO KNOW THAT AM NO LONGER A VERY YOUNG WOMAN ALTHOUGH I STILL LOOK VERY ATTRACTIVE,AM NOW IN MY FIFTIES.I REALLY DON'T KNOW HOW WE ARE GOING TO MANAGE A RELATIONSHIP.BUT IF YOU THINK IT CAN WORK THERE IS NO PROBLEM.

I DO NOT QUITE UNDERSTAND WHAT YOU SAID ABOUT SWITZERLAND.PLEASE YOU MUST REPEAT THAT CALL AND MAKE SURE YOU HAVE A DETAILD DISCUSSION WITH THEM AS PER MY INSTRUCTIONS IN MY SECOND MAIL TO YOU.

EGGY,BELEIVE ME WHAT I AM DOING IS LEGAL AND I DON'T THINK THAT I WILL BE INVOLVED IN ANY TYPE OF SCAM LIKE YOU FEARED.THIS IS WHY I HAVE BEEN VERY CAREFL EVER SINCE MY HUSBANDS DEATH.I JUST NEED YOU TO HELP ME WITH THESE THINGS SINCE WE HAVE STARTED ALREADY.YOU MENTIONED SOMETHING ELSE ABOUT YOUR SURNAME,IS ANYTHING WRONG WITH THE USE OF YOUR SURNAME?

FINALLY PLEASE EGGY,I WANT YOU TO KEEP EVERYTHING THAT WE ARE DOING SECRET FOR MY INTEREST.I WILL BE EXPECTING YOUR RESPNSE. BEST REGARDS, MARYAM.

I felt things were going quite well.

Darling Maryam (do you have a pet name that you liked to be called?)
I'm so glad you think we can have a future together. Unfortunately I can't say

☞ **bitton** (*v, South Gloucestershire*) The moment after you've replied to a scam email and realized it was indeed a scam. *I think I've just been bitton, I offered to help Saddam's mistress move $450 million from her stash in Kuwait via my bank in Fotheringhay.*

the same for your colleagues in Zurich, who seem a bit rude, to be honest. How about if I call you and talk directly to you? What number can I reach you on? I yearn to hear your voice. You say you are in your 50s – I'm a strapping 25 – but I think older women are very desirable, especially if they're on the run!

You mention your computer boy. He's not your boyfriend, I hope? I get jealous easily!

By the way, I keep getting emails from other people also called Maryam Abacha, saying that they also have money to give me. How do I know which one is the real you?

Eggy

DEAR EGGY, THANKS AGAIN FOR YOUR MAIL.TODAY THE CUMPUTER BOY WAS ABLE TO OPEN THE ATTACHMENT AND I SAW YOUR PICTURE,YOU ARE GOOD LOOKING YOUNG MAN.BUT DON'T YOU THINK THAT WE ARE DRIFFTING AWAY FROM OUR ORIGINAL OBJECTIVE.I DON'T MIND A RELATIONSHIP WITH YOU ONLY IF YOU CAN KEEP IT SECRET DUE TO MY CONDITION.BUT I THINK THAT WE SHOULD CONCLUDE WITH THIS PROJECT FIRST.

CAN YOU COME TO NIGERIA?I WILL REALLY LIKE TO SEE YOU BUT THAT WILL BE AFTER WE HAVE COMPLETED THIS PROJECT SO WE CAN HAVE ENOUGH MONEY TO SPEND. RIGHT NOW ALL MY EFFORT AND CONCENTRATION IS ON THIS PROJECT.

SO PLEASE DO WHAT YOU CAN TO HELP ME.TRY AND CONCLUDE WITH THE SWISS COMPANY AND GET AN APPOINTMENT WITH THEM ON THE POSSIBLE DATE THAT WE ARE GOING TO GO THERE.THIS IS IMPORTANT TO ME EGGY.

FINALLY PLEASE DO NOT GIVE MY E-MAIL TO ANYBODY AND I ADVICE THAT YOU SHOULD NOT REPLY TO ANY OF THOSE,BECAUSE IT MIGHT BE A PLOY TO FIND OUT WHAT I HAVE WITH YOU.BY TOMORROW AM GOING TO CHANGE

MY E-MAIL ADDRESS AND I RECOMMEND THAT YOU CHANGE YOUR OWN TOO IF WE ARE GOING TO CONTINUE COMMUNICATION.

I WILL BE EXPECTING YOUR RESPONSE.

BEST REGARD

MARYAM.

And so I'm confident that by the time you read this I will be flush with cash and living on a desert island, surrounded by bodyguards and people wearing the Aso-Oke. Of course, I'm aware that the risk is high: Many of those persuaded to visit Nigeria by such folk end up fleeced, murdered or missing. But I'm sure that won't happen to me.

Quite a few folk wrote in begging me not to go, which was touching. Sadly, four years on, Nigerian email fraud is as bad as ever. One group that tries to monitor such things, the Dutch-based Ultrascan Advanced Global Investigations, said that in 2005 some $3.2 billion may have been lost to what they call Advance Fee Fraud. This involves more than 200 scam rings operating not just in Nigeria but across Europe, Asia and North America. For more, check out www.ultrascan.nl/html/419_advance_fee_fraud.html. Remember: scammers online are just like scammers offline. They're trying to trick you with sob stories, hard luck tales and promises of gold easily won. Do online as you'd do offline: Walk on by.

viruses and firewalls

Viruses have been the bane of computers since the early 1990s. But they've evolved, just as their medium of transmission – the Internet – has evolved. Which is why I felt I had to keep writing about them, even though I knew it wasn't what people wanted to read, which is why I seem to have begun most of my columns on the subject in the same way. Here's how I saw the problem in June 2000:

If you're sick of hearing about computer viruses, stop reading now. But then don't blame me if you get an email with X-rated attachments and a pop-up message on June 20 reading: "I'm proud to say that you are infected by Fireburn!"

Yes, virus watch isn't over yet. May was probably the worst month yet for viruses, but that's no reason to lower your guard. The next biggie may not be "Fireburn," which already has been caught and analyzed by tech gurus (and which doesn't do anything worse than fire up an online chat program and make X-rated remarks to other chatters on your behalf), but it's bound to be sneakier than its predecessors. So you should start getting used to having such viruses around.

Part of the problem is that as computers get easier to use, they get easier to infect. Virus writers can concentrate on a handful of programs like Microsoft Word and Microsoft Outlook, confident that lots of people use them. Particularly dangerous are macros, or little batches of commands, that allow virus creators to hide viruses in documents, or even in a Web page. It's this technique that the recent "ILOVEYOU" and "Resume" viruses used. Or take the "KAK worm" virus, which uses JavaScript – lines of code that help make Web pages more interactive. The KAK worm may even be worse than the macro viruses because it can infect your computer even if you don't actually open the infected email in Outlook, but just have it sitting in your preview window.

If you were unlucky enough to get hit by the ILOVEYOU bug last month, the pros wouldn't have been much help. Most antivirus software works by storing a directory of all virus "signatures" – bits of code that are particular to each known virus. That's not much help with a new virus, which almost certainly will look different. The result: Antivirus software is always one step behind the virus writer. "Remember that most antivirus companies offer free downloads of their software. So the bad-guy virus writer downloads them and makes sure the new virus is undetected," says Bruce Hughes, manager of the Content Security Lab at Virginia-based computer-security consultant ICSA.

In the face of this, you don't have much choice but to wise up. There are individual antivirus programs out there, but they may not in themselves be enough. And remember: So far, viruses have been sneaky only in the way they get past your defenses, not so much in what they can do to you. Those that get in destroy data and try to reproduce themselves. But as yet, most don't, for example, invade a spreadsheet and start changing vital figures without your knowledge. Now, that would be fun. Says Anthony Kuo, senior product marketing manager of Trend Micro Inc., an antivirus-software manufacturer, "Antivirus is and always will be an endless battle."

It was and it is. Here's how bad it had gotten by February 2003:

After spending the best part of Sunday afternoon removing 231 viruses from a friend's computer, I was ready to give Steve Chang, chief executive

☞ **tendring** (*n, Essex*) The feeling that you've probably got a virus on your computer but you're not sure.

of Taiwan-based anti-virus developer Trend Micro, a piece of my mind. Turns out I picked the wrong guy.

When I suggested that the manufacturers of anti-virus software – the programs that try to block nefarious bits of computer code from entering your computer and wreaking havoc – had done a poor job of protecting us, he disarmingly agreed. "I don't think we – not just Trend Micro, but the industry – have done a good job. We're always one step behind the virus makers, we're just trying to catch up," he told me in a phone interview. Not quite the positive spin I was hoping for from one of the oldest players in the anti-virus industry. So what's the problem? Well, there are lots of parts to the problem, and none of them makes for pleasant reading.

First, anti-virus software only works if it knows what to look for. That's fine if it's a virus that's been around for a while. The software writers take a piece of the virus – a line of code is usually enough – and add it to a library of similar pieces. A file, or email, coming into your computer is then run through that library to check for matches. If there's a match, chances are that file or email is infected and the anti-virus software tries to remove the virus. But what happens when the virus is new, like the SQL Slammer virus, which crippled Internet servers across the United States and Asia last week? The most harmful viruses (or worms, or trojans, they're all pretty much the same thing) do their damage before the anti-virus folk have a chance to update their libraries, let alone get the update to the user. By then the damage is usually done.

A few years ago there was talk about a more biological approach. Instead of running everything through a library of known viruses, why not look for patterns of behavior in existing viruses, and flag any similar behavior as a possible virus? This so-called heuristic scanning hasn't really happened, Chang says, because it threw up too many false alarms. At best, this approach could catch about 80% of known viruses. But it also caught a lot more. "The problem is the more you fine-tune this behavior, the more you pay for the false positives." The result: angry users, and IT managers quickly turn the thing off.

So we're left with the library approach, which is horribly inefficient.

The more viruses there are, the bigger the library. Trend Micro's own PC-cillin has 365 virus patterns, meaning every file that runs through the virus scanner has to be matched against 365 different patterns. The result: You notice your computer slows down when you have a virus checker running, so you turn it off.

Things aren't going to get any better. While 2002 was a quiet year for virus writers, they've got off to a busy start this year. A virus, called Sobig, which appeared in early January and is still going strong, attacks Microsoft's Outlook email program, wrests control of your computer, and mails itself to your contacts. MessageLabs, a British company that tracks viruses, has caught more than 100,000 copies.

So what to do? Manufacturers must start selling anti-virus software that's friendly and seamless to the user. As Chang suggests, if anti-virus software is peddled as a "utility" it's unlikely to be much help to folk who have no idea what a "utility" is. (When was the last time you defragmented your hard drive? Checked your registry for errors? Those are what we call utilities.) One thing I'd like to see: a more standard way of alerting users to the fact that they don't have anti-virus software running when they start up their computer.

Sadly this didn't really happen, and antivirus remains a mysterious alchemy of a business, perhaps intentionally so. Trying to demystify the process a little, I recruited one Brian Johnson, an American IT consultant for his advice about how to defend your computer:

By the time you read this, a worm called Blaster may well be history. If not, you might want to read on. (Even if it is history, read on anyway.)

Blaster was a malicious piece of computer code that infected as many computers as possible with the aim of launching a coordinated attack on Microsoft's Windows website. Blaster made use of a bug in Windows that Microsoft had spotted and fixed, but whether or not your computer was vulnerable in large part depended on whether you had downloaded the patch and had things like firewalls and anti-virus programs running, were wearing galoshes and a sou'wester (I've always wanted to use those words in a column) and pointed your computer due north when it rained.

Well, sort of. To me, all Blaster brought home was how hard it is to protect your computer, and more importantly, to know whether it's protected. So after receiving an interesting and illuminating email about Blaster from a reader of my blog, Brian Johnson, of San Jose-based IT consultants Centerbeam, I asked him to put together a checklist of things you should do to protect your computer. Here it is.

Maybe the best way to describe the overall strategy of protecting your computer is to think of layers of defence, like the fortress of Helm's Deep in Lord of the Rings. When the bad guys – the Orcs – broke through one layer, the army inside fell back behind the next layer.

LAYER ONE: Stop problems before they reach your computer

- Turn off your computer when you aren't using it. It's very tempting these days to leave your computer on and attached to your always-on broadband connection. Don't. Turn off your computer when you leave your home. Quite simply, if your computer is off, it can't be hacked.

- Use a firewall. Windows XP has a built-in firewall, but if you aren't on XP, or want an additional layer of protection, then try Zone Alarm (a free version is available at www.zonelabs.com).

LAYER TWO: Immediately identify and stop a risk when it arrives at your computer

- Get virus protection: Invest in a high-quality program such as the one offered by McAfee (www.mcafee.com). But remember: Virus-protection programs tend to look for the threats they know. Be sure to set up your virus program to automatically check for updates, otherwise new intruders will not be caught.

☞ **clenchwarton** (*n, Norfolk*) The feeling when you try to reboot a computer after a serious crash, not knowing whether the problem was caused by something going horribly wrong or whether it's just a temporary glitch.

LAYER THREE: Don't allow intruders to work

- If a virus or worm makes it past your firewall and your virus-protection program, there's still another level of defense: Don't knowingly allow the critter to work.

- Get your system patches up-to-date: The easiest way to do this on a Windows XP system is to go to the System Update (in the Control Panel) and make sure this function is turned on and that it is checking daily for new updates.

- Don't open unknown email attachments: Pay attention to the email that hits your inbox – and don't click on it as soon as you receive it. Don't open suspicious attachments (especially with file extensions such as: .vbs, .exe, .bat, .wsh) and get in the habit of first saving all attachments, scanning them with anti-virus programs before you execute them.

LAYER FOUR: Be able to escape

- Boot Disk: The current beastie that's on the loose has been known to completely crash a system so that it can't even be booted. This is a reminder that it's a good idea to create a boot disk, something you can boot the system with and at least recover your undamaged files. To make one, right-click on your floppy drive and follow instructions.

- Back-ups: Back up to as many different media as possible – CD-ROM, diskette, USB drive, external hard drive, or even online. Keep your back-ups someplace other than next to your computer.

Finally, Brian concludes, resign yourself to the fact that taking these steps is part of the price we pay for the convenience of personal computing. In this day and age, it is inevitable that your system will come under attack. So, you can pay the price now, or some day regret that you didn't.

This is all excellent advice, and for once I can't think of anything to add. Do all of it and nasty bugs like Blaster won't get you.

Despite this, firewalls remained something of a mystery to most users, which is why I dedicated a whole column to it in July 2004:

Judging by the letters I get from readers, nothing seems to concern folk more than the security of their computers. So this week I'm going to talk about the most basic, and most misunderstood, part of securing your computer: the firewall.

First, what the heck is a firewall? Security specialist Bruce Schneier, founder of United States-based Counterpane, says the term comes from early coal-powered trains where an iron wall was built around the engine furnace to prevent fires from spreading to the passenger cars. In computer terms, it's a gate that tries to prevent viruses, evil programs or anything that's not been invited in from getting into a computer or a network. So what's the difference between anti-virus software such as Norton or McAfee and a firewall?

I asked Jerome Briot, whose Paris-based security-software company Sistech (www.thegreenbow.com) makes a firewall program called TheGreenBow. "Anti-virus software and firewalls have totally opposite logic," he says. Anti-virus software lets everything in except what it knows is dangerous, based on a blacklist it has in its pocket. (This blacklist is the updated virus library that you get when your anti-virus software updates itself every so often.)

A firewall, on the other hand, blocks everything except what you, or your system administrator, allows. "Anti-virus is responsible for searching for 'malicious' programs or processes on the PC, like a police force," says Briot. "A firewall is more immigration, or frontier control." Anti-virus software has a list of suspects and is keeping an eye out for them. A firewall is an immigration inspector, suspicious of everyone and banning anything that doesn't have the proper papers.

Now we know the difference, does that mean it's a question of either/or? Can we users just opt for an anti-virus or a firewall? The short answer: No. Good anti-virus software doesn't do a bad job of keeping the nasty stuff out – so long as you keep your software updated. With viruses spreading so rapidly these days, the period between a virus appearing and the anti-virus company updating its list – not to mention the delay until you get around to downloading the update for your own software – is getting dangerous. During this period you'll have to rely on your firewall. As Briot puts it: "This is where a personal firewall has a role to play: to stop worms and Trojan horses when the anti-virus has no patch to identify them."

So will a firewall catch everything? Sadly, no. Most firewalls work by giving permission to applications, or programs. Once that permission is given, anything the application does is OK as far as the firewall is concerned. Think of it as the immigration guy, having let the application into the country, not giving a hoot about what the application may get up to. So, say you've given your email program permission to access the Internet, anything nasty that happens to come in via email is not going to be noticed by the firewall.

Actually, some firewalls are getting better at this. They look not just at allowing or refusing applications, but detecting changes in those applications, and inspecting data as they go in or out. But you should never think of your firewall as a reason not to be vigilant about opening suspicious emails or clicking on links you're not sure about. As Daniel McNamara, an Australian systems administrator points out: "People seem to think a personal firewall is the magic bullet against all attacks."

There's another problem: What happens if something gets past the firewall? A few years ago firewalls wouldn't help you, as they were only monitoring inbound traffic (think of an immigration officer not caring about folk leaving the country, only monitoring immigrants). So, if a keyboard-logging program was installed without your knowledge, it could be sending out details of your passwords, unchecked by the firewall. That is still the case with the Windows XP built-in firewall, but with most other firewall programs, outbound traffic is also monitored and blocked unless it has your permission. Bottom line: With a decent firewall, your data are pretty safe.

☞ **brize norton** (*n, Oxfordshire*) The inevitable slowing down of one's computer that comes with installing Symantec's Norton Antivirus or Internet Security software. (*see also* **Chipping Norton**)

What most folk don't really tell you about is what to do if you get infected. The following month I took a shot:

If your computer is infected by a virus, Trojan, worm or some other nasty slice of code, never fear: Worst comes to worst, you can call on a 60-year-old retired Australian lab technician who goes by the online nickname of Pancake.

Though he wouldn't put it this way himself, Ed Figg (his real name) is living proof of the failure of anti-virus companies, firewall manufacturers and Microsoft to keep us safe from viruses. Given that we each spend about $100 a year for software to protect our computers, you'd think that would leave us safe. But no. Ed the Pancake, and dozens like him, spend up to eight hours a day online as unpaid experts helping other users with problems – most of them viruses that have slipped past their computer's defences. So what should you do if you think it's happened to you?

In a perfect world you would invite Ed round for a cup of tea and get him to fix it for you. But there are some things you should do before bothering him. Here are some tips from the experts:

- First, you need to know what you're infected with, because the treatment may be different for different problems. As Josh Daymont, director of research at Internet-security company SecureWorks puts it: "Cleaning up a Trojan or virus from your home PC can be as simple as downloading and running a program from the Internet or as difficult as defusing a complex bomb." If you have an anti-virus program installed, run a thorough check. If you don't have one, visit TrendMicro's free HouseCall (housesecall.trendmicro.com) service and run a scan that way. If you're not connected to the Internet, get a CD-ROM with a relatively new version of an anti-virus program and install that. Some programs will let you run a quick check for the most-common infections before you install them.

- Now, assuming you have found an infection and know what the virus is called, make a note of it. Then try to get your anti-virus program – or HouseCall – to clean it. Chances are the software will do the trick. If the software says it's cleaned everything, reboot and do another scan, just to be sure.

Now for the bad news. Anti-virus programs don't always do what they promise. That's because they were designed when viruses were few and moved slowly. That's no longer true. As Justine Troy of Internet-messaging security company MessageLabs puts it: "What seemed to be effective protection a year ago is far from it today."

Viruses can now, for example, embed themselves into an open file. If the file is running, the anti-virus program can't get into it. The best thing to do is to close down the file in question. This is easier said than done, and unless you really know what you're doing you could do more damage than good. As Ed the Pancake says: "A lot try it on their own and then when we take over we have no idea as to what files they have removed and what are still hidden." So, should users not even try? "If their own virus program finds and takes it out, OK," says Ed. "But if not, get help. A wrong file removed could lose you the whole lot."

By help, Ed means people like him. Or, if you have access to it, phone support from your anti-virus software maker. Indeed, nowadays that should come as standard. As Terri Adkins, director of special projects for eAcceleration Corp., a provider of anti-virus protection, puts it: "Only with unlimited, live telephone support, can any AV software live up to the promise of total protection."

In short, if you're not sure what you're doing, get help. Because there's more bad news: Not all anti-virus programs will find every kind of infection, let alone clean them. There are a number of reasons for this. One, says United States-based software developer and consultant Alan Canton, is that the bad guys "have reverse-engineered the major protection programs and have learned what these applications look for." They then write code to dupe the anti-virus program. The result: Your average anti-virus program is like a policeman on the beat while a crime is going on under his nose.

Another reason is that viruses can actually attack and disable the anti-virus software – a bit like bribing the policeman to look the other way. Yet another possibility is that the virus is very new: "Nowadays, it is possible for a network worm to spread around the world in less than 20 minutes," says Nick Scales, chief executive of British Internet security company Avecho. "The best response from the traditional anti-virus companies to a new virus is one hour, and then they have a delay of minutes to days or even weeks before each individual user has updated himself to be protected." That's a bit like the policeman who finishes his cup of tea before leaving for the scene of the crime.

Then there's an even darker possibility: The virus may have been cleaned, but not before it has dumped what is called its payload. Think of the virus as the car that's dropped off the villains. The police nab the car and the getaway driver, but the bad guys are already hiding in the bank. They're the payload. Anti-virus software may remove the virus, but it is not always up to the task of cleaning the payload – which could do anything from using your computer to send spam to logging your passwords.

I know this sounds scary. What's the point, I hear you ask, of anti-virus software if it doesn't clean up properly? Good question. In the worst-case scenario you may have to start from scratch and reformat your hard drive. But it shouldn't have to come to that. Remember the golden rules: Keep anti-virus software and a firewall running, and keep them up to date. If you get infected, do all you can to learn about the infection and try to clean it up using anti-virus software. If you can't, there are people on the Internet who can help. Just ask for Pancake and tell him I sent you.

I wrapped up the column, and I wrap up this chapter, with some guidelines:

Here are some more tips that may help you get rid of viruses and keep them from coming back:

☞ **hanging houghton** (*n, Northamptonshire*) When your computer doesn't exactly crash, doesn't exactly keep going for no clear reason.

- **Do it yourself.** If you know the name of the virus that is infecting your computer, try downloading a tool specifically designed to do the job.

- **Get help.** There are several forums offering fast help, including: Cyber Tech Help (www.cybertechhelp.com), Xstudio (www.xstudio.ca/pcsupport) and Wilders Security Forums (www.wilderssecurity.com). For paid help, check out the Alliance of Security Analysis Professionals: www.a-sap.org/

- **Back up and keep your software handy.** If things go wrong and you do have to start from scratch, it helps if you are prepared.

- **Be vigilant.** As Symantec, makers of Norton Antivirus, put it: "Double-check before you double-click. If you receive an email message with a suspicious attachment don't open it even if you know the sender. Never open attachments from unknown sources or attachments you are not expecting and turn off automatic opening of email attachments."

- **Get to know what's going on in your computer.** The toughest viruses to delete are those that load themselves into memory. So, if you want to find them and squish them, it pays to know which programs are legit and which aren't. As Alan Canton the software developer explains: "Before users suspect any kind of infection they should open the Windows Task pane (by pressing ctl-alt-delete) and become familiar with the names of all the programs that are running. After a few days this familiarity will increase.

  They might print out a list for future reference. If a user thinks they might be infected, he or she should take a look and see if there is something in the Task Manager that does not look right or was not there before. They then type the name of the program (i.e. BadProgram.exe) into Google and they will know in a second if they've caught a bug and what to do about it.

☞ **felsted** (*n, Essex*) When your computer reboots for no discernible reason.

- **Install a firewall.**

- **Remember to update.** Reader Michael Clark from Berkeley, California, asks whether "it's enough to occasionally use the Symantec antivirus 'live update' to keep my computer safe? I seldom go to the Microsoft updates, patches, though perhaps that is naïve". With due respect, yes, it is and yes, it is.

As Bill Franklin, chief executive of spam- and virus-free email service 0Spam.Net says: "Applying Microsoft patches to the operating system as well as products like Office is very important. These patches usually close certain security holes and change product settings to keep you out of trouble."

Nothing has changed to make me want to alter that advice. Although Microsoft's own operating system now contains a firewall, and, at least for U.S.-based users, the company now offers OneCare (www.onecare.com) a service which will, for a price, protect your PC. I've not tested it but it sounds good. Although of course the fact that the company is both leaving you vulnerable because of its product and charging you protection against it does bring to mind mafioso comparisons I'd rather not get into here.

credit card fraud

Credit card fraud – the art of stealing credit cards, or their details, and then using them to buy stuff either online or offline – is big where I live. Indeed, any resident of Indonesia will tell you how hard it is to buy anything online outside the country with an Indonesian credit card and/or an Indonesian shipping address. Seems we're pariahs to the rest of the world, because of the country's bad reputation. But while Indonesia is a big part of the problem, it's a great place to understand how it works, and how to minimize the risk you'll fall victim to it. Here's a piece I wrote in June 2001, based on an interview I conducted with an Indonesian fraudster who asked to be called 'Bagus':

I don't want to alarm you folks any more than I have in previous columns about life online, so those of you who don't have or use credit cards can skip to the end.

There is a puzzle and it is this: Depending on who you talk to, credit-card fraud over the Internet is either a very serious problem that is going to destroy the future of online commerce, or nothing worse than credit-card fraud elsewhere (less than 1%, according to the major credit-card issuers.) So who's lying?

I suspect the problem looks different depending on where you are standing. The big credit-card issuers, which have long gotten used to coping with fraud, aren't particularly fazed by the rise of online credit-card abuse – for them it is just another medium. Those promoting online commerce and e-marketing argue that an online credit-card transaction is as secure, if not more so, than doing the same thing by fax, phone or letter, countering the media hype of credit-card fraud. For online retailers, they have an interest in playing down the problem – even when they have to foot most of the bill from fraudulent charges – for fear of scaring customers into unplugging their modems. And for customers, while the idea of having someone use their credit card is a scary one, most are likely to see fraudulent charges wiped if they complain to their card issuer.

So where does the truth lie? For a glimpse of how bad it could get, look at Indonesia. There, credit-card fraud is a growth industry – and a wake-up call to anyone who thinks that online commerce is safe as it stands.

Let me introduce a 23-year-old Indonesian we will call Bagus. A few years ago a friend gave him a stash of stolen credit-card numbers, hooked him up to an online chatting channel and showed him how to trade those numbers for more numbers with other chatters. He quickly gathered hundreds of credit-card numbers – including expiration dates, names and billing addresses, as well as security features such as CVV2s, three digits printed on the backs of some credit cards.

Since then Bagus, an architecture student, has bought books, MP3 players, CDs, laptop computers and other hardware from retailers such as Amazon or from auction sites such as eBay. Friends have ordered everything from guitars to motorbikes to sets of Italian soccer shirts. These items are then shipped to rented addresses in Indonesia. "All my friends do it," Bagus says.

Now this isn't just an Indonesian problem. Most of these transactions involve credit cards belonging to citizens outside Indonesia. These are obtained either through sophisticated hacking into retail databases or old-fashioned methods, such as trawling through dumpsters for receipts. How they get the details doesn't really matter; the faceless, underpoliced Internet is the perfect place to turn them into products.

Players such as Bagus say they avoid using Indonesian credit cards because police are more likely to follow up those cases. That doesn't mean there isn't a problem with online fraud in Indonesia. More than 70% of

Internet credit-card transactions attempted in Indonesia are fraudulent, according to BCA, one of Indonesia's biggest banks, which has just set up an online banking service.

But the problem is more serious. Indonesia is merely the base for an organized Internet fraud ring, similar in operation to Bagus and his friends but on a much bigger scale, according to BidPay.com, a New York-based online payment service. The ring uses stolen U.S. credit-card numbers to register Internet domain names, thereby assuming the identity of a website administrator – the online equivalent of a doctor, lawyer or other upstanding citizen. It bids for items on auction sites, using stolen credit-card details and a respectable-looking email address. Then, a member of the ring contacts the seller and asks for the item to be shipped to a friend or relative in Indonesia. The number of such fraudulently registered domains: 11,000 at the most recent count, says BidPay's vice president of international operations Marek Bradbury, "which we consider to be just the tip of the iceberg."

It doesn't stop there. The gang uses the domain names to establish its own websites to relist the items and sell them to unsuspecting buyers, in the process obtaining more credit-card numbers. Quite a wheeze, and it may explain why auction fraud accounts for the majority of online fraud. And it is growing: Auction fraud cost customers about $4 million last year, according to the U.S. Federal Trade Commission's Internet Fraud Complaint Center, while in the first quarter of 2001 losses from complaints reached $3.2 million alone.

In other words, credit-card fraud is the backbone of a mini-industry that knows no borders. Arguments that such fears are exaggerated because online transactions are secure miss the point that the faceless Internet is a perfect hunting ground for creative fraudsters, and the credit card is their perfect weapon. Retailers, credit-card issuers and software manufacturers are coming up with some interesting counter gambits, but first everyone must agree there is a problem and that credit cards, in their present form, make it too easy for folks like Bagus to steal stuff online.

OK, those of you without credit cards can start reading again.

A year later things hadn't gotten any better so I returned to the scene of the crime, this time with a visit in October 2002 to the Indonesian policeman in charge of cracking down on the problem. Perhaps inevitably, he wasn't hugely happy with the piece I wrote about him, but I felt it conveyed some of the problems he faced:

I rather like living in a country where the parliamentary speaker is still at his desk after being found guilty of corruption, where the central bank chief worked all the way through to his appeal against a similar conviction (he won), and where a man suspected of leading the destruction of a political party headquarters in 1996 has just won re-election as governor of the capital, largely because the person backing him is the president – oh, and head of the party whose headquarters he allegedly trashed. To me that's what makes Indonesia interesting. But not half as interesting as when the head of the country's cybercrime task force blames Indonesia's rampant online credit-card fraud on a surplus of, and I quote, "sexy naked ladies".

There I was, in a cramped, ice-cold office with a policeman clad in black, listening to Julio Iglesias MP3s and discussing why Indonesia is fast developing a reputation as the world's worst online credit-card scammer. The policeman was Police Superintendent Brata Mandala, chief of the Information Technology Sub-Directorate of the Directorate of Special Crimes of the National Police Headquarters. And the way Mr. Mandala sees the problem is like this: You can't really blame all these kids for trying credit-card fraud if it's so easy and so available. It's like a sexy naked lady, you see? If she's there, being all sexy and naked, you can't really blame a fellah for trying his luck, right?

Now I'm not going to start disagreeing volubly about the appropriateness of such remarks with a plain-clothes policeman in the middle of a Jakarta police station bristling with weaponry and handcuffs. In fact, in a way, I could see his point. Given that his department has absolutely no resources to speak of – the laptop he uses is his own (the office computer is apparently only up to pumping out Latino ballads), he has one dial-up connection and he's put in a request for $300,000-worth of equipment which he appears resigned to never getting. You can't blame him for trumpeting the few successes he's had and venting some of his frustration at how slow things move, such as it taking seven months to get an affidavit from the United States, by which time the alleged perpetrator's changed his name or skipped the country. With a distinct lack of role models at the top, you might forgive Mr. Mandala for being somewhat less than disgusted with the country's youth trying pot luck with some stolen credit-card numbers.

After all, the underdressed lady is accessible enough. Folk ("fraudulent low-life criminals," as one online retailer terms them) can easily obtain card numbers from the Internet, or even make them up, using freely available software. With a free, disposable webmail account they then order stuff online, trying hundreds of different cards until they get lucky. They then sit back until their goods – anything from a drum set to a motor-racing helmet and body suit – arrive. No wonder the scammers' email addresses translate into insults or taunts – "I'm a ghost" being the only one printable here.

Still, it's beginning to bite: The misdeeds of these youths, and the apparent holes in Mr. Mandala's dragnet, are forcing retailers to abandon shipments to places like Indonesia in droves. Amazon continues to ship stuff to me, possibly because I've been a customer for aeons, but other retailers get distinctly stand-offish when I say that my present home is Jakarta. When I tried to order some CDs from a small New York-based store called Insound, I found that its website did not list Indonesia as an option. When I complained, a guy called John said that 95% of the fraudulent orders that cross his desk are from Jakarta. Ouch.

Now, while some retailers must share the blame for Mr. Mandala's naked-woman syndrome – in not running the most basic checks by, say, using free software to verify that the originating country and bank of a credit card match the customer's shipping address – I can't blame those who won't deliver to Indonesia. They are the ones who end up paying if an approved transaction turns out to be fraudulent – along with extra fees called chargebacks. All this on top of paying for the shipment of the goods in the first place. Not surprisingly, they're hurting.

If naked-lady points are being passed around, credit-card issuers earn them in heaps. They play down the problem because they know online retailers can't afford not to offer credit-card payment as an option, and that they don't pay the consequences if something goes wrong. This is changing, but only slowly. Issuers are now coming out with mechanisms that add an extra layer of security – an online equivalent of the customer signing the docket – that may give all parties some peace of mind, and will eventually transfer some of the transaction costs back to the issuer. This should do away with a lot of amateur credit-card fraud, but it probably will only be a minor battle in a long war against online fraud. Still, at least the ladies are putting some of their clothes on. Mr. Mandala will be delighted.

Has anything changed? Not really.

This retail isolation can also be seen in the virtual financial sector. Internet payment gateways such as Paypal have practically banned Indonesian users from creating accounts. But you can't really blame them CNET blogger Vishnu K. Mahmud wrote recently that "as a result of these indiscretions, Indonesia as a whole has been blacklisted by a majority of the online vendors. In consequence, setting up shop as well as collecting payment worldwide for Indonesian Internet entrepreneurs becomes an impossible task. Internet commerce and transactions make the whole task of transferring money and services over the web easy. But Indonesia is not participating." Which is sad. In countries such as Indonesia the scammers still largely operate outside the law, although this is gradually changing in some countries. Russia, one of the criminal centers, in June 2006 sentenced six people to up to six years in prison for credit card fraud. The six were accused of making more than 5,000 false credit cards and selling them over the Internet. But in some ways credit card fraud is a poor relation to phishing, which I'll explain in the next chapter.

phishing

One of the scams that wasn't really around when I started the column, but which has become big news since, is something called phishing. I started exploring it in late 2003, simply because I couldn't believe that the scamsters were getting so smart. At the time it was considered such a fringe activity when I tried to give a talk about it to a conference of bankers a year later they gave me such blank looks I thought maybe I had the wrong room or they only spoke Spanish. Here's how I introduced the topic to readers in early 2004:

You're an avid reader of this column, I know, so you don't need reminding about what a dangerous place the Internet can be. And the usual advice you'll get from folk is: "Don't do anything online you wouldn't do in real life." It's not bad advice, but it doesn't always work because online life is not like real life.

In real life, for example, someone is unlikely to go to the trouble of printing up a letter that looks as if it's from your bank, or from a reputable company like Microsoft, asking you to update your account details because your password/license/credit card/standing order has expired. But they will on the Net. It's called "phishing" (pronounced "fishing") and, in the past couple of months, it's become the favored way of scammers to part you from your cash.

This is what happens: You'll receive an email that looks as though it's from your bank, or a website you do business with, such as eBay, and you'll be told there's a problem with your account. (Or, more ingeniously, you'll be warned about online scams like, um, phishing.) You'll be requested to log into your online bank account, and verify your password. The email looks and feels genuine – there are familiar logos on display. The email address it was sent from looks almost right. The images showing up in the email could well be from your real online banking site. Even the link for you to log on to your account may look right: Hover your mouse over it, and, in the status bar at the bottom of your screen, all you may see is a link to the bank's real website.

So you believe it must be OK. You click on the link, and hey presto, the familiar banking log-on window appears in your browser; behind it may well be the bank website itself. You double check. Is the link showing up at the top of your browser window legitimate? Yes, it is, so you heave a sigh of relief, congratulate yourself on your good sense and proceed to log in. You hit Enter, and still everything seems OK. The familiar banking website acknowledges your password. You're in. And safe.

Not so fast, mister. You've been phished. What has probably happened is this: The link that looked so innocent in your email actually contained a link, buried somewhere inside it, that took you to a site controlled by the scammer. So while the main banking website that appeared in your window may have been legit, that log-on window that hovered above it – the one you typed your password into – was not. The scammers probably captured your name and password, grabbed it for themselves, and then passed it on to the legitimate website. As far as you were concerned, you signed in as normal. Chances are your bank account will be emptied pretty fast after that.

Even big-name banks are being hit This has been going on for a while, but in the past few months it's grown a lot worse. "People were doing this at least a year ago, but it seems to have taken off in the last eight weeks," says Mike Prettejohn of Britain-based Internet-services company Netcraft, which offers banks and other companies a way to check whether their websites and customers are being targeted by such fraud. "A year ago people were doing a lot of things with PayPal requests, but now they're concentrating on the banks."

There are no reliable statistics on this, but big-name banks in Europe, Asia and North America have been hit. One industry group, the United States-based Anti-Phishing Working Group, estimated that more than 60 million fraudulent email messages were sent out over two weeks in mid-December, and identified more than 90 different kinds of attack. The group estimates that about 5% of recipients respond, which is not a good sign.

So what's to be done? Well, banks are doing what they can to educate users. Regular readers know the drill: Keep anti-virus software up-to-date, keep your firewall running, be extremely skeptical of any email coming from someone you don't know. Other measures are worth taking: Keep different passwords for each online account you have, so if a scammer gets one password, he doesn't get into them all. If you think a bank or any commercial website looks a bit lax, don't do business there. And remember: Banks never send you emails asking you to do things, so don't respond to emails that do. (This, sadly, is not always true of other sites that ask you to enter credit-card details. I recently got an email from Google Answers – a place where you can ask specialists questions in exchange for payment – telling me my credit-card information was not correct, and asking me to update it. I don't see how Google and other sites can get around this, but be very wary of any such email.)

But it's not the end of the world, says the director of the Australian High Tech Crime Centre, Alastair MacGibbon: "We see it as striking at the confidence of the banking customers, so we treat these matters very seriously. But we don't think that it actually threatens the Internet as a way of banking, and we don't think it's the only crime that occurs online," he says. He's right. Phishing won't kill online banking. But it's a reflection of how quickly online crime is evolving, and how life online is different to normal life. Consider the Internet as a party in a bad neighborhood: You may meet some nice folk there, but it pays to keep an eye on your wallet and be wary of whatever is in the punchbowl.

At the time I included some tips about how users might be able to spot phishing emails:

There's a key element in making the phishing scam so effective: Experienced users will inspect a link before they click on it. If a hyperlink appears in HTML email – the same fancy formatting you'd see on a Web page – then the real link will be hidden inside the text.

To see the hidden hyperlink and find out where you're really being taken when you click on it, move the mouse over the hyperlink. You'll see – usually at the bottom of your email-program window – the full address appear. That's always a good thing to do in any situation, but it makes especially good sense if you're reading something that may be dubious.

Now, this is the sneaky bit. There are a couple of tricks the scammers use to disguise the link to their website, and to make you think it's genuine. They both use a rule in links: If there's an @ sign in the link, browsers will only read letters AFTER it. It doesn't matter what's before it, including a website address. So, clicking on, say, www.legitbank.com@http://www.dodgyville.com will take you, not to LegitBank's website, but to DodgyVille's.

That's the basic rule (and I know it's a dumb one, but I didn't make it up). To allay your suspicion at seeing the dodgyville.com bit of the link, the scammers put lots of nonprinting characters (gobbledygook which the email program won't recognize and will replace as white space) into the address, so it will appear thus: www.legitbank.com@http://www.dodgyville.com. Now you probably won't see the real link because the blank space will nudge it off the end of your screen.

Another trick is to make use of a bug that's in Internet Explorer, which hides all text after the special character group %01. At the time of writing, Microsoft hadn't fixed the flaw.

The bottom line here: Don't be fooled by a Web address, just because it looks kosher. Sniff it, view the email in normal text (i.e., not HTML), call your bank, do anything before clicking on a link you're not sure about.

Such links may not just take you to a log-on page: Some will try to load viruses in your computer (usually designed to steal passwords and whatnot). Scary or what?

While all this is still true (and the advice is still worth following), things have moved on. And not in a good way. The big problem has been that the bad guys seem to be good at finding out and teaming up with other bad guys. As I explained in a piece a few months later:

Consider this: At any given time, there may be hundreds of thousands of home computers around the world waiting for instructions from someone who isn't their owner. These are called "zombies," and they may explain why you get so much spam and why your computer sometimes does weird things you didn't ask it to.

Here's how: Your computer is connected to the Internet. Say I had infected your computer with a worm, which then dropped an extra bit of code into your operating system. Your anti-virus software may remove the worm, but it may not find the code. The code is called a "bot" – short for robot – and it would remain inside the operating system, occasionally checking back to me for instructions. Your computer has now become a zombie. But why on earth would I do that?

It's too early to be able to say for sure. But we may soon get some clues: Last month a 21-year old German, known only as Axel G, was arrested on suspicion of creating something called Phatbot, a bot that has infected and now resides in, according to some estimates, 750,000 computers around the world. This arrest may shed some light on the purpose of bots. Phatbot is by no means the only bot out there. According to some reports, Phatbot is descended from worm called Agobot, sometimes called Gaobot. And, depending on which anti-virus manufacturer you believe, there have been between 450 and 900 variants of Agobot.

So we've established that there are more than a few bots out there. Also that, if Phatbot is anything to go by, they have infected a lot of computers, turning them into zombies. But why would someone do this? Is it just a bunch of adolescents messing about for a lark? Partly. The Internet is a great place to show off if you're geeky programmer who doesn't get out much. But there's more to it than that. There's good money involved. What seems to happen is this: If my bot sits on, say, 10,000 computers, allowing me to control them, I could parcel all those zombie computers together and sell them. This is what's called a botnet: Access to thousands of Internet connections. The going rate, according to Internet watchers, for a connection to a zombie is about 10 cents. So whoever controls Phatbot could, theoretically, make $75,000 from selling his botnet.

But who would buy it? Spammers are likely clients. If you want to email millions of Viagra ads in one go without anyone being able to trace you, a botnet is a great way to do it. Zombie computers act as intermediaries between the spammer's computer and the recipient, meaning not only that the spammer can get his mail out quicker than if he were just using a handful of his own computers, but also they help to disguise where the spam actually came from. Handy if you're in a country where spamming is illegal.

That's not all: In the past year dozens of gambling websites in Europe have been targeted by criminals demanding protection money of up to $50,000. Pay up, they say, or we'll bring down your website on Cup Final day, or some other major gambling event. Those who don't pay up are suddenly hit with simultaneous visits from hundreds of thousands of computers, all of them zombies. This is called a "distributed denial of service" attack, and that's exactly what happens. The gambling website is put out of service, just when customers are trying to place their bets. Unsurprisingly, some websites have quietly paid up, preferring to lose a few thousand dollars than lots more in lost business.

Then there's phishing, emails that impersonate your bank's website or another institution and lure you to give up your online banking password. Such scams rose 178% during April, according to the Anti-Phishing Working Group. All those emails have to be sent out somehow, which is probably where zombie computers come in. It's like a criminal being able to case the joint, not just of a few houses but of a whole city, all at one time all while he's sitting snugly at home.

Now, in case you've forgotten, these are not just other people's computers doing this. Chances are it could be yours, or that of one of your employees or a family member. Millions of computers are constantly connected to the Internet, and unless they're well secured, they will be probed several times a minute by other computers looking for a way in. Not all of these probes have sinister intent, but many of them do. And while having a bot on your computer may not be the end of the world, it's not a nice thought to think that your data is vulnerable, and that your PC could be helping someone else deliver pornographic spam, attack other computers or bring down online casinos.

So what can you do? Well it's the old mantra: Install anti-virus software on your computer, keep it updated, and make sure that your Windows has all the latest patches by activating the automatic-update feature. Install a firewall, and if it doesn't stop your computer from connecting to the Internet, have it on the most secure setting.

Lastly, if you haven't been doing this for a while, it might be worth checking that you're not already infected. I'd suggest you use an online virus checker the first time around: Trend Micro's HouseCall (housecall.antivirus.com) does a pretty good job and it's free. The bad news is, if you're infected, you'll probably need a professional to make sure your computer is thoroughly clean. The world of bots is not pretty.

It's still not pretty. Botnets are still big, changing hands for large amounts of money, as a conduit for spam and bad stuff. What worried me, and still worries me, is that the tools we have for combatting this stuff aren't always as good as they could be: Here's what I wrote in April 2005 about the first serious software designed to protect us:

What hope do we have against the evil phishers if the programs designed to protect us don't work?

Phishing, the art of duping users into giving up passwords, PINs and bank-account details via ingenious emails, is the fastest growing scam on the Internet. In the first week of October 2004, the Anti-Phishing Working Group, one of several industry bodies formed to address the issue, reported catching a whopping 161 different phishing scams. In the last week of January this year, the group identified more than 950. I could find seven references in the main print media to phishing in 2002; the next year there were 406. In 2004 there were 10 times that number. That's a lot of scams, and a big jump in column inches (many of which were contributed by yours truly). So, surely, we're finally winning against these guys? Surely we know all their tricks, and can avoid them?

Sadly not. Between $100 million and $1.2 billion has been lost globally to phishing attacks in the past year or so, depending on whom you believe. That's a lot of cash. Especially if it's yours. There are bad people out there and they are smarter than most of the people holding your money. And, perhaps more important, smarter than most of the people promising to protect you.

Here's an example of why. Last month, I received an email purporting to be from the U.S.-based Charter One Bank, now owned by Citizens Financial Group Inc. I have accounts at neither, but apart from that I could find little in the email to indicate that it was fraudulent. The link I was being asked to click on – usually the suspicious part of the email – went to Charter One's real website, and, although the address was long, it didn't raise any serious question marks. As a result, clicking on the link in the email message took me to a website that was clearly legit. Nothing about the site looked dodgy, although the form, requesting my banking details, passwords and PIN numbers didn't quite jell with what I knew about banking security. Banks don't usually ask us to input all that stuff online, after all. But this was the bank's own website, for goodness sake.

This is scary enough: If I'm looking hard at a website and I can't tell whether it's legitimate or not, what hope does my Auntie Ethel have? But that isn't the scariest bit. To be certain, I fired up some toolbars – pieces of software that latch onto my Internet browser and warn me if something is amiss with a website. These toolbars look at the site you're trying to visit and will peer closely inside the link to see whether it's what it says it is. Four of the toolbars reported back that I was indeed at Charter One's website. But, and here's the rub: I wasn't OK. I was looking at a scam website within a legitimate site, fooling the toolbars, and nearly fooling me.

This, for those of you interested, is called script injection. What the scammer has done is to exploit a hole elsewhere on the Charter One site, which allows him or her to inject a small window, or frame, into the Charter One page. That frame contains the form requesting all my details. While the form isn't technically on the Charter One website, as far as I'm concerned it looks like an honest banking Web page. And, scarily, that is also the conclusion of four out of the five anti-phishing toolbars I relied on. Only one, from United Kingdom-based Internet security company Netcraft Ltd. (www.netcraft.co.uk), threw up a warning message. The rest would have allowed me to breezily fill in my account details.

So what does this tell us? First off, phishers are smart and we are dumb. This weakness in the code that programmers use to build websites isn't new, and banks have known about it for a while. Netcraft's Internet services developer, Paul Mutton, tells me that he had notified Charter One about this hole a week earlier but the bank apparently didn't take any action. (Charter One didn't respond to my email requests for comment, although the hole was removed shortly after I notified the bank about it.) Banks have got to be smarter about this, and realize that they must constantly monitor their own websites to see whether they are vulnerable.

This is just the beginning: Institutions will eventually have to figure out more secure methods of protecting the assets of their customers, and of communicating with them. It's no good telling customers that they'll never be asked to give away personal details online because phishing scams are ingenious enough to bypass that with a plausible explanation: In the Charter One case, by connecting the request for a record update with last year's purchase of the company by Citizens Financial Group.

Lastly, don't trust software to keep you safe. Anti-phishing toolbars might be a good idea as an initial line of defense. But, as my tale illustrates, they aren't foolproof. This script injection was just one breach in what will be an increasingly sophisticated online war. Phishers will get smarter, leaving us confused and anxious.

My advice: Educate yourself, if you can, about what is happening. Download the Netcraft toolbar. If that all seems a tad overwhelming, follow some simple rules: Don't respond to any email, click on any link or open any attachment until you've picked up the phone and called the institution involved.

And, finally, always bear in mind that only a fool will offer you foolproof protection from scammers.

Netcraft is still doing the best job, in my view, of monitoring phishing and providing some protection against us. At the time of writing they're detailing a complex attack on Citibank customers that finds a way around what is called two-factor identification – basically two layers of security: a password, and one of those widgets that throw up numbers that change every few seconds. Phishers have found a way around that, and they will continue to find a way around defenses so long as there's money in it. It shouldn't stop you banking or paying your bills online but, just as you wouldn't use an ATM without exercising some caution about your surroundings, passsers by, the time of day etc, so should you exercise caution when doing business online.

spam

I seem to have written about spam more than any other subject. I didn't for the first year, partly because it didn't strike me as very interesting subject, and partly because I didn't really feel I had anything useful to offer readers. (I still don't.) But then I realized it wasn't going to go away and that it was getting sneakier. No longer was spam just like junk mail – pick it up, glance at it, throw it away – but that it could actually ruin our day, slowing us down and making us feel harried and pestered, even in our own den. Part of the trouble has been that people who should know better have long underestimated the problem, and the spammers. This was how I saw it back in February 2001:

I'm here to tell you that spam – unwanted mass emails peddling rubbish to anyone silly enough to leave an email address lying around on the Internet – is a thing of the past. If you believe that, you'll believe anything. Trust me, your inbox is too valuable to be left uncluttered for long.

Jupiter Research, an Internet-commerce consulting company, late last month declared "the end of spam as we know it". Around the same time, the European Commission said the spam phenomenon is "now in decline". Amen. But in the first few weeks of this year I've received more unwanted email than in the whole of last year; offering me printer-cartridge refills, a tip for a hot stock that on closer inspection was a dead duck, and a list of one million emails so I could do a little spamming of my own. Clearly, if spam is on the way out, it isn't going quietly.

So why the difference of perception? The industry consensus on spammers is that they are "unscrupulous characters who think nothing of breaking the law" (the European Commission's words), and who are now wilting under the threat of legal action and jail. This much is true: The U.S. Federal Trade Commission, for example, prosecuted more than 100 cases of spam-related fraud in 2000, and it promises more.

The problem is this: Spammers are dying out because the Web is getting more sophisticated. Replacing them are legions of "email marketers" that employ much cleverer methods to get your attention. This, the European Commission report says, "is where the real action is". What is the difference? "Strict application of privacy policies and the use of email lists based on full consent are now *de rigeur*," the commission says. In other words, spammers send you stuff you didn't ask for, email marketers only send you stuff you did.

Hmmm. This is all a tad too ingenuous for me. Permission-based marketing sounds all very well, but it is liable to abuse. When you mark a check box on a company website agreeing to receive email updates, does that also include, say, promotional material about other companies' products? And, such so-called opt-in boxes aren't necessarily sacrosanct. Online-auction house eBay angered some of its six million users last month by – apparently accidentally – changing users' preferences so that everyone was automatically signed up to receive more promotional material.

It may have been a one-time problem but the case illustrates how valuable those checked opt-in boxes are. And it's not just for the privilege of swimming in junk email. Allow a marketer to access your inbox and he has something approaching a window into your soul. Early this month the Privacy Foundation, a U.S. think tank, illustrated how email can be configured to allow the sender to eavesdrop on email and monitor what the recipient does to it – including receiving any comments added to any forwarded copies. That's worrisome, but not particularly common.

More disturbing is another feature the Privacy Foundation calls "Web bugs" – invisible images embedded in an email or Web page that monitors who reads it. Receive an email with a Web bug inside it and the person who sent it can find out whether you have read it and use it to track when you visit their website. Not exactly Big Brother, but sneaky – and according to foundation chief technology officer Richard Smith it is "pretty much industry standard practice."

To me, such snooping – illegal or not – is unethical and undermines the notion that users will be open to a trusting relationship with marketers and will be happy to receive carefully targeted email promotions. Say you are a car freak, the thinking goes, and you'll be happy to trade a little personal data to receive stuff on the latest model of windshield wiper. The prospect of this makes the industry salivate. Email advertising, according to Internet advertising giant Doubleclick Inc., is growing faster than other parts of the market, such as banner ads on websites. By 2005, Jupiter Media predicts advertisers will send 268 billion email messages – 22 times greater than the number sent last year.

This in turn will feed moves to make email more eye-grabbing. For examples of what the email of the future may look like, check out LifeFX at www.lifefx.com, where software-driven talking heads will read out your email. Nice work, but the faces have an unfortunately sinister air about them, especially when they smile. Having some creepy disembodied head try to sell me a new kind of deodorant might put me off email altogether.

Jazzy or not, promotional email will become tiresome to many. So is there an antidote to an inbox bulging with unwanted avatars and under heavy surveillance by the advertising industry? Yes. Don't give out your email address too readily, or employ spam-busting email shields such as SpamMotel (www.spammotel.com). As demand for privacy grows, expect to see products that will – at least, in theory – act as an intermediary between shopper and retailer. For an early example of that, check out Qode (www.qode.com), a gadget that scans-in product bar codes and then will hunt online for the best price, promising all the while to maintain your anonymity.

The only question: Do you trust it? I'm starting to get nostalgic for those unscrupulous spammer characters.

This turned out to be half right, half wrong. LifeFX didn't make it (thankfully), although you can still check out their weird faces at www.lifefx.com/indexunsupported.html. Qode is still around. Web bugs are now everywhere, as part of an increasingly sophisticated spamming universe. Here's what I found 18 months later:

It must be tough being an email marketer these days. Despite their best efforts these tie-wearing folk, who engage in the highly respected business of collecting email addresses and then sending out carefully targeted missives with provocative titles – usually appealing to one's greed, manhood, paranoia or propensity to gamble – are getting lumped together with sleazy ne'er-do-wells, known as spammers, who collect email addresses and then send carefully targeted missives with provocative titles, usually appealing to one's greed, manhood, paranoia or propensity to gamble. It's shocking, simply shocking, that the two groups could be confused with one another.

Take, for example, a company called Members' Select, part of the Kendare Group, which has this month thoughtfully, and without my asking first, sent me about 30 emails offering easy weight loss, down comforters, a chip to boost mobile phone reception, a free PDA, two free mobile phones, a free Hello Kitty gift, cheap long-distance calls, free movie tickets, to double the speed of my computer, to pay me to drive my own car, and to include me in a program that's changing the way we fall in love. That's on top of asking me questions I have recently been asking myself, such as "Did you know you could legally own a cable descrambler?" (Answer: "Yes. But first, what is a cable descrambler?") or "Jeremy, are you losing control?" (Answer: "After all these emails, yes, a little.")

Now my cynical friend Jim says I've clearly hit Spam Central and I should get out as quickly as I can. Rubbish: I am sure these fellows are professionals, and have only the highest respect for my privacy and shopping interests. The only page on their website, for example, is a 1,800-

☞ **lubenham** (*n, Leicestershire*) A product advertised through spam that sounds as if it will solve all sexual dysfunctions. *Your wife is not satisfied. You need lubenham. Really* word privacy policy that offers reassuring words about what to do if they decide to change their policy. "By continuing to use the site or remain active in the database following an announcement of any changes," the announcement reads, "you will be deemed to have agreed to such changes." Now, this is absolutely fair and decent and open, in my view, and I say, "Tosh" to those folk like Jim who argue pedantically that since I didn't actually sign up to be a member in the first place it's somewhat tough to expect me to know about all this, let alone agree to it. Still, to silence those naysayers I fired off an email to the Members' Select help desk asking them to clarify, as well as following their instructions to remove my name from any future mailing list. While I haven't heard back yet from the help desk, I'm pleased to say that I keep getting tantalizing offers, which is proof they haven't forgotten about me.

Jim says I've ended up on this list because I made the mistake of once subscribing to something completely different, in this case Blink.com, a Web page bookmarking service. Blink later metamorphosed into "a consumer-oriented rewards service and the most sophisticated solution for the management of Web-based content and research" – I'll confess I'm not quite sure what this means – and was in May bought out by the Vendare Group, which might explain why Members' Select and another Vendare venture, a gambling site called Jackpot.com, have taken a touching interest in my consumer choices. Cynical Jim says my email address is now finding its way through a sleazy cabal of online marketing firms and I'd be better off unplugging the computer and setting fire to it.

To such negativism, I'd counter that these guys are marketing pros. Blink, for example, claims among its advertising "partners" respected folk such as American Express, eBay and L.L. Bean, while the Vendare Group's Jackpot lists Sony, Doubleday, TV Guide and Chase as advertisers who have, as its website puts it, "illustrated a rapid acceptance of Jackpot.com's business model." I'm not quite sure what that means either, but it's clear evidence that these people are definitely not just sleazy spammers.

Sure, Jim's rejoinder is that spam has just grown up and got a real job: email marketing. And that we, Internet users, can kiss goodbye to the days when we might innocently read on a website that "your privacy is extremely important to us," think it means just that, and hand out our email addresses secure in the knowledge we won't be spammed to blazes. But don't listen to Jim. He's just jealous he didn't get a chance to buy a Hello Kitty cable descrambler and matching slippers.

Jim, sadly, was probably right. Infuriated that legit-sounding folk were invading our inbox, I decided in 2003 to try out some self-defense weaponry:

A milestone, of sorts, was passed last month. According to MessageLabs, a United States-based company that studies these things, the Internet for the first time handled more spam email messages than normal emails. In other words, for every legitimate email sent, there was at least one spam, or unsolicited junk email, sent. Compare that with a year ago when the ratio was about one spam for every 20 emails. A year before that? One in 1,500. Spam was never pretty, but it's getting ugly, and something has to give. But what?

Spam is a business, and understanding that is halfway to embracing a solution that works. Why, for example, does MessageLabs spend so much time counting spam? Because it sells services and software that help companies avoid it. In fact, spam is, I suspect, much more profitable for the folk who clean it up than the guys who put it out. Think about it: It costs a spammer very little to send one email, and only one in 10 million to generate a sale to stay in business, but God knows how much in lost man-hours for you or I to receive it, open it, read it, feel slightly nauseous, discard it and then wander over to the water cooler to complain to colleagues about it. There are conflicts of interest here that make me slightly uncomfortable advising you to buy products to keep out what shouldn't be in your inbox anyway.

So here's my solution: It's simple, costs you nothing and will improve as you get more spam. Most anti-spam software looks for things it recognizes as spam-like: words like "Viagra," for example, and filters it out. But this isn't always that effective – replace "i" with "1" and you have v1agra, or add some invisible formatting code in the middle of the word, so the word looks the same to a reader, but different to a spam filter. So as spammers get more cunning, filters have to get smarter. This is why using logic, rather than keywords, makes sense. Enter an 18th-century vicar called Thomas Bayes from the English town of Tunbridge Wells. He devised a probability theory that has become a useful tool in gauging whether email is spam or not.

Briefly, Bayesian filters look at the content of email (including the headers, in most cases, and the hidden code in emails, called HTML, that organizes fonts, colors and pictures), slices it into bits – words and chunks of code – and judges the probability of each bit being evidence of spam. It will then scrutinize the 15 most interesting bits and add up their probabilities (0.99, for example, meaning 99% likely it's spam) and then cast judgment on the email. The more you prod it along – yes, this one is spam; no, this one looks like spam but is actually my Auntie Edith suggesting I have plastic surgery – the better it gets. And of course the more email you get, the more it has to play with. Bayesian filters don't just look for matches, they look for patterns of behavior that give spam away.

For starters, try POPFile (popfile.sourceforge.net) which will work on most operating systems and with most email programs. If you're squeamish about manual tweaking, check out Spammunition for Outlook (free from www.upserve.com/spammunition/default.asp) or SpamBully for Outlook or Outlook Express (www.spambully.com).

On top of that, try a trick of my own: Ask colleagues or friends to assign agreed tags to subject lines and set up your email program to recognize those tags and filter them into special folders. [Meet] for example, could be used to relate to meetings, [Budget] for stuff related to how much money you plan to waste that year and [Fire] for emails alerting staff they're being downsized. Such emails would then leap past any filters and be easy to search for. Spam's not going to go away soon, but with good filters you need never see it in your inbox again. Or go to the water cooler.

My trick never really caught on, I must confess. Getting friends to do anything is an uphill task, but if you use that trick in outgoing messages it does help filtering responses into the correct folder, unless respondents insist on changing the subject field. Spammunition hasn't been updated since then, but it's still available. SpamBully is now into version 3 and costs $30. And I still use POPFile.

For some people, Spam is war. In December 2003 I wrote about a team of Dutch bloggers who decided to take the law into their own hands:

It's now open war in the spamming world. On December 2, a new version of an email virus, called Mimail-L, appeared, apparently the work of a vengeful email marketer trying to disable organizations that track and oppose spam. The virus (or worm, to be exact) will mail itself to everyone in your address book, and will take over your computer as part of a coordinated attack on anti-spamming websites. It's not the first such worm, but it's potentially the nastiest.

This is more proof of the collusion between spammers and virus writers. But it's also part of an accelerating war between spammers and the people who hate them, and who know enough about technology to do something about it. Take the recent case, for example, of three Dutch bloggers called Bas Taart, Retecool and Bumble, a Florida-based spammer called John and a website called www.customerblast.com.

It's November 18, and Bas gets an email from the Customer Blast website, offering 75 million email addresses for only $1,000, a list that is "clean, deduped, and verified twice." Just another piece of spam, you might think, but for Bas Taart it's the final straw, and he does what many of us nontechies may dream of doing, if only we knew how: He spams back. Visiting the Customer Blast website's feedback form, he composes a few lines of computer code (called a script) that will fill up the form with garbage and send it to the Customer Blast website – every second. He then posts this script to his own website (www.bastard-inc.com) and invites anyone else to download and use it. Two Dutch bloggers pick it up and start publicizing it, leading to about 5,000 people bombarding the Florida-based Customer Blast site.

Then, things got interesting. Customer Blast, instead of complaining or suing, retaliated. According to Bas, the company – or someone operating on its behalf – started doing the same thing back to him and the other two bloggers. Email addresses listed on their website – including those belonging to dozens of folk who had left comments on their websites – started receiving hundreds of emails, causing their email programs to crash. One of the Dutch bloggers was hit so badly his website went off-line. Cyber war had broken out.

Bas and the others fought back. He put the original script back online, along with a Web page that was divided into frames, or cells, each of them a reloading copy of Customer Blast's homepage. With thousands of people helping, the traffic to Customer Blast's homepage would have been massive. Customer Blast was blasted off the Net, and at the time of writing, is still offline.

So how did Customer Blast feel about all this? Finding out was not easy. Spammers have learned to cover their tracks these days, as laws against spamming get tougher, as more and more people complain and as folk like Bas and Bumble go postal on them. After a bit of sleuthing (checking the registration of more than 50 websites, dialling a dozen or so numbers and having some surreal conversations with strangers, along the lines of "Excuse me, are you a spammer?") I tracked down the guy behind Customer Blast, a 38-year old resident of Florida called John Hites. He's a big fish in the spamming world: *The New York Times* last month listed him as the world's fourth-most prolific spammer.

At first, John wasn't keen to talk to me, but on the second try he opened up a bit, if only to tell me he was no longer involved with Customer Blast. "That's all been sold, man, that's gone," he said. And while he seemed to know about the attack, he didn't want to talk about it much, saying such blitzes are routine. "Those are pretty easy to beat," he said.

Anyway, John is getting edged out by legislation and a growing backlash by a public who feel abused by spammers. John is disarming about the public's view: "I agree with them, and that's why I sold the company. There used to be a time when it wasn't that big a deal, but now the majority of the public says they don't like it, it's going to go pretty much by the wayside," he said.

But the war goes on. A new United States law outlawing certain kinds of spam is likely to come into effect on January 1 and it may put people like Hites out of the game, but my worry is that may just push spammers further offshore, to countries where Internet-service providers are under no pressure to close down spammers. China, Korea, Pakistan and India are becoming popular hosts, or relays, where the email passes through. There will always be folk willing to handle spam and the Internet knows no borders, so it doesn't matter where they are based.

Not that I think vigilantism is the answer either. The First Dutch Cyber war – which is still going on – may have thrown Customer Blast off the Internet, but it has also aggravated the problem by turning both sides into outlaws. Who knows where it will go next? As even Bas, the Dutch blogger, reflecting on his actions, concedes: "I'm 30, I'm married and I'm an information-technology professional. I never tried to get total anarchy or anything. I never imagined it getting out of hand the way it did."

That revenge fantasy may have been a one-off. But in mid 2005 it became the business model of a company that believed treating spammers with their own medicine might work. Here's what I wrote about Blue Security in June:

It's every email user's fantasy: Getting back at spammers by bombarding them with the same rubbish they send us. But would it work, and is it right?

A new company, Blue Security (www.bluesecurity.com) thinks so. Launched this month by two Israelis, it promises to "start deterring spammers" and "reclaim your email experience". And it's already caused a fair smattering of controversy.

In a nutshell, this is how it works. Blue Security tries to get as many ordinary people like you and me to sign up for its service. When we do, two things happen: First, we download a piece of software to our computer. More on that later. Second, we're assigned a BlueFrog email account. But these are not really for our use; they're what are called in the industry "honey pots", designed to lure the target – in this case spammers – into a trap. Blue Security does this by publishing the email account on as many Web pages as it can and then waiting for the spammers to find them. When spam starts to arrive, they dissect the emails to figure out who really sent them. It does that because most spam doesn't come from the person it says it comes from; figuring out the identity of the real sender is harder, sometimes impossible. Then, acting on your behalf, Blue Security goes through a process of "warning" the spammer to stop his or her activities. If that fails, and more spam arrives, then the piece of software on your computer goes into action. It will visit the Web page of the spammer and start complaining – by filling out a feedback form usually found on most spammers' product pages.

This may not sound like much of a revenge attack, but imagine if tens of thousands, even hundreds of thousands, of Blue Security members all did it. It would, according to Blue Security, slow down the spammer's website and make it hard for the pest to keep doing business. Eventually, in theory, the spammer would be so frustrated by this vigilante response it would agree never to send spam to Blue Security members and the "complaint visits" would stop. This would be done by the spammer downloading special software and a list of all those people who had signed up for the Blue Security service. The software would go through the spammer's list of email addresses and weed out all Blue Security members.

Signing up for the Blue Frog is, at least for now, free. Blue Security hopes to make its money by selling the service to enterprises. If, say, a large company signed up for the service it would add all the addresses of its employees to the Blue Security member list, ensuring that all those people would be removed from the mailing list of any spammer that had agreed to Blue Security's demands. In this case, for example, when these users sign up, they are able to submit their own email addresses as well as their honey pot address. All addresses would be included on the "don't spam me" list.

So why do some people think this isn't the right way to go? Well, the main concern is that this might not be legal. Blue Security is careful in its language, and says it has cleared the process with U.S. lawyers, but some critics suggest that by actively trying to prevent a website – the spammer's – from operating, Blue Security may be launching what is called in the trade a Distributed Denial of Service attack. It would be a bit like a community taking objection to a shop legally selling alcohol and blocking the doorway so customers couldn't get in and the shop staff couldn't make deliveries. A Distributed Denial of Service attack is illegal in most countries, as is putting a shop you don't like out of business by blockading it.

Other criticism is more technical, and I won't bore you with it. But the bottom line is, people think the spam-busters won't work. They point to the fact that most spammers move operations quickly, so shutting them down in one place won't deter them. Another is that spammers tend to operate via computers in a place like China, run by companies that explicitly sell their services because they are "bullet-proof." In a word, this means they don't care if their customers are spammers. Another complication, according to Joel Smith, co-founder of email-security provider AppRiver LLC, is that spammers tend to split their websites across different computers, some of them hijacked machines, or "zombies," that belong to unwitting individuals.

Robert Haskins, who works for Internet monitoring company Renesys Corp. and has written a book on spam, says: "There has been a lot of talk about and work on the general concept of fighting spam by using vigilantism over the years, and it just doesn't work."

Blue Security rejects these criticisms, saying it has carefully researched its approach and that it isn't illegal, unethical or ineffective. Says Eran Reshef, CEO and chairman: "We have no intention of taking spammers out of business. The only thing we want is for them to understand there is a community of users who don't want their messages."

I have some sympathy for their position. It's true that spam is just as much a problem as it ever was. And the irony here is that while spam filters are doing a great job of catching most of the rubbish being fired at our inboxes, only a few offensive emails need to get through to irritate us.

But still I don't think Blue Security's approach is the right one. By trying to beat them at their own game it merely takes the spam war to another technological level and will push the spamming world further into the Badlands. A few spammers might agree to Blue Security's terms, but the rest will find a way to get around it.

So if this kind of thing doesn't – or shouldn't – work, what should we do? Most analysts and legitimate email marketers I spoke to would like to see plans bear fruit for an improved kind of email system – where the sender is authenticated. As Internet security analyst Ambika Gadre of email filtering company IronPort puts it, "[email] grew up in an academic environment where everyone trusted each other. It wasn't designed to be used in this way."

In the meantime, if spam really bothers or offends you, I'd suggest you sign up for an ISP or email provider (not always the same thing) which promises to keep all the spam and viruses out of your inbox.

Sad truth is, however satisfying it is to imagine bringing spammers to their knees by giving them some of their own medicine, this isn't the way the Internet should be going.

This time I was right. Deluged by a counterattack a few months later Blue Security folded. The spammers have not only won, they've expanded their operations. My last offering on the subject, in June 2006, was about the rise of something we might call web spam:

Ever since email came along, there's been a battle to keep spam out of your inbox. But now, you also need to look out for Web spam.

The issue popped out of the shadows a couple of weeks ago when marketing bloggers noticed something strange happening on several big search engines, including Google. Two websites, the mysteriously named t1ps2see.com and eiqz2q.org, suddenly started dominating search results from "loansaver" to "old mayline table." Google indexed more than seven billion pages belonging to them; Alexa, a site that charts Internet traffic, briefly ranked the first site as more popular than WSJ.com. Neither site offered more than a few links and ads, and neither existed a few weeks before. So how come they were suddenly rubbing shoulders with the Internet big boys?

Both websites belong to a 25-year-old Moldovan named Evgheni Tariuc, who has declined to disclose exactly how he did it. "This is a commercial secret," he said in a recent interview via instant message. But we can piece together most of what he's done. In brief: Register hundreds of websites, fill them with some text he grabbed from the Web, get them to link to each other (in order to boost their rankings in the system that Google uses to measure popularity), and then sit back and watch them ride up the search results. Google eventually cottoned on to this and stopped it, and has said that the number of links was exaggerated by a glitch in its own software. But there's no question that Mr. Tariuc scored a major coup.

Welcome to the world of Web spam. It's similar to email spam in that it's an attempt to get your attention by fair means or foul. But while email spam aims at your inbox, and tries to persuade you to click on a link that will lead you to buy the spammer's product, Web spam's target is your browsing. Web spammers hope to skew search results so that you go to their sites. They make most of their money not from people buying their products, but from those people clicking on what are called "sponsored links" – ads, essentially – such as those served by Google's AdSense division, that can be found on Google's search results pages and many other websites and blogs. Services such as AdSense work as middlemen, delivering ads on behalf of advertisers to Web pages relevant to the product being sold. Go to a travel website and you'll find the Google AdSense ads are all about travel.

Why should this bother you? Well, Web spam will only be profitable if spammers can boost their sites' rankings on search engines such as Google, meaning they are constantly trying to manipulate those rankings in their favor in this way – a practice that might be called "spamvertizing." This means, says Norwegian Internet consultant Ann Elisabeth Nordbø, who runs antispam website spamhuntress.com, that it's becoming harder to find what you want, since with some search results "the first four pages are dominated by throwaway sites that were spamvertized in order to get them ranked highly."

There's a whole industry, known as search-engine optimization, dedicated to trying to boost the rankings of websites on search engines. While much of it is legit, some of it crosses the border between good honest promotion and, well, sleaze. Because it's often not just about making the most of the way Google and other search engines rank websites. It can also be about creating content that has nothing to do with actually informing visitors, and everything to do with getting them to click on ads. In the t1ps2see.com case, for example, the "content" listed in search results that makes the site look appealing to users doesn't actually appear on the pages they link to, says Ms. Nordbø. "The...freebie sites are there to give content to the search engines," she says. "But when users land there, they're whisked to a target site" through little bits of code that reside on the Web page. Bait and switch, basically.

This is creating a strange situation. Web spammers rely on two things – search results and context ads. The most popular of both of these services are run by one company: Google. This, according to some critics, has made Google somewhat reluctant to a) improve its search engine to remove these tilted results, and b) crack down on the Web spammers that make money both from and for AdSense; after all, the advertiser pays the third-party ad-serving company, wherever its ad appears. Says Ben Edelman, a researcher at Harvard University and something of an expert on sleazy Internet ad tactics: "Puzzlingly and disappointingly, Google pays out substantial funds to partners engaged in this kind of Web spam – making the Web less useful and more cluttered for users and search engines alike." A Google spokesperson says the company doesn't comment on specific cases, but that the company "takes appropriate action in response to publishers found in violation" of its policies, "which may include terminating their AdSense account(s)."

Web spam may not be as obvious a nuisance as email spam, but it still needs to be stopped. It's not just about wasting our time with fake websites, or stumbling upon offensive content because of misleading links. It's more about curbing what Ms. Nordbø calls "the trashification of the Web." We've come to rely on search engines to get us around the Web, but if we find they're taking us down sleazy alleys, or to websites that claim to offer us objective advice about teenage pregnancy or dry-stone walling but instead trick us into filling their tip jar, then we'll all start to feel the pain.

The Internet is full of spam of one kind and another. And I don't think it's going to go away. In the end it's going to be down to ordinary citizens to clean up the mess, I suspect. It's like litter. Some countries get the idea that litter is bad, so no one litters. Other countries are still inundated by it, because enough people don't get it for litter to be the norm. Spam is no different. We're going to have to start throttling the spammers where they feel it most: their pockets. This can only be done if we never, ever, open a spam email or click on a link in a spam email, or a spam website. The reason why spam is such big business is that it works: There are enough of us who buy their stuff to make it worthwhile. One day we'll learn that and stop. Only then will the trashification of the Web cease.

passwords

Passwords are the Achilles Heel of every security system. Here's why it's scary, from a column called "Cracking a Password Becomes Child's Play With New Programs" from February 2001:

If you have ever used a computer, chances are you have used a password. Chances are that the password was your spouse's name, your child's name or that of a much-loved pet. Chances are that password could be cracked in about one second flat. Chances are you use the same password to access all your other online accounts, including your bank, your medical records, etc. Chances are you don't like the way this is going. Am I right?

I don't want to alarm you, but passwords are at the heart of computer security and they are the weakest link. Most people use passwords they can easily remember. This makes it increasingly easy for ne'er-do-wells to get a hold of them because as computers get faster, and more people use them, the tools available to crack passwords improve. Now, with small programs you can download from the Internet, cracking a password is child's play.

Opening a Microsoft document, for example, is relatively easy. A program such as MoneyKey from Passware (www.lostpassword.com), will decipher the password for a Money file instantly. A file from its main rival, Intuit Inc.'s Quicken, can be opened by constructing a fake password. Improved measures in Microsoft Office, according to LastBit Software's Vitas Ramanchauskas, make it harder to crack longer passwords but his software still guarantees eventual success.

Here is the problem. In the real world, we limit access to our property with keys. In the computer world we have to use a nonphysical, virtual key, which is the password. The thinking goes that as only you know the password, your online property – your data – is safe. But of course it isn't that simple.

There are myriad ways the ne'er-do-wells – we'll call them crackers – can get their hands on your password. One is shoulder surfing, which involves the highly technical process of walking past your computer when you are typing in your password. The online equivalent of this is something called "password sniffing," which entails using special software to monitor network activity. If the cracker knows that the first thing you do when you dial into the office is type in your username and password, it doesn't take a genius to realize that capturing and deciphering that data could prove fruitful.

This is one reason why many passwords are encrypted, using supposedly complex formulas, or algorithms. This makes it harder, but not impossible. The password for a Microsoft Word version 8 file, for example, is encrypted through a multistage process, according to Crak Software (www.crak.com), a password-cracking site. The encryption process uses a 128-bit binary number, or key, meaning that in theory there are 128 bits of entropy – or uncertainty – in the encryption code. On paper that sounds invincible: centuries should pass before someone can decrypt your password.

In practice there is less to crack than meets the eye. Such high-bit encryption systems measure only the maximum entropy in a code. In fact, passwords are usually shorter than the length required to make use of all the permutations available. That quickly reduces the workload for a cracker. Making his job easier is the fact that most users don't want to remember a complicated password, so it is probably a recognizable (and memorable) word that may even be guessable.

Computers, too, are getting more powerful, meaning that brute force techniques can be used against passwords. Helping the cracker are

☞ **porlock** (*n, Somerset*) A word you use as your password that you think is unbreakable, and yet can probably be guessed by a five-year old on crack.

wordlists that can be thrown at the password to check for possible matches: a complete English wordlist might involve 150,000 guesses, which would take a few seconds on a normal computer. Failing that, pure brute force can be applied, where every combination from "aaa" to "zzzzzzzzz" can be tried. This may take some time – say a week on a Windows NT system – but security consultants hired to test networks say they can run an attack for several days before a systems administrator might notice. L0phtcrack, a password cracking program, decoded 90% of all passwords at a large high-technology company in less than 48 hours using an off-the-shelf PC.

And in case you think all this is way too theoretical, here are some recent cautionary tales. In the past week dozens of websites have been hacked into, including Intel Corp., the Idaho state government, the messaging provider ICQ, the U.S. Financial Institutions Commission, Sony Corp.'s Taiwan site, the New York Times, Compaq Computer Corp., Altavista, and Hewlett-Packard Corp. (for a list of such hacked sites, see www.attrition.org/mirror/attrition). Early this month hackers broke into the World Economic Forum website, retrieving 800,000 pages of data including email addresses, credit card numbers and passwords of luminaries from Microsoft's Bill Gates to Palestinian leader Yasser Arafat.

All such attacks would involve either bypassing the password security or cracking the code. According to the *Guardian*, a British newspaper, the Atari website of games manufacturer Hasbro was broken into by hackers in late January using the default username and password "test". Weeks later the site still displays a sign saying it is "undergoing routine maintenance".

The commercial wing of this business offers password-cracking services for files you can't open – no questions asked. OfficePassword, from LastBit Software (www.passwordtools.com), promises to recover 75% of all Microsoft Office passwords within one day. Watching such programs whirring away on your Microsoft Word file is a sobering experience: your computer can be very fast when it wants to be.

Of course, this all means you are going to have to be a bit more savvy about passwords. One solution: keeping them on your hand-held digital assistant. There are programs to help: 4T Nox (www.fortsoft.com), for example, stores passwords and user names on your Palm device. But be warned: Palm passwords can be hacked. And even FortSoft had to release an update earlier this month when it discovered the program's own password wasn't being encrypted properly.

The lesson: there is no such thing as a safe password. I warned you that you wouldn't like the way this was going.

That said, it is possible to dream up better passwords, although it requires some effort and a decent memory. Read this piece I wrote in October 2002 called "Try Cracking This Code":

Passwords. People are always banging on at you to change them, keep them secret, don't put them on a sticky on the side of your screen, don't use your pet Komodo's name and all that, right? Jeez, would they just lighten up already?

Well, I hate to be a killjoy but they have a point. With more financial transactions being made online – from air miles to banking, to bill-paying, to book-buying – more and more of our personal data is at risk of being compromised. The development of the Internet relies on people like us feeling comfortable hanging out there. I'm not going online shopping, banking or gambling if I don't think my data, bank account and credit cards aren't safe. This means privacy, and security must be assured. And yet all this information is deeply compromised – not only by other people, but by ourselves.

You may not think your password protects much: Most of us believe we don't have that much that other people would want to expend a great deal of effort to try and take from us: "Who's going to go to all that trouble to get my email password, for crying out loud?" I hear you cry.

The problem is that, for a ne'er-do-well, a password is a foot inside the door to a much larger treasure trove. If they can get your password, they might be able to hack into a bigger network; or, in your case, if they

☞ **nostell** (*n, West Yorkshire*) The one (hopelessly insecure) password you have for everything that needs a password.

know the password to your Yahoo! mail account they might figure – with good reason, I'd wager – that it's the same as, or similar to, your password to other, more lucrative online treasures, like your online bank account. A chink in the amour is all that is needed.

What to do? Passwords are very easy to crack if they're simple. The longer and more complex your password, the harder and longer it's going to take someone to crack. If the program, or website, you're signing into allows you to use 14 characters or more, use them; if it allows capital letters and other characters, use them. It's the difference between a ne'er-do-well taking about 30 seconds to crack a password like "johnbrown" and days, even months, if it's "j()7* n_b50%N."

The trick is to make up something you can remember. A great password forgotten is no use. So here are some tips:

- Base the password on mnemonics or acronyms, not words or names. Use your favourite song titles, movies, football teams as starters. It's got to be something that you know a lot about, but not something that other people can find out about you – such as your birthday, your place of birth, or your kids' names. The first letters of the movie The Year of Living Dangerously, for example, could be used in conjunction with its two main stars, Mel Gibson and Sigourney Weaver, to read "tyoldmgsw."

- That's just the start. Now you have something you can remember, but it's still just basic letters. You need to turn some of them into numbers, punctuation symbols and capitals. Try turning the o into a similar-looking zero, the l into a one and the s into a five. That would give you "ty01dmg5w" which is a lot better, and still easy to remember, since the numbers are similar to the letters they've replaced.

☞ **hinton parva** (*n, Dorset*) The hint to help you remember a password which leaves you none the wiser. *It says "My favorite teacher at school" but I don't remember which one I put. Total hinton parva.*

- This, sadly, is still not good enough. The people who write hacking programs are on to this kind of trick, so your password is still vulnerable. It needs an extra trick or two. Try capitalizing the family-name letters, alter the 0 to similar-looking bracket marks (), and move the numeric characters one key to the left on your keyboard.

If your passwords are as good as that, then you should be safe. But there's still a weakness, and it's still human. Never give your passwords to anyone, don't reuse them for different accounts, and change them every few months. Store them on your personal digital assistant if you like, but remember that, even if it's in a well-encrypted file, all your valuable info is just one password away from being accessed by someone. If they steal your device, chances are they're eager enough to try to crack the password protecting all your passwords. Passwords are better kept in your head, triggered by things you'll never forget.

Now, if you'll excuse me, since I've told you my password I've got to go make up a new one.

Nothing has changed since then to make me think otherwise, although given we now have to remember so many passwords, it's worth building an inner sanctum of unique passwords for the things that matter – bank accounts etc – and easier ones for the less important web sites and email accounts you use. Just make sure there's no possible connection between the two, or between any of the passwords for your important data. Remember: if a bad guy can get one of your passwords, you don't want him to be able to guess any of the others.

privacy

Privacy is a tough subject to write about. In a way, we don't have any privacy anymore. If you doubt me do a keyword search on me (or you, if you prefer) on Google, and pretty soon you can find all you need to know about me. But that doesn't mean we shouldn't still be aware of what privacy is, nor on how it can so easily be surrendered. I tend to think now that privacy is something we should always fight to preserve – against governments, against companies, against our employers – even while we acknowledge the war is already lost. Here are some examples of it that I've written about over the years, illustrating, I hope, how our privacy can be undermined in the most surprising ways. Take this column, for example, from September 2001:

In days of old, applying for a job was a pretty private affair. Check out a job ad, send the employer a CV, attend an interview. Now, protected in these online days by the anonymity of the Internet, it should be even more private.

It isn't.

The Internet isn't anonymous. You leave a digital trail everywhere you go, and filling out a CV on the Web is not quite the same as sending one directly to a potential employer. Indeed, according to the Denver-based Privacy Foundation (www.privacyfoundation.org), there is a danger that by applying for jobs online, your information – including detailed work histories, salary information and other sensitive data – might become a commodity that may end up in the hands of all sorts of people you never know about.

The Privacy Foundation's report released last week about the activities of the online recruitment site Monster.com, owned by TMP Worldwide Inc., is an instructive glimpse into how the Internet can work against the user and how commercial imperatives threaten to undermine the trust needed for the Internet to function.

The site works like this: Apply for a job posted on Monster.com and you are invited to create an account, which in effect means filling out a resume. You won't be alone: There are more than 8 million resumes stored at Monster.com, the report says. That resume information will then go to your prospective employer.

So far so good. However, now – unless you have chosen a `private posting option' – your resume may also be accessible to all employers paying to access Monster.com's online database. This means a lot of eyeballs. According to the survey in January 2001 by the Society of Human Resource Managers, cited in the Privacy Foundation's report, the number of human resource managers in the U.S. who use the Internet to find job candidates is growing annually. This is fine if you are hoping for exposure, but could be somewhat unnerving should, say, your present employer use the service.

Not only that: The Privacy Foundation's author, Pam Dixon, noticed that a resume filled out at a corporate website could end up on a third-party site such as Monster.com anyway. To demonstrate this, Ms. Dixon used a pseudonym to apply for a job in human relations at H&R Block, a financial and tax advisor, by creating a profile for herself. Immediately afterwards, she logged on to Monster.com and found exactly the same profile. Nowhere on the H&R Block site was an affiliation with Monster.com mentioned, according to Ms. Dixon, and links to the H&R Block's privacy policy didn't work at the time. (H&R Block, Ms. Dixon says, plans to terminate their arrangement with Monster.com for separate reasons. Monster.com says that any resumes submitted to an affiliated site are viewable only by that company and the individual job seeker.)

☞ **yelland** (*n, Devon*) A person who talks loudly in an otherwise quiet office. *We've got a yelland in the next cubicle, talking about the soccer day in day out. Can't hear myself think.*

This sort of incident is scary. Resumes are sensitive documents and to be cavalier with them borders on reckless. But it doesn't stop there. The report also claims that resumes that appear on Monster.com may also have been trawled from elsewhere on the Web, almost certainly without the author's knowledge. Ms. Dixon points to company documents submitted in court for a copyright suit last year that show Monster.com was working on software that would hunt for resumes from other Web pages throughout the Web and be stored at Monster.com without the resume owner's consent. (Monster.com didn't address the issue in its reply to the Privacy Foundation report and it isn't mentioned in its privacy policy. A company representative couldn't be reached for comment.)

Moreover, according to former Monster.com employees Ms. Dixon interviewed, even those applicants who submitted resumes directly to Monster.com may not have control over them. Several employees told her that recruiters are occasionally given access to old, inactive resumes that job seekers have requested be removed from the database.

Monster said in its reply to the Privacy Foundation that all deleted resumes were "permanently removed from the system", but acknowledged copies were kept on backup systems. The company's online privacy policy also notes that copies may be retained in separate databases of employers and recruiters, for which Monster.com sheds all responsibility "for the retention, use, or privacy of resumes in these instances."

By now I would be pretty upset if I had posted a resume to a company only to find it sucked into some grand database. But there is more. Using standard technology in Web browsers, Monster.com may build up a detailed profile of you, your location, employment and job interests. While most of this information is aggregated en masse as general, demographic data rather than sorted individually, users may still be alarmed at how their activities online can be monitored.

Ms. Dixon's work is pretty thorough. And it raises some important questions. As she concludes, "if job seekers and the personal information they provide becomes a commodity without adequate privacy protections, online sites may lose job seeker trust and a valuable tool will be tarnished."

I couldn't agree more. As long as my personal data is going to be valuable to someone else, in whatever form, I'm going to be mighty careful to whom I give it.

Privacy isn't just about your personal data. It's about the choices you make – especially if you live in a democracy. I found myself getting concerned about voting systems in 2002, as people talked more and more about using the Internet, and technology, for elections and polls. Here's something I wrote in March 2002, called "The State We Could Be in":

Voting in your underwear? Sounds an appealing proposition: the chance to exercise your constitutionally protected right without actually having to leave your home. You could be watching Frasier while working out which candidate you want to mess things up for you for the next three/four/25 years, based on criteria such as which one most closely resembles a Teletubby/Frasier's brother Niles/your Aunt Maudlin.

Yes, the lure of Internet voting is coming around again. In May, soccer enthusiasts will be able to vote for their favorite players in the World Cup via a joint South Korean and Japanese project (mvp.worldcup2002.or.kr; the site is not fully functioning yet). This is just an online poll, of course, and doesn't add much to the mix except to try to introduce a new social group (soccer fans) to the concept of online voting. Elsewhere, however, online voting is already kicking in: Some towns in Britain are undertaking pilot projects allowing voters to choose their local councilors via the Internet, or even via SMS, in borough elections in May.

I don't want to be a killjoy, but this kind of thing gives me the heebie-jeebies. The arguments in favour of online voting make sense – faster counting, less human error, attracting younger, hipper voters with mobile phones and Internet connections in their hatbands, higher turnouts, you can vote in your underpants, etc., etc. – until you actually think about it. Computers, we've learned since we plugged one PC into another, are notoriously insecure. Viruses are now so sophisticated and prevalent that many security consultants advise their clients to update their anti-virus software every day. What are the chances of a voting system not being a juicy target for people writing these nasty little vermin programs?

Another argument wheeled out in favor of Internet voting is this: The Web is now managing billions of dollars of transactions successfully, so why can't it handle voting? There's a simple answer to this, as security consultant Bruce Schneier of Counterpane Internet Security (www.counterpane.com) explains: The whole point of voting is that it's supposed to be anonymous, whereas any financial transaction has attached to it details of payee, recipient and other important data. This makes it much, much harder to protect any voting system from fraud, much harder to detect any fraud and much harder to identify the guy conducting the fraud. What's more, if there was evidence of fraud, what exactly do you do in an online vote? Revote? Reconduct part of the vote? Chances are that faith in the overall ballot has been seriously, if not fatally, undermined.

Some of these problems could be done away with via ATM-style machines that print out a record of the vote. That could then be used in any recount. But it's still not enough: As online voting expert Rebecca Mercuri points out, there is no fully electronic system that can allow the voter to verify that the ballot cast exactly matches the vote he just made. Some nasty person could write code that makes the vote on the screen of a computer or ATM-machine printout different from that recorded. This may all sound slightly wacky to people living in fully functioning democracies. But (political point coming up, cover your eyes if you prefer) democracies can be bent to politicians' wills, and one country's voting system may be more robust than another's.

Scary stuff. Florida may seem a long way away now, but the lesson from that particular episode must be that any kind of voting system that isn't simple and confidence-inspiring gives everyone stomach ulcers. The charming notion that the more automation you allow into a system, the more error-free and tamper-proof it becomes, is deeply misguided. The more electronics and automation you allow into the system, the less of a

☞ **mickleover** (*n, Derbyshire*) Ads that get in the way of browsing. *I was reading this article and then I got a mickleover so I left the site.*

role election monitors can play.

Internet voting, or something like it, may well be the future. I'd like to see it wheeled out for less mission-critical issues, like polling for whether to introduce traffic-calming measures in the town center, or compulsory kneecapping for spitters, say. But so long as computers remain fragile, untamed beasts that we don't quite understand, I'd counsel against subjecting democracy to their whim. Even if I am in my underpants.

Underpants or no, my husky voice wasn't heard, and the U.S. went ahead with electronic voting systems. With more problems. Here's one I spotted in November 2003:

Here's a half-decent plot for a movie: A grandmother who runs a small PR outfit (whose homepage barks at you affectionately) stumbles on some documents that strike at the heart of the democracy we cherish. Fearlessly, she takes on the forces of darkness. Not bad, eh? Shame it's true, and that the story has yet to have a happy ending.

The tale revolves around electronic voting: the compelling notion that you can get rid of bits of paper, punch-cards, ballot boxes, hand counts, even the voting booth itself, and replace it with touch-screens and servers. To follow the story, we need to understand a bit about why this is, as it stands, a really bad idea.

Democracy is based on trust. You turn up to vote because you think the procedure isn't rigged. But your trust isn't blind: You want to know that the process is monitored by independent folk who understand how the system works, and who you trust to keep an eye on things for you.

With electronic voting, all this gets harder, not easier. The more digitized you make voting, the more complicated it gets, the harder it is to monitor, and the easier it is to mess with it. Some ne'er-do-well could tamper with the smart card he is given to vote with, and cast multiple votes. An election official could replace the memory cards storing the tally with one of his own. A hacker could break into the computer storing the votes and alter the outcome. Election monitors would see none of this, or else they might, but just not know what they were seeing. You get the picture? Electronic voting is not as simple as it looks. And after all that, you still need a paper trail that people can go back to if, for any reason, the electronic system – or voters' faith in it – breaks down.

Which is where our story begins. It starts with Bev Harris, a 52-year-old grandmother from Renton (population: 50,000), just south of Seattle, who was getting interested in the whole e-voting thing. What she found out quickly was that it's all very secret. There are a handful of companies making voting machines in the United States, and none of them is about to hand over its equipment for public scrutiny. Their argument: "security through obscurity." In other words, if people don't know how something works, that makes it secure.

Anyway, Ms. Harris started looking around the Internet and came across the homepage of Global Elections Systems Inc. – a voting-equipment maker bought out by rival Diebold Inc. in 2001 – which included a link to an FTP site (FTP is a way to download files from one computer to another). There she came across 40,000 files, all unprotected by any password. After some agonizing, she downloaded them all to her computer – it took 44 hours – and started rummaging through them.

All this happened early this year. She sent the files to experts, academics, activists and journalists, who started picking through the material, which was quickly posted around the Internet. What they discovered was somewhat scary: The voting system inherited from Global Elections Systems by Diebold seemed to have some serious flaws: A fair bit of it was based on off-the-shelf programs, such as Microsoft Office, and had dubious security features; a study by Johns Hopkins University tested the software from the FTP site and concluded "this voting system is far below even the most minimal security standards applicable in other contexts." Douglas W. Jones of the University of Iowa, who had tested a predecessor of the Diebold system in 1997, realized that no one had taken note of his dire warnings then that the machines used a woefully inadequate encryption system. His conclusion: "entirely unacceptable." An independent study done for one of Diebold's clients, the state of Maryland, concluded: "The system, as implemented in policy, procedure and technology, is at high risk of compromise."

All pretty scary, particularly if you take into account electronic voting is no longer a pipe dream. South Korea will introduce electronic voting for all elections from 2005. Japan, Taiwan, Hong Kong and Australia have launched pilot projects. Companies like Diebold are moving fast to take advantage of some $4 billion of U.S. federal funding for states to replace their old punch-card and lever-voting machines. This before any oversight committee has been formed to set any standards for certifying the machines (including for example, the need for a paper back-up). Diebold already has some 33,000 touch-screen machines in place throughout the U.S., and, along with its competitors, is aggressively pursuing a promising market.

It's also aggressively pursuing its critics: In September Diebold's lawyers demanded dozens of websites remove material originating from the FTP site on grounds of copyright, including sites which just link to the material. This has spawned a protest movement as students put up dozens of mirror sites – websites that post copies of the FTP material – and a legal response from the Electronic Frontier Foundation, a civil liberties organization, which earlier this month filed for a temporary restraining order on Diebold. The case will be heard on November 17.

Diebold has rebutted many of the charges made against its system, arguing in part that the material downloaded was not representative of its product. The Johns Hopkins report has been partially discredited because of this, but, despite doubts about the origin of the documents, other academics have supported many of its more damning conclusions. Rebecca Mercuri, a research fellow at Harvard's John F. Kennedy School of Government and a leading expert on electronic voting systems, is careful not to read too much into the documents, given their provenance. But so long as officials, and companies like Diebold, keep everything secret things will only get worse, she says. "This whole system of the way our voting systems are being constructed and tested is preposterous and does not inspire confidence in the security, auditability, reliability, or recountability of our elections."

And you thought democracy was boring.

Forget democracy. Think about shopping: A technology called RFID is gold for retailers keeping track of all sorts of things – including you. Here's what I wrote in August 2003:

In the end, it comes down to this: Would you, O Shopper, strolling the aisles in your local supermarket, consider a beep telling you that you just passed your family's favorite peanut butter:

a. an appalling intrusion into your privacy and an unacceptable degree of customer profiling?
b. manna from heaven, in that now you won't get bawled out by the kids for again forgetting to buy that heavenly paste?

Whether you and I answer a) or b) is going to determine whether a new kind of technology called RFID makes it out of the warehouse and on to the retail floor.

Okay, so what am I going on about? RFID stands for radio frequency identification, and in the past couple of weeks it has caused a bit of a rumpus. (More about this later.) RFID is basically a way of tagging a product, a bit like a bar code, only smarter. Bar codes, swiped by a reader (one of those gun things the checkout person wields), reveal what the product is and who makes it. Then the register can match it with a database to determine price and get an idea of how the product is selling.

Not bad, and the technology has been in our shops for a decade or so. But there are some things bar codes don't do: They don't say anything about which batch the product is in or how long it's been on the shelf. They can't identify each product individually. Someone actually needs to point a reader at the thing, or drag it over a till with a reader built in, for the bar-code data to volunteer itself. In short, bar codes are relatively dumb.

This is where RFID comes in. What if a tag on each product contained a lot more data, such as when it left the warehouse, or whether it's been kept in a place that's too hot or cold? What if the tag was smart enough

☞ **snitter** (*n, Northumberland*) The person who always talks to co workers in a whisper.

that you didn't need to point a reader at the product for the information to leap back at you? What if you were able to press a button on the computer in your office and "ping" all the products in your warehouse for an instant inventory? This is basically what RFID offers.

And of course, retailers and suppliers are pretty excited about it. In fact, it's already in place in quite a few industries, including, for some strange reason, the livestock community. A lot of pets also get RFID-tagged these days, so when they stray they can be identified and returned to their owners. As folk agree on standards, and prices of the actual tags fall, this kind of thing is spreading. Fast.

So where is the hoo-ha? The problem comes when you deploy it in a shop. These RFID tags are very efficient. They can store a lot of data, for a long time. If you buy a pair of shoes, the tag in those shoes could contain data about when and where you bought them and how much they cost. That's now. In the future, the same tag could have stored information since you bought them, such as where you've been with them, how often you've changed the laces, whether you have foot odor issues (theorizing here, but it's possible) and whether you might have been breaking the law in them.

Needless to say, it's a sticky area. In early July, British supermarket chain Tesco caused a stir when it used RFID tags on Gillette Mach3 razors at one of its stores to trigger an in-house security camera. Why razors? It turns out that they are popular with shoplifters, because they're small and they're expensive. Check out eBay: I counted more than 50 brand new Mach3 sets at a fraction of their retail price.

Privacy groups are upset, and bound to get more so if retailers start introducing technology like this without explaining it first. And it's not just theft. You and I are not going to be too happy if we find out that our shopping habits are being monitored any more than they are already.

There could be benefits. Some washing machines and refrigerators already come with RFID readers that can advise users on how to wash, store or cook tagged products. But what I don't want is an RFID tag on every product, banknote and stored-value card I have, transmitting information about me that allows shop clerks, bank tellers, policemen and my mother to know where I've been, what I'm wearing, how much money I have in my pocket and what diseases I'm entertaining. That's not about to happen, but the technology allows it. And some retailers would love it.

We as customers need to figure out what we're comfortable with. Finding the peanut butter is well and good, but we'd better be careful we know what comes along with it.

Not a lot has changed since then. But you don't have to go out to face these kinds of problems: Just access your email. I love services like Gmail, Google's email service, but I refuse to put any emails in there that are remotely personal. Here's why, in a piece I wrote in May 2004:

Privacy is one of those things you either obsess over, or don't see what all the fuss is about. You're either someone who gets indignant when a shop assistant asks you for your home address at the checkout, or you're not. You either hate the idea that your credit card is a mine of information about your shopping habits, or you couldn't care less.

This debate is timeless, but the Internet and in particular two recent new phenomena have brought it into focus. The first is a crop of online networking services that range from automatically updating your contacts' details, such as Plaxo Inc.'s address-book software to networking websites like Friendster and LinkedIn, which allow you to hook up with other users with similar tastes or business interests online. The other phenomenon is something called Gmail, the soon-to-be-launched email service from the soon-to-be-listed search-engine company Google.

All these services may involve storing your personal data – contacts or emails – on the companies' computers. In the case of Gmail, Google will scan your email content so you can organize it better and so that they can deliver "targeted" ads to the Web page on which you're reading the email. If your emails contain the word "horticulture," ads from florists may appear. In the case of Plaxo, people fret about the fact that your whole address book could be stored on Plaxo's computers. Networking services, meanwhile, have access not only to lists of who you know, but all the personal information about them and your contact with them. This, the privacy folk argue, is just asking for trouble. Are they right?

I sought the advice of experts on this, from lawyers, privacy advocates, technology gurus and executives. They all had quite different responses: some for, some against. Clearly this is not an issue with a simple answer, but here's what I think:

While I'm excited that technology and the Internet are making our lives easier, I don't think we're very well equipped for the pace of change and its implications. Technology is all about leveraging the power of a computer to do things on a scale we couldn't do by hand, or couldn't even do with a computer a few years ago. If I trawl, for example, through one of your emails I'm not going to build up much of a picture of you or your buying habits. But if I trawl through 100, or 1,000 – or one gigabyte's worth – then I could get a pretty good idea. Do you really want your email provider to know that much about you and to share it with advertisers?

Humbug, say the skeptics. Chris Winfield, president of 10E20, a Web-design company in New York says: "Yahoo!, Hotmail and AOL routinely scan your emails for viruses. How is this different to Gmail scanning your messages to display ads?" I disagree: These services are not compiling data from the content, they're filtering out emails based on certain limited criteria: Does this look like spam? Does this smell like a virus? Others argue this is no different to, say, a department-store loyalty card. "Why is Gmail's process considered an invasion of privacy, when no one even thinks about a store knowing what type of underwear you wear?" says Julian Field, chief technology officer of U.S.-based software company Fortress Systems. I respectfully disagree: It's more akin to allowing your phone company to listen in to your phone conversations and play jingles at you based on what you're talking about.

Some say all this comes down to trust. Do we, the users, trust the person to whom we're giving our information? Or do we consider selling some of our privacy – targeted ads, for example – worth the price? That may seem a simple enough equation: After all, if Google is offering us one gigabyte of online hard-drive space, what's a few targeted ads for all that storage? These companies all have privacy policies, they say they respect our privacy, they vow they won't sell any of this information.

But what happens, for example, if the service is sold? Plaxo makes clear in its privacy statement that the information will be part of assets transferred, raising legal questions about whether the new owner need abide by Plaxo's privacy agreements. Plaxo says the information will be transferred "subject to all terms and restrictions" of its privacy policy. There are also problems of abuse and incompetence: Companies that renege on user agreements, or face external attacks on insecure data. Plaxo has acknowledged two vulnerabilities on its computers that could have allowed hackers to snatch data. Both were fixed and no data was lost, Plaxo says.

Another problem on the issue of trust: The exchange of privacy for value implies that we understand what we're signing up for. When was the last time you read a user agreement before clicking the "Accept" button? Did you understand all its implications? I read through Plaxo's and it sounded fine until Australian academic Roger Clarke pointed out some grey areas, such as what happens to data stored under earlier versions of Plaxo's privacy policy, and what happens to data after a user cancels his subscription. Stacy Martin, privacy officer for Plaxo, says the company will soon update its privacy policy to reflect some of Clarke's and other people's concerns.

Critics of the privacy enthusiasts argue that if you don't like it, you can always go elsewhere. "You can't complain about something that is free," says Divan Da've, chief executive of New York-based Internet consultants Integrated Systems Management. "Don't like it? Don't use it. Just don't spoil it for the rest of us." While true, this is not a useful argument, for the simple reason that we don't have as much control over these things as we used to. Call it "passive privacy loss." What control do I have over my contact data if someone else has decided to store it on Plaxo? Whose privacy is being abused if a salesman stores all his company's business leads online? What happens to the emails that I send to a Gmail user? Are we who have not signed up for these services subject to the same privacy rules that apply to users?

The bottom line: We need to think not about what is happening but what could happen. It's not enough to say, "There's no problem yet, so why make it into one?" Technology is always one step ahead of us, the users. Don't believe me? Think spam that we can't control; think pop-up windows that we can't get rid of; think of phishing emails that look so realistic we are duped into giving up our banking details. Now think about storing all your emails in one place, with a company known for its brilliant search technology.

Once you've handed over your personal data, you can't always get it back. What happens to it a few years from now? Think of all those computers containing discarded information, sold off second-hand. Think about new technologies that may be able to establish links in supposedly anonymous data to figure out it's you, and to decide your unhealthy interest in flowers makes you too environmentally radical for employment. It's not just about protecting your unlisted phone number, though that is part of it. It's about helping to preserve a private space free of commercial and government intrusion.

The good news is that companies like Plaxo seem to be serious about addressing legitimate concerns, and are trying to talk the more radical critics down from their pedestals. But it's a long haul, and Plaxo and everyone else in the game of winning the trust of users would do better not to hide behind legal ambiguity but build technology that, as much as possible, leaves control in the hands of users.

Privacy is basically protecting your identity. Scammers want your identity so they can impersonate you and buy stuff. But companies also want to know as much about you as possible because then they can sell you stuff you might want to buy. It might sound like a fair exchange – who doesn't want to be sold stuff they want? – until you realize that may also mean drugs for the medical problem you'd rather keep to yourself, legal services for the lawsuit you'd prefer to keep quiet, and extra overdrafts for the slight liquidity problem you're not telling your spouse about. A lot can be learned about you online, and protecting yourself is not as easy as it may appear. Here's one way I wrote about in December 2005:

The Internet is great. Most of us can go anywhere, do anything, read anything, see anything, say anything, download (more or less) anything; and all of this can be done apparently anonymously. As a famous 1993 New Yorker magazine cartoon had it, with one mutt at the computer keyboard explaining to another at his feet: "On the Internet, nobody knows you're a dog." Actually, much to the disappointment of canine surfers everywhere, this isn't exactly true. The Internet will quickly figure out that a) you order weekly supplies of Lick Your Chops (Adult Dog Maintenance Formula) from PetFoodDirect.com, and b) you regularly visit canine dating service AfterBark.com. Your dog status has been rumbled.

The truth is, you aren't as anonymous on the Internet as you thought you were. It is possible for companies, organizations, governments and individuals to collect extensive details of your identity, interests and activities merely by watching you surf. Just by linking your computer address (where your computer hooks up to the Internet) with the data you send and receive, and the footprints (or pawprints) you leave on the websites you visit, they can build up an extensive profile of you.

As Lance Cottrell, Internet anonymity advocate and creator of a program called Anonymizer, puts it: "There is generally a perception that activity on the Internet is anonymous with the possible exceptions of credit cards and identity theft." In fact, it isn't like that: "In reality," says Mr. Cottrell, "time spent on the Internet is probably the least private time one spends in any activity. Almost all sites are involved in detailed user and usage tracking. While most of this isn't for any nefarious purpose, the amount and detail of information gathered and stored is mind boggling."

This is because, over time, a detailed dossier is being gathered, explains Mr. Cottrell. "The issue isn't the single click and information related to that, but the accumulation of data over tens of thousands of hits and pages spread over years and hundreds of websites." This information is being gathered not just by the sites being visited but by other related businesses such as advertisers.

☞ **boothby pagnell** (*n, Lincolnshire*) The space above a cubicle that coworkers feel entitled to lean over to talk to you, ignoring any semblance of according you some privacy.

While many users install firewalls and run antivirus software to ensure we don't get fooled into giving away our personal details, Mr. Cottrell is talking about something different. Security isn't always the same thing as anonymity. Keeping your personal data secure is one thing – it's akin to keeping your wallet, credit cards and ID card safely away from pickpockets. Anonymity is different. In the real world we can walk around without letting people know who we are – we can browse in a shop without registering our name at the door. On the Internet we don't have quite the same choice: By default, we aren't only leaving our calling card in most places we visit, we're also telling each of them where we last came from, where we're going, our hometown, what we bought, and lots of other juicy tidbits. All of this, coupled with personal information we may have submitted to job-hunting sites, say, or medical newsgroups, gets stored away for years, exchanged, leaked, stolen, or sold.

You might not think you're leaving much of a trail that could be abused by Web watchers, but security experts disagree. "Who is to say the profile they build is really accurate?" says security consultant Matthew Tanase. "What if this information falls into the wrong hands? How secure is the information and what is the potential for abuse?"

So what can we do about it? Well, it depends on how much effort you want to put into it. For a start, your computer address. A lot can be told from this, especially if you use the same computer and the same Internet connection over a long period. Masking this address is the first step to Internet anonymity. This can be done by simply visiting a website that cloaks your address so the places you visit only see the website you're visiting from. It's a bit like going into a shop with a grocery store bag over your head. The shop can tell only that you've got some link to the grocery store. Apart from that, nothing. For examples of these websites, check out Anonymouse.org or Proxify.com.

But this doesn't help with the data itself. Disguising your address doesn't necessarily disguise what you do – and the data that passes between you and the sites you visit. This is where Mr. Cottrell's Anonymizer comes into its own. Anonymizer (www.anonymizer.com) removes anything from the data your computer sends that may identify you – or your computer – to the website you visit. It also prevents that website from trying to reach your computer to get more information, or dump files on your computer that may help it remember who you are the next time you visit. Anonymizer encrypts the data you do transmit so that other people can't see it; it also warns you when you are visiting websites that may contain nasties trying to get into your computer. (A new version of Anonymizer's Anonymous Surfing package costs $30 for a one-year subscription.)

Another option is the USB drive StealthSurfer II, which is great if you use other people's computers a lot. Plug in the StealthSurfer (www.stealthsurfer.biz) and use its onboard software – including a browser, email program, password management program and a version of Anonymizer's software. All the data will be encrypted and none of it will be left on the computer you're using – only your key drive.

Using the StealthSurfer might be too fiddly for some people. But if I've scared you enough about all this, it does offer you an all-in-one package that should give you some peace – and keep your "dog-ness" a secret.

acknowledgements

First off, I'd like to thank Mark Hanusz, owner of Equinox and my publisher. Without his faith, enthusiasm, professionalism and know-how, this book would be just a pile of clippings in a drawer.

Going further back, I'd like to thank Reginald Chua, then editor of the then *Asian Wall Street Journal*, for not stamping on my idea that I try to pick up where the great Stan Sesser left off with a personal technology column. Thanks also to a succession of editors I worked with at that time, including Abby Pesta, as well as those patient editors and bureau chiefs who allowed me to straddle both technology and Indonesian coverage, among them Abby's brother Jesse and Raphael "Rocky" Pura. At the *Far Eastern Economic Review* I was blessed with great editors in Michael Vatikiotis, David Plott and not least Helen Przygodzki, who helped steer me through three wonderful years and allowed me to explore the further reaches of what was possible in a column about technology. Thanks too, to Poravit Sreshthaputra who designed its home and to Selçuk Demirel, who became our sole illustrator (and whose illustration graces the cover of this book.) Lastly, with the column back at *The Asian Wall Street Journal* (now *The Wall Street Journal Asia*) I am indebted to editor John Bussey, as well as *Personal* (and now *Weekend*) *Journal* editors present and past, S. Karene Witcher and the ever cheerful Janelle Carrigan, for making a corner of their section a home for the column, with illustrations from the talented Ingo Fast. Deputy *Weekend Journal* editor Richard Lord has taken up the task of steering the column for the past year, yet another safe pair of Dow Jones hands.

Although this book is based on columns I've written for the Journal and Review, I'm also grateful to the BBC World Service for giving me a chance to sound off on a regular basis in a recorded segment that goes out once a week on Business Daily. This may not have helped listeners, but it's definitely helped me try to understand the problems ordinary users face, which is what Loose Wire is supposed to be all about. Particular thanks got to Manuela Saragosa for making it happen in the first place, and to Jonathan Frewin and Alex Ritson for mentoring me through the whole recording-my-voice-so-it-doesn't-sound-like-an-axe murderer-in-a-public-toilet thing. I've got them to thank for aircon-less afternoons sweating under a blanket in my study trying to locate the source of a buzz that renders the recordings useless.

Friends who helped make this possible by helping me over the years with ideas, comments, infrequent praise and less infrequent snorts of disgust, in no particular order, are: Dean Yates and Mary Binks, Sophie Khan and Colin Stewart, Tessa Piper, Bert Hofman, Kurnya Roesad, Shanty Harmayn, Ditta Amahorseya, Jim Della-Giacoma, Sidney Jones, Wicak Soegijoko, Helen Przygodzki, Sydney Low, DL Byron, Buzz Bruggeman, Andy Abramson, Halley Suitt, Timothy Roche, Jo Kao, Andrew Thornley, Gráinne McCarthy, Matt Stephens, Don Greenlees, Puspa Madani, Richard Paddock, Sean Foley, Melody Kemp, Chris Hill, Indi Soemardjan and Meutia Chaerani, Ellen Hutabarat, Jerry Justianto, Rene Pattirawadene, Gen Kanai, Johnny and Mona McDougall, Mieke Kooistra and Guy Janssen, Kate Duff, Warren Caragata, Dharmawan Ronodipuro, Mark Keenan, Phil Baker, William Daniel, Ong Hock Chuan, Rin Hindryati, Poppy Barkah, Richard Oh, and of course my old friend Robin Lubbock and his long-suffering spouse Joy Hackel. Family support courtesy of my mum, whose contacts provided the inspiration for Ethel Girdle, and my brother Adam and his family.

Thanks too to Andy Abramson, Phil Baker, Poppy Barkah, DL Byron, Jim Della-Giacoma, Kate Duff, Jonathan Frewin, Roy Grubb, Jonathan Grundy, Graham Holiday, Chris Riemer, Jim Rothbarth, Pito Salas, and Peter Ungphakorn for reading drafts of this book, most of them under surprisingly little duress.

Lastly, of course, there's my wife Sari who has over the years patiently endured my mood swings, listened to my half-baked and rarely realized ideas, and read through many a column draft, laughing dutifully in the right places as I lean menacingly over her shoulder. Without her the columns would have been even more turgid and the book still on some remote backburner next to the inflatable car idea and my other unfinished book projects.

index

note: all software programs are listed under the category "Software"

OTHER TITLES BY EQUINOX PUBLISHING

NON FICTION

PEACE IN ACEH: A Personal Account of the Helsinki Peace Process
Damien Kingsbury
979-3780-25-8
2006, softcover, 236 pages

The Legacy of The Barang People
György Busztin
979-3780-37-1
2006, softcover, 120 pages

AT HOME ABROAD: A Memoir of the Ford Foundation in Indonesia 1953-1973
John Bresnan
979-3780-34-7
2006, softcover, 236 pages

DREAMSEEKERS: Indonesian Women as Domestic Workers in Asia
Dewi Aggraeni
979-3780-28-2
2006, softcover, 272 pages

THE PEPPER TRADER: True Tales of the German East Asia Squadron and the Man who Cast them in Stone
Geoffrey Bennett
979-3780-26-6
2006, softcover, 392 pages

SRIRO'S DESK REFERENCE OF INDONESIAN LAW 2006
Andrew I. Sriro
979-3780-20-7
2006, softcover, 592 pages

THE SECOND FRONT: Inside Asia's Most Dangerous Terrorist Network
Ken Conboy
979-3780-09-6
2006, softcover, 256 pages

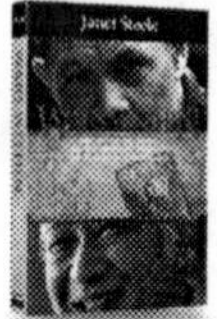

WARS WITHIN: The Story of *TEMPO*, an Independent Magazine in Soeharto's Indonesia
Janet Steele
979-3780-08-8
2005, softcover, 368 pages

SIDELINES: Thought Pieces from *TEMPO* Magazine
Goenawan Mohamad
979-3780-07-X
2005, softcover, 260 pages

AN ENDLESS JOURNEY: Reflections of an Indonesian Journalist
Herawati Diah
979-3780-06-1
2005, softcover, 304 pages

BULE GILA: Tales of a Dutch Barman in Jakarta
Bartele Santema
979-3780-04-5
2005, softcover, 160 pages

THE INVISIBLE PALACE: The True Story of a Journalist's Murder in Java
José Manuel Tesoro
979-97964-7-4
2004, softcover, 328 pages

INTEL: Inside Indonesia's Intelligence Service
Ken Conboy
979-97964-4-X
2004, softcover, 264 pages

KOPASSUS: Inside Indonesia's Special Forces
Ken Conboy
979-95898-8-6
2003, softcover, 352 pages

TIMOR: A Nation Reborn
Bill Nicol
979-95898-6-X
2002, softcover, 352 pages

GUS DUR: The Authorized Biography of Abdurrahman Wahid
Greg Barton
979-95898-5-1
2002, softcover, 436 pages

NO REGRETS: Reflections of a Presidential Spokesman
Wimar Witoelar
979-95898-4-3
2002, softcover, 200 pages

FICTION

ELLIPSIS
Laksmi Pamuntjak
979-3780-30-4
2006, softcover, 98 pages

SAMAN
Ayu Utami
979-3780-11-8
2005, softcover, 184 pages

THE SPICE GARDEN
Michael Vatikiotis
979-97964-2-3
2004, softcover, 256 pages

ILLUSTRATED

THE KING, THE WITCH AND THE PRIEST
Pramoedya Ananta Toer
979-95898-3-5
2001, softcover, 128 pages

IT'S NOT AN ALL NIGHT FAIR
Pramoedya Ananta Toer
979-95898-2-7
2001, softcover, 120 pages

TALES FROM DJAKARTA
Pramoedya Ananta Toer
979-95898-1-9
2000, softcover, 288 pages

MODERN MALAYSIAN:
A Tribute to Felda's Craftspeople
Sh. Sakinah Aljunid
979-3780-32-0
2006, hardcover, 160 pages

MADE IN INDONESIA:
A Tribute to the Country's Craftspeople
Warwick Purser
979-3780-13-4
2005, hardcover, 160 pages

TRAVEL

BANGKOK INSIDE OUT
Daniel Ziv & Guy Sharett
979-97964-6-6
2005, softcover, 176 pages

A CUP OF JAVA
Gabriella Teggia & Mark Hanusz
979-95898-9-4
2003, softcover, 144 pages

JAKARTA INSIDE OUT
Daniel Ziv
979-95898-7-8
2002, softcover, 184 pages

KRETEK:
The Culture and Heritage of Indonesia's Clove Cigarettes
Mark Hanusz
979-95898-0-0
2000, hardcover, 224 pages

THE NATURAL GUIDE TO BALI
Anne Gouyon
979-3780-00-2
2005, softcover, 448 pages

ACADEMIC

SOCIAL SCIENCE AND POWER IN INDONESIA
Vedi R. Hadiz & Daniel Dhakidae
979-3780-01-0
2005, hardcover, 304 pages

PEOPLE, POPULATION, AND POLICY IN INDONESIA
Terence H. Hull
979-3780-02-9
2005, hardcover, 208 pages

COMMISSIONED

TWENTY YEARS OF WELCOMING THE WORLD
Melia Bali Villas & Spa Resort
2005, hardcover, 160 pages

CELEBRATING INDONESIA:
Fifty Years with the Ford Foundation 1953-2003
Goenawan Mohamad
979-97964-1-5
2004, hardcover, 240 pages

CLASSIC INDONESIA

THE RISE OF INDONESIAN COMMUNISM
Ruth T. McVey
979-3780-36-3 (sc)
979-3780-35-5 (hc)
2006, 510 pages

INDONESIAN COMMUNISM UNDER SUKARNO:
Ideology and Politics 1959-1965
Rex Mortimer
979-3780-29-0 (sc)
979-3780-27-4 (hc)
2006, 464 pages

JAVA IN A TIME OF REVOLUTION:
Occupation and Resistance 1944-1946
Benedict R.O'G. Anderson
979-3780-14-2
2006, softcover, 516 pages

Printed in the United States
67059LVS00005B/36